THE
LIGHT
WITHIN
MY
DARKNESS

MARCIA ORCUTT

Paperback: 978-1-63767-375-1
eBook: 978-1-63767-376-8

Ordering Information:

BookTrail Agency
8838 Sleepy Hollow Rd.
Kansas City, MO 64114

Printed in the United States of America

With gratitude,
to
Dr Donald C McNeil Ph D
and
Fr Jason Giombetti

for being like candles
on my continuing journey

shining your light
into my darkness

gently guiding me in the ways of truth

allowing the One Light that ignites every flame
to gradually unveil my
hidden face

so that my light might also begin to shine
and reflect The Light of Truth

may I always remember that I, too, am a candle
unable to light my own flame

I do not burn for myself.

"I learned a long time ago the wisest thing
I can do is be on my own side,
be an advocate for myself and others like me."

Maya Angelou

A LETTER FROM THE AUTHOR

*R*eading The Light Within My Darkness may be difficult, however, living through sexual abuse is horrific. The damage done often remains with the victim throughout his or her life. Repressed memories may take years to return. I shared some of my story in my initial memoir, From Darkness To Dawn/ A True Story of Recovery From Postpartum Depression which I republished as both From Darkness To Dawn and Becoming The Dawn (the same book with different titles) to more accurately reflect some of the information as more memories came back to me. This letter, along with some grammatical corrections, are the basic additions to this republication of Becoming The Dawn with its new title to avoid confusion. Becoming The Dawn had a rocky start. It was battered around in the marketing world due to my poor decisions much like my poor start in life. This, however, does not stop me from trying once more, as I believe the message of this book is too important to ignore.

As I continue in my recovery and on my journey in my deepening relationship with God I have returned to the church of my childhood, the Catholic Church. Through the grace and the power of the sacraments, I have encountered Jesus and have received His great love, compassion, and healing as only He can give. I speak throughout my memoir about the mother/daughter bond between myself and my daughters and how important this was for me to keep going while I was so depressed. I did not have this bond with a person during childhood however my relationship with Jesus today surpasses any I could have had. This relationship encourages me to grow, change, and to become the best person I can be. When repressed memories come into the light today or self-destructive thoughts enter as they still do, I have a defense system. My thinking has changed. I ask God to remove these thoughts. Today I value my life because I believe God cares and values me and each of us, for who we are, not for what did or did not happen to us.

Recently I had the opportunity to spend a few days by the ocean. During my time there I spent much quiet time reflecting and watching the ocean. This beach was extremely rocky. As I walked and picked up some rocks, I was struck by how smooth their surfaces were. I thought back on my life journey. Previously I had written I thought of myself as a broken shell that could never be put back together. Now, years later, my thinking has changed as my healing has continued. Like the tide (and as I do the work I need to do), God's grace continues to wash over me. My rough areas and brokenness are mending. I have survived the storms of my life. I no longer crumble handling ordinary life events that once threw me. And like a rock, I can stand firm on my faith and not rely on substances when difficulties come my way. Lastly, I am one of many rocks. I need God and others. I am not an island. I depend on God.

Deep in my soul, as I rest in God's presence, I often experience periods of peace. In the past my hope was that I would get through the day or that I might feel less depressed. Today my true hope is that one day I may be with my Lord and Savior, Jesus, where every tear will be wiped away and I will no longer care or ask why this horrific evil happens.

I share my story in the hopes that others like me may be encouraged to seek treatment; allow Jesus to enter their brokenness and join them in their healing journey; raise awareness of this evil; and remind survivors that shame for the abuse that happened to them is not theirs to bear.

Please join me if possible in praying for victims and for those who commit abuse of any kind. It is not my intent to have anyone believe as I believe. I am asking you to be willing to turn the page and let the water wash over you as you continue to read.

Thank You,

Marcia Orcutt
4/29/21

PREFACE - FROM DARKNESS TO DAWN

*A*s my journey and healing have continued since I first wrote From Darkness To Dawn (A True Story of Recovery From Postpartum Depression), my underlying issues and understanding of these thirteen years of severe depression have become clearer. Today, several years later, after remembering many more repressed memories of sexual abuse by different people in my life and journeying through much more pain, I have decided to republish my memoir to more accurately reflect those years and the causes of my depression.

Although I was initially diagnosed with post partum depression after my second daughter, Sarah, was born in 1996, I did have a history of trauma that I had not remembered as the professionals had begun to suspect from my symptoms. I now know that the severe depression I experienced after Sarah was born was a symptom of my Post Traumatic Stress Disorder (PTSD) which was triggered by both Sarah's birth and by my older daughter's, Emily's, age (2), at the time. My PTSD is an emotional illness caused by the sexual abuse I suffered earlier in my life.

I did not know the extent of the abuse when I originally wrote the book nor could I know because I wasn't ready or able to deal with the issues.

When I remembered the initial repressed memories I describe in From Darkness To Dawn, nine years into my severe depression, I began to heal.

A huge part of my healing is my growing relationship with God. I struggled with God for a long time. However, it is the assurance of God's immense Love for me that gives me the strength to continue to face the truth in my life.

This book provides a glimpse of how sexual abuse affected me emotionally, cognitively, physically, socially, and spiritually throughout my life without me knowing why I felt the way I felt; or why I thought the way I thought; or why I believed the things I believed; or why I acted the way I acted.

Once I became aware and learned though, I realized it was my choice, my responsibility, to make a better choice not only for myself, but for my children, so that I could be the mother I hoped to be to them, so that I could pass on to Emily and Sarah something different than what was passed on to me. I had the opportunity to see in the light and learn the truth, and out of love I needed to do my work to heal so I could pass that healing to my two daughters who are now in their twenties. This is probably the biggest way I do not regret the thirteen years I lost from being more fully present in my daughters' young lives. I have made many mistakes as a mother but by doing my own therapeutic work, I have the opportunity to hopefully interrupt the unspeakable, unbearable, and unthinkable cycle of abuse that often passes on to the next generation.

I continue to learn about my PTSD. I am learning new ways to cope with my symptoms. I am learning new ways to think about myself and the world. It is a lot of work and sometimes I am in a lot of pain. At times I don't feel like going on. I have been in that place too many times. I have spent too much time in my life running away from my pain, running from my reality, or running from myself. I can't afford to run away anymore. The next time I run might be my last time.

Instead, I run toward God, the people I trust, and the people I love. I do the same things today I share in this book, the things I was taught during this thirteen year very long and very dark journey. The difference today is, I believe in the God I run to and I believe the people who say they care, really do care.

I still need to stop many times, slow down, and quiet my anxious thoughts. Many times, I sit on my bench in a quiet chapel, and as I sit with God present, I try to be still. In the stillness, He speaks to me and calls me by name. He invites me to surrender, again, to let go, of many things, gradually, because that is how I am able. Jesus takes all I offer. He can handle all, I can't. He restores my dignity. He enables me to walk, with my head and eyes raised to the sunlight. I can write my name to this book and not be ashamed of my past. More importantly, I am no longer ashamed of who I am. I know and believe I am a child of God made in His image.

How do I know this? God tells me as I sit in the silence with Him. I also know this through the people in my life who are present for me and who treat me with the respect and dignity and love I never thought I deserved or could show myself.

For just as much as this is a book about abuse, it is a true story about love and forgiveness, patience and family. It is a story about the greatest gift, Jesus, and about how very much He loves us.

I share as honestly as possible how good and loving God has been to me and how He makes Himself present in my life (that

I am aware). I share freely from His love that flows in. I pray it freely flows out.

I offer this book as my prayer of praise and thanksgiving to God. There is so much I do not understand. Today I try to sit with this "not knowing" and surrender this also to God trusting that He knows all. I try to let it go. I try to put one foot in front of the other, no matter how haltingly I walk. I cannot deny where I have been because if I do, I will most likely pass that darkness along. I am learning there is a more loving and better way to live.

I was shown it is in The Light of the dawn of each new day… there is freedom in God's love for me…for any of us… who want it…

I invite you to share this often difficult and dark but true journey with me …

Marcia Orcutt
September 20, 2019

PROLOGUE

*A*s I lie in the maternity ward, I feel as if a tidal wave has rushed in unannounced and swept over me. I am lost in the middle of a storm that will not quit. The thunderous wave comes crashing down on me emotionally, physically, and spiritually; attempting to destroy anyone close to me in its path. It is pulling me out to sea. I am sinking underwater. I close my eyes more tightly, holding my breath since I have no oxygen tank. I am deathly afraid that sharks will attack me. I have no boat or life preserver.

I attempt to open my eyes. This has to be a terrible nightmare. I struggle to get out from under the enormous waves that threaten to drown me. I have just given birth. I must get to my baby girl. "I am coming," I call to her. I scream as a thunderous wave fills my open mouth full of salt sea water. I gasp for air and struggle as I spit out the water. I attempt to kick against the current to rise to the surface. "Stephen," I call out, "Can you hear me? Where is Sarah? Bring Sarah to me."

As I struggle to open my eyes and shake the water from my hair, I realize this is no nightmare. It is my reality. It is my present truth.

I had no idea at the time that one of life's most blessed events would be the start of the deepest and darkest spiral of my life. Our second daughter Sarah, a beautiful seven pound, eleven ounce baby girl had just been born. But in the midst of this miracle of birth, something dark and threatening seems to have been born inside of me. I have become a stranger to myself.

CHAPTER 1

THE DESCENT

9 was at the beach for a walk with my husband. The two of us were each lost in our own thoughts as we listened to the waves break onto the shore with the incoming tide. I love the ocean. It has been a source of comfort for me; a place I come to relax, read, daydream, and in recent years since our first daughter, Emily, was born, a place of fun. My husband Stephen loves to swim, unlike myself, and he spent much time with Emily in the water or on the beach with her pail and shovel, building sand castles and tunnels. My heart was overflowing that day. I was about to give birth to our second child anytime now. I thought to myself that my life was so different, so changed, like the ocean can be.

My life changed course eight years ago, the day before I turned 29; the day I put down that drink. Walking on the beach, I sensed that I was finally on the right road after a long time of trying to find myself. I had felt a gentle spark burning within me. One thing I have not done is to dwell on my past.

The night our second daughter, Sarah, was born, was a glorious event and beautiful night equaled only by the birth of Emily two years earlier. My husband and I had waited with anticipation for this moment, just as we had for the birth of our first daughter. However, something went dreadfully wrong this time. Not with the pregnancy or the birth itself. There were no complications and no drugs were given during childbirth. Sarah's birth came easily, with labor lasting only five to six hours. Stephen was beside me during the delivery, dressed in a yellow hospital gown and face mask. I focused on his blue eyes as he attempted to calm my frantic breathing. We repeated, "One, two, three, one, two, three" just like we learned in our prenatal classes. I tried to focus on the ocean; picturing the sun reflecting off the blue water. Soon, I told myself, we would have our own bundle of sunshine. With these thoughts, I knew I could endure these passing pains of childbirth; realizing the joy that was to come would be worth every minute. I thought of Emily, asleep at home with her nana. I thought of how much love and joy we had experienced as a family over the past two years. Emily was also born on a September night.

When I heard our newborn infant's cry, I laid my head back on the pillow, exhausted but content. The doctor proudly proclaimed, "Congratulations, you have a new daughter," as the nurse placed her in my arms. As I held Sarah for the first time and looked into her blue eyes that were just like her father's, I cried; unsure if these were tears of joy or sadness. I loved my daughter, Sarah, I was sure of that, but I was confused about my feelings. I felt overwhelmed. Was I exhausted from the six hours of labor or was something else happening with me? I had Emily two years ago and I didn't remember crying so much. Beneath the calm surface of the ocean an emotional storm was brewing and growing in intensity.

We brought Sarah home and attempted to enjoy life as our family grew from three to four. Although we met each day's basic challenges, I never seemed to have a peaceful moment or time enough to juggle each child's needs while also finding time to spend time with my husband. And how could I get just a moment or two for myself? A moment just to slow down and brush my own hair, have a cup of tea, or talk to a friend.

I seemed to be crying all the time and I had a lot of trouble sleeping. My moods would change drastically and without warning.

Before Sarah was one-year-old, I was diagnosed with severe clinical postpartum depression. I was thirty-seven.

This was the start of a thirteen-year journey that I can only describe as a living nightmare. The attempts made to heal my depression failed time and time again. Over the years, I had tried different medications in varying dosages, along with combinations of medications; electroconvulsive shock treatments; ongoing therapy sessions two to three times a week; group therapy sessions, and in-patient hospitalizations. Being depressed was hard enough to deal with, but knowing that my illness was affecting my family terrified me.

Each time I left them to go to my numerous appointments I felt like I had to choose between spending time with them or taking care of myself. I felt selfish, thinking I would never get this precious time back. I felt my young daughters would resent the time I didn't spend with them. The waves never stopped coming. The hopes and dreams I once had for my daughters and our life as a family seemed to be drowning in a sea of despair. I could not understand what had happened to me. Or why.

I never passed that swimming class at the YWCA when I was a teenager. My fear of going underwater held me back, and this fear has kept me from swimming all these years. It is unbelievable how powerful this fear can be.

I also had a huge fear of asking people for help that I developed during childhood.I had many fears that controlled me, many which began to surface and hit me all at once, similar to ocean waves swelling with increasing force as they gather strength before incoming storms.

I was distraught to learn that I was facing a tsunami that was leaving a path of destruction and devastation in its wake.

I am a mother. I am walking with my precious daughters. I cannot walk for myself right now, but that is okay. I walk, trying to trust that the spark lit within me eight years ago did not go out entirely when this depression overcame me. I cannot feel this spark within me, but I feel connected to my daughters. I trust this connection. I hold onto their tiny hands. Onto their voices. Onto their hearts. When the intensity of the waves increase, I hold on tighter. I am not willing to let go of them without doing my best to fight for them. My disease would fight me on this point over and over.

What will happen to my daughters? I knew how important it was for Sarah to feel loved. And I knew how important it was for me to feel loved. Thinking of this agitated me. I felt the waves stir within me. When I heard Sarah cry I hurried to her side. "Mommy's here," I said in a soothing voice as I placed her at my breast. I looked into her blue eyes and told her "Mommy loves you so much." When she cried during the night, I could barely drag myself from my bed at times. I put Sarah in our bed between Stephen and myself; often nursing her and letting her fall asleep between us as I protected her with my arm around her. I was too exhausted emotionally and physically to take her back to her crib. I believed I was trying to transfer as much love as possible from my body to hers while I remained submerged in my feelings of guilt over not being the mother I thought she deserved. I loved her dearly, and I wanted more for her than I thought I could give her.

Many times throughout these years I felt like I was kicking my legs against the current in a vain attempt to safely make it to shore. As I rushed to get to Sarah so I could nurse her, my thoughts were consumed. "She needs me" was all I could think. I must get to her before she is too hungry. I longed to place her by my breast and nurse her, mother to daughter. I will give her what she needs at this time in her life, satisfy her most basic need for food. I secretly hoped that my mother's milk would satisfy her greater need for love. This deeper, yet most basic need seemed to call to me at a deeper, basic human level. So deep that I could not ignore it. I could not worry about who would be there for me. Sarah and Emily needed to come first.

I knew that reaching out for help would be a start. Reaching out scared me, but drowning scared me more. The thought of losing my daughters and husband because of my own emotional frailties terrorized me. My sisters initially offered to help us care for Sarah and Emily. As they lived out of state, one sister offered to take our daughters to live with her family. While we appreciated the gesture deeply, we were concerned about establishing our own bonds with them, especially Sarah as she was still an infant. We loved them and wanted them to be cared for, but we also felt like our love was essential for their development. Having no way of knowing how difficult or long my depression would last, we decided to keep our daughters with us and get help to care for them as needed.

Out of necessity and desperation, I put one foot in front of the other. I tentatively reached out my hand. I sent my S.O.S.

CHAPTER 2

A LOOK BACK

*A*s much as I wanted to move forward, I needed to revisit my childhood and adolescence. Part of these years were turbulent, causing me to keep them below the surface of my memory. This had not served me well. It seems best to be upfront about my background and some of the poor choices I made before I continue. They are a part of the fabric of my being however much I wish they weren't at times.

I had often focused on the negative ever since childhood. I had four sisters, two older and two younger than me. My oldest sister, Mary Ann, died when she was fourteen, and I was born two years later. I often felt I was her replacement, and a rather poor one at that, and that I was always living in her shadow. My mother had high goals for all of us. Whenever I came home from school and handed her my spelling or math test, she often asked "Why did you get one wrong?" I never felt good enough. I felt like my oldest sister should have lived and I should have never been born. Despite how hard I tried, I could never seem to please my mother. When I closed my eyes, I would picture my mom's face. She looked disappointed in me when she saw my school grades each day. I responded "I'll try to do better tomorrow," but deep down I wondered how much harder I could possibly try, and how much disappointment my mother could handle. It seemed that no matter how hard I tried, I just couldn't get a perfect score. My mother wasn't too happy with me, I decided, but I was unable to tell her this. Instead, I continued struggling to obtain this elusive perfect score. Yet, even when I achieved it, I never seemed to feel happy about it.

My mother made the decisions and was the disciplinarian in our family. She seemed to control everyone in the house, including my father.

My father seemed to be passive. Certainly, he was present in our house, sitting in his favorite chair or puttering around in the garage when he wasn't working. He was very silent. When he did speak, he rarely spoke about his feelings. Neither did my mother, but I could easily tell how she felt both from her tone and the volume of her voice. My parents seldom interacted with one another except for their arguments, which seemed to happen frequently. Following these arguments, my dad would not speak to my mother for days, sometimes two weeks. This produced awkward moments, especially at the dinner table. Many meals were spent in silence.

Just as my dad had his predictable way of responding to these arguments my mother had her way. These arguments often took place late in the evening when my sisters and I were in bed, supposedly asleep. As much as I tried to block their arguments out of my mind, I could never totally shut them out. I hid my face in my pillow but the hurtful words penetrated through. "You're drinking in the basement, I know what you are doing down there." It was always my mother's voice screaming at my father. I could never quite make out my father's response.

My mother's response to my dad was to say, "I am only with you because of the children." She walked to the hallway closet, retrieved her coat, opened the garage door, got in her car, backed out of the driveway and drove away. This entire time I lay as still as possible, trying to make myself invisible in my bed upstairs in my bedroom. Honestly, I think I was trying to disappear. I was trying so hard to protect myself from this reoccurring nightmare. But I failed every time. No matter how hard I pressed my pillow against my ears and shut my eyes I never could block out my parents' screaming voices from entering my young head. I remember thinking, "Why stay here if you don't even like him?" But at the same time, I feared that my mother would be gone when I woke up the next morning. My mother always returned, however this did little to relieve my fear of abandonment. I also felt sorry for my father that my mother left us. I was angry with her for leaving. I felt sorry for my father that my mother said she didn't love him. I felt like someone should protect my dad. It never occurred to me that he should be protecting and defending himself, that he was the adult. It also failed to occur to me that he should be protecting me since I was the child. I felt responsible for him in some way. I didn't understand why I felt like this. I was aware of these feelings and they scared me, causing me much anxiety. I was too afraid to tell anyone how I felt. Who would I tell anyway? I never interacted with my dad and I was afraid to interact with my mom. Fear controlled and ruled my life. So I did what came easily to me; I kept my feelings to myself.

Or so I thought.

My feelings were overwhelming me and I needed an outlet. I found it in food when I was ten years old. I began relying on food to provide me with comfort and security rather than trying to get these things from forming intimate relationships with people. I was no longer willing to risk that at this young age. I never questioned why. Food seemed to be an obvious and better choice. Perhaps it did not even seem like a choice, but why not?

Thinking back, I am not sure if I ever really thought about this. At ten years old, I never dwelled on this, but it entered my mind now.

Turning to food for my security was a relationship that lasted for over twenty years. It initially worked but went on to deceive me. I initially thought this relationship would fulfill me by enabling me to be the thinnest person in my family, allowing me to be noticed, especially by my dad. Ultimately, this relationship with food violated all those promises I thought it made to me; leaving me physically hungry for food and emotionally starved for affection, and spiritually shut off to anything of the spirit. My fears eventually engulfed me. My addiction had overcome me. I had become afraid of living, and my life became a form of spiritual death.

My mother seemed to have a need for my sisters and me to be alike, to have the same interests, and to always agree with her. The problem was that I did not agree. I could not accept my mother's way of thinking or her way of viewing the world. I had a huge problem. I lived in that house; that was my family and my parents were my parents. Although I loved them, I just never seemed to fit in. Before I was too old I began to feel like I was not part of this family. None of my other sisters seemed to have the same issues I was having, or if they did they never talked about it. I was also an extremely sensitive child and would easily cry. Again, I seemed to be the only one doing this, which only added to my sense of not belonging.

I continued avoiding my issues by not eating - I would bring my lunches home from school and hide them in my bedroom closet. Then I would wait for trash day and sneak the rotten food out into the curbside trash, hoping to avoid being caught by either parent. This became time-consuming, and I became fearful that I would be discovered. The dreaded day finally arrived when my mother found the lunches. She confronted me with a stern demeanor, "What are your lunches doing here in your closet? Your father works long and hard to pay for this food. It isn't for you to waste. What's wrong with you? Don't let me find any more food here again." My mother was obviously angry. I cried and said, "I'm not hungry at lunchtime, that's all." I was afraid to tell her the truth. Despite the warning, my eating behavior did not change. I continued to hide my uneaten lunches, saving them under my bed or pushing them farther behind in the closet. There were not too many safe places to hide things in that house. My mother always had a way of finding them! My mother eventually noticed that I was losing weight when I was in college, but by then my anorexia was out of control. My mother told me to eat but nothing else was done about my illness. Perhaps my parents were overwhelmed or simply did not know what to do about my anorexia. I do not know because unfortunately, we never discussed it. I suffered in silence for many years before I sought treatment. I did not understand if what I was doing with food was wrong or shameful. Today I know it's neither. After much physical and emotional pain and treatment, I know my eating disorder is an illness, which needs to be treated, like any other illness.

It became difficult for me to separate my home from my family, or perhaps it was as if my home became an extension of my family. The house took on a life of its own, especially when I was a child and could not ask anyone what anything meant. My mom often stated, "What happens in this house stays in this house." I began to believe it. I wondered if the house had ears, and if it did, what did it hear? Did it hear the same arguments between my parents that I tried so hard to block out at night when I was trying to fall asleep? Did it hear me crying myself to sleep whenever I heard my mom leave? Did it hear me crying when I ran up to my bedroom after bringing home another 98% spelling paper and still felt like a failure?

What if this house had eyes? What did that mean? Did it see me hiding my food in my bedroom closet? Did it see me trying to sneak it outside on trash day? Did it see me pulling the bed covers over my head as I tried to make myself disappear when my mother was looking for me? Worse, did those walls see my fear and my confusion and insecurity? Did those walls see how much I hated myself? Did they see how much turmoil I had inside of me?

Could they read the words I wrote in my diary when I sat on my bed and penned my most personal thoughts in what I thought was a private book? Could they read through the lines and interpret the feelings I carried close to my heart that tore apart my soul?

It was difficult to find a place to be alone in that house. My mother seemed to have a constant need to know what was happening and where everyone was, while I seemed to have a need for solitude. These two needs seemed to clash. And we did, many times. I thought I was wrong. I thought I was a mistake. The real mistake was that I was too afraid to talk about how I felt. How could I? I thought the house had eyes and ears and would hold my secrets, along with everything else it had heard and seen. What would be the point of exposing my innermost self? I was in enough pain. Talking about my true self would not reap any rewards. What would be the point?

I could not risk it. I was too afraid. Besides, I have another uneaten brown bag lunch in my possession. Where can I hide this one? I have more important things to think about.

The few times I dared speak my truth, I knew I was not heard. Just as my parents' arguments seemed to be absorbed into the walls and the next day all appeared to be well, I wondered what other things these walls had seen and heard. How much could the house contain? Could it contain me? What secrets was it holding, and why? I wondered. I began to think of my home as an unsafe place to speak and confide my thoughts and feelings. I envisioned the house growing and becoming one way on the inside, but another way on the outside. I was truly confused. Did this reflect who I was becoming?

I thought that our house would absorb everything I said and spread my secret into the walls. It had heard and seen so much during the years and had no way to release it. No wonder the walls are that awful moss green color, I think. But sometimes, like now, I think of it as a putrid green like the color of vomit. These walls are infected. The secrets they hold are too much and they have no way to come out. It's almost as if mold has grown inside between the insulation of the walls. The walls were meant to hold the secrets in. They did, and as time went by these secrets grew in the dark, turning the walls a sickly green color. The walls were once a pale green and reflected the sunlight, but as time has passed, what they have seen and heard has festered. Since it is a closed system with no way to release, what has remained in the dark, stays in the dark, so the secrets that have grown into mold have oozed out into the walls and changed them to the moss green that seemed to damper my spirits.

The one cheery room in the house was the kitchen, which was red and white. We had many happy times here despite the silent meal times. We often sat after the meals and talked about nothing in particular as we grew older. My father worked in the evenings and was usually missing from these after dinner gatherings. This room had white curtains, which seemed to gleam in contrast to the moss green ones in the living room and the formal dining room.

When I left my house to go to school or my one girlfriend's house, I felt a slight sense of relief, but I was generally a burdened child. I spent many happy times playing with my three sisters growing up. We didn't have many toys but we didn't need them. We played dress up and many make-believe games in the basement and outside in our yard. The yard had a gorgeous apple tree and an artificial cherry tree with beautiful pink blossoms that carpeted the lawn each May. My sisters and I played bride and groom, making ourselves gowns from blankets. We put the blossoms in our hair and on the carpet. One of my favorite make believe games was playing school. We also played house, pretending we were the moms. Of course, our doll was the baby, and we had a doll carriage we pushed around. We spent many hours playing in this way and reading books. My mom played with us when there was a thunderstorm and the power went out. We played cards around that kitchen table with a candle burning. My dad played with us on Sunday evenings; my sisters and I called it bat and ball. We played in the backyard after Sunday night supper as dinner was always at noon on that day. We shared many good times despite my inner turmoil. But my inner turmoil was there as I grew. My food addiction helped keep the feelings manageable. Or hidden. Or disguised.

I was confused about my home and family. At times there seemed to be happiness and open activity, while at others there seemed to be such oppressiveness and fear. Control. Either - or. Black and white. Which was it I wondered. I never considered that perhaps it could be both.

My fear told me I was involved with the problems and unhappiness in our family, but it made sure I did not ask. I didn't think I wanted to know the answers because I was afraid I couldn't handle them. Instead, I kept silent and continued to stuff my feelings and hide my lunches. Despite doing well in grammar school and high school, I felt insecure and fearful. I went off to college, looking like a success to my family and to others, but inwardly I thought and felt I was a failure as a person. I was in a horrible place emotionally but even at this age I was too afraid of being rejected, criticized or judged. I knew I was too fragile, so I listened to the lies my fear told me. Food was no longer effective even though I was addicted to the routine. So I sought an alternative. It was too easy to find.

CHAPTER 3

A NEWFOUND FRIEND

*M*y first day of college, I felt like I had entered an exciting new world. After I said goodbye to my parents, I went to the college quad for the freshman get together. The trees were deep green and had not yet started changing to their fall colors. The grass was a lush green and dotted with colorful blankets and folding chairs. Students were gathered in the center of the quad; laughing and talking as if they had known each other for years. I hurried over to join them. There was a beer keg in the center, although at the time I had no idea what it was or that I would come to love it. I just knew I wanted to join the other freshmen and belong.

"Hi, do you want a beer?" someone asked.

"Sure," I replied. I had that first one then another. I wanted to belong, and I thought everyone was drinking. I know today that was not the case. I loved how I felt when I drank that beer. I didn't particularly like the taste, but I liked how I felt afterwards. I felt freer to speak and meet new people. I was less conscious about myself. I felt less afraid. What a relief that was! Without realizing it, I was back in line for another drink with my twelve-ounce plastic cup. I lost track of how many refills I had that day. Whatever magic this beer had, I wanted it. That was the beginning of my short drinking career. I did not drink every day I was in college, but when I did, I enjoyed myself.

While orienting myself to college life, my parents' home was intentionally set on fire. Part of our home was destroyed and my parents and two younger sisters had to live in a trailer for several months while our home was rebuilt. I was untouched by this trauma since I was not home at the time. More importantly, I was so detached from myself and my feelings I could no longer feel an appropriate response to the tragedy, nor could I allow myself to express my feelings to anyone. In my mind, the timing of my introduction to alcohol could not have been better. It enabled me to further separate myself from my feelings in a way that denying food had failed to do.

Several years after graduating from college there was nothing social about my drinking. I had a good job, but when I was alone I drank to block out reality and ignore the pain I felt when I was sober. Drinking was no longer a choice for me. I needed to drink. I drank to numb my feelings, the same feelings I tried to get rid of with food. I felt empty inside. I felt as if I had no identity or sense of who I was, no sense of self. As a child, I thought my dad would or should give this to me. Now, as an adult, I was not only still that lost child, I was now an alcoholic who needed to drink to survive. The alcohol no longer numbed my painful feelings. My life revolved around trying not to drink. I found myself drinking despite not wanting to drink, and then hating myself more each day because I broke my promise to myself.

I only ate what I needed in order to survive. My food intake consisted of oatmeal for breakfast, an eight-ounce container of low-fat yogurt with an apple for lunch, and a large bowl of hot air popcorn for dinner. Some nights I would allow myself a second bowl of popcorn. This was accompanied with two to three light beers, one hundred calories each. I easily became drunk on three beers because my food intake was so restricted.

My world had become extremely small. I lived alone. I worked, came home, drank, then went to bed.

I tried to stop drinking on my own for two weeks but I couldn't stop. I became desperate. My life seemed hopeless. I felt like I was a bad person. I knew I had become someone I was not meant to be. I was full of fear and self-doubt. These feelings were familiar ones that I had lived with most of my life, but now they were magnified. The self-hate, the loneliness, and the despair I felt overwhelmed me. I thought, "I will be twenty-nine tomorrow but I have nothing left to live for. I can't stop drinking. There's no point in going on. I am going to kill myself." These thoughts scared me enough to reach out and tell a longtime friend, "I think I have a problem with drinking." Fortunately, that friend told me, "You do not have to go through this alone. There is a recovery group you can attend."

I began going to this group and I continue to attend today. While there I learned about my disease of alcoholism. I learned to take responsibility for my disease and my actions. I learned how to live one day at a time without a drink. Today I know that I have been given a daily reprieve from drinking based on my spiritual condition. I need to surrender my alcoholism to God on a daily basis. My recovery from alcoholism started me on a new and difficult journey. When I went to my first meeting I felt like I was home. I heard, "Welcome. It's good to see you here." For the first time, I felt like others truly understood me. I began to make friends, and felt I had finally met people I could share my problems with who would not judge or ridicule me. I came to understand that I drank to avoid facing my deep-seated insecurity and fears which drove my thoughts and behaviors: my fear of not fitting in with others; my fear of not having enough food or money or a job; my fear of confrontation; my fear of rejection or abandonment; my fear of losing what I had; my fear of what people thought of me; my fear of not being good enough; my fear of not being loved or lovable, which to me was one of the worst feelings of all.

Drinking initially allowed me to suppress these fears and emptiness inside of me. Now I had a program of recovery and a higher power to ask for help. Living sober, I had to learn to handle my fears and feelings in a more positive way. This would be a life-long process.

I asked God to help me stay away from a drink each morning and thanked Him at night. I tried to turn my will over to Him. I had a problem; I knew I was afraid of God. I did not trust that God cared for me or about me. I listened to others speak about a caring God, and I wanted to believe that God would help me, but the shame and guilt I felt convinced me that God wanted to punish me. As time passed I started becoming open to the idea of a loving God. That was as far as my fear allowed me to go. But that was enough. That was all God needed.

I felt like my life had turned around when I became sober. I began experiencing the joys of life with my husband and Emily. I was not naïve; I knew I had a lot of work to do. I had a spiritual program of recovery and God to help me and keep me sober one day at a time. This was a new way of living and that was truly what it was and is today — a new way and approach to life.

No one was more startled than I was when I became severely depressed after Sarah was born. I had tasted the sunshine after these initial years of sobriety. I felt like it was stolen from me. I fell headfirst into severe postpartum depression along with its terrifying companions including anxiety, severe sleep disturbances, suicidal thoughts, mood disturbances, an inability to concentrate, and irritability.

At the end of my drinking, I wanted to end my life. I briefly thought about it, and that scared me enough to ask for help. That was the grace of God to me. Now I was sober and I had so much in my life; but I found myself in a darker and bleaker place than where I was when I was at my lowest place drinking. How had this happened? How could I answer this? What could I possible say? I felt like a cruel joke had just been played on me. My dark and negative thoughts began to spiral out of control and were picking up momentum. I knew from my past experiences with drinking how bleak and destructive my own thinking could be. I couldn't worry about how I ended up here, at least not now. I was conscious of one thought, "I need help." I didn't need to speak this aloud. It was evident to my husband that I was ill. I needed a therapist and a psychiatrist. It was not easy or something I wanted to do. There was always a part of me that resisted reaching out for help, a part of me that thought I didn't need help or that I didn't matter.

My question became, "Was I willing to walk through my fears for my daughters and my husband?" I knew at the beginning that I wasn't willing to walk for myself. I felt like all the life had been sucked out of me like a deflated balloon. I had no way to pick myself up, and was forced to allow others to help me. It was this or I was headed for further destruction.

CHAPTER 4

SURVIVING THE SHOCK

I don't know if it was a blessing or a curse, but there are parts of these years I do not remember. I was told my memory loss, now considered permanent, was the result of the twenty electroconvulsive shock (ECT) treatments I received early in my treatment. I recall going as an outpatient for the last four or five treatments. According to my husband, only the initial treatments seemed to have any kind of positive result. Somewhere in the course of the treatments I had a very adverse response. My depression and overall mental stability became worse than when I first began the treatments. Despite our concerns, my psychiatrist stated it was necessary to complete the series of treatments and assured us my adverse response was nothing to worry about.

The entire process traumatized me. My husband had been asked to go home. I laid in the prep-op ward with an eggshell colored curtain surrounding me. Each time I was asked, "When was the last time you ate, when was the last time you drank, what medications are you taking" while the nurses prepared me for my treatment.

They spoke to one another, "She doesn't have good veins, she has valves in her veins, we will have to use her hand again for the IV. This won't be easy."

I closed my eyes and tried to keep from squirming as they poked and prodded, trying to insert the IV.

"I think I found one. Look, the IV is running clear. That was easier than I thought it would be this week."

No one was more relieved than I was when that IV was inserted.

As they left my side, I felt I was endlessly waiting to be taken into that sterile, cold surgical room where my brain would be "shocked" another time. I remembered thinking *what am I hoping for anyway?* At that point my hope had been to survive that shock treatment and go home to my family. I could see no further than that. I had no other dreams. My illness had stolen them from me this early in my journey.

While I waited, I envisioned the horror of what awaited me on the other side of those double doors and curtain. I shuddered to myself when I heard the footsteps of the orderly as he approached my stretcher to push me into the long narrow corridor that led to the operating room. We waited there in silence for my turn. I thought to myself, *what could possibly be an appropriate thing to say to me?* I thought of *Good Luck,* but even I knew I needed more than luck. I was left alone with my thoughts.

I was frozen with fear as I envisioned the scene which would soon unfold: a surgical assistant will hook me up to a heart monitor while another will place a blood pressure cuff around my upper arm. Following this, another medical assistant will attempt to place an oxygen mask over my mouth. This was one of the most terrifying moments for me because I'm claustrophobic. As soon as I saw that mask coming towards my face I wanted to jump off the stretcher and shove the assistant's hand away. Since my arms were immobilized from the cuffs and tubes I couldn't do this, but the thought remained. I begged each time, "Do you have to put that mask on my face and mouth? I feel like I will die when you do that. Isn't there some other way?" Most of the time we reached a compromise. They waited to place the mask over my mouth until after the anesthesia started to work. So sometime between my counting backward from ten to one the mask made its way onto my mouth. Once the anesthesia was administered I was less aware but I was not completely put to sleep. I remembered hearing the doctors and assistant's voices in the background as I counted "three, two, one." I felt jolts to my head, a sensation I cannot forget. This would be repeated perhaps three times. The entire process was over quickly once the actual "shocks" were administered. The process and side effects remain.

I focused on the details of the oxygen mask. I was horrified at the thought of the entire process, wondering what was to become of me. I thought to myself, *shouldn't this be written down in my chart somewhere?* The ECT treatments were horrific enough. I thought the rest of the process could be more personal. This detail was important to me since I was there alone. I was in the hospital for my 15th or 16th ECT treatment and was severely depressed. I was scared. My brain was being shocked. What had become of me?

As I recovered from the anesthesia, I was returned to the recovery ward. When I awoke out of my stupor I was hooked up to machines that took my vital signs. A nurse came over and asked, "How are you feeling?" I asked myself the same question. Disappointed yet again, but not surprised, I said "I don't feel any different." She wrote some notes in my chart and asked me in a cheery voice, "Would you like cranberry or apple juice today, saltines or graham crackers?" She called my husband and told him to come and get me in an hour or two; scheduled my next ECT appointment; and told me my psychiatrist would get the results of today's treatment within the next twenty-four hours. When my husband arrived she told me to enjoy the rest of my day. I silently thought to myself, *Yeah, right, enjoy the rest of my day. Easy for you to say.*

Even though I can only recall four or five treatments, the impact they made on me will forever be etched in my memory. As I wrote about them, my heart sped up. I don't relive these moments too often. Truthfully, I never think about these moments. I did now because my story would not be complete without them. Why would I think about them? They were absolutely terrifying. I felt alone and lost. I certainly didn't feel like a woman or lovable or lovely. I had lost my dignity. I had lost myself. Despite the assurance given to us with each horrible treatment that I would be less depressed, the ECT treatments were not successful. If anything, I was more depressed and anxious than before I started.

For years, I blamed the psychiatrist for these failed treatments and for my permanent memory loss. After many years and much thought I have come to realize several things. One is that treating depression is complicated. Although there was a treatment protocol, it is not an exact science. Many different factors influence treatment, and it often takes time. I was severely depressed. It was this psychiatrist's professional opinion that the ECT treatments would help me. Secondly, my husband was often part of my treatment decisions. We both needed to trust the psychiatrist's judgment.

I also vividly recall the "One Way" sign in the hallway whenever I was wheeled into the operating room. I asked myself, *Am I coming back, what happens if something goes wrong when they are shocking my brain?* It was not easy for me to talk to my therapist or confide in my husband about my fears. I had many of them churning around in my mind during this time. These fears added to my depression. I left the ECT treatment series several months later a changed person, and not for the better. I couldn't understand how that could be possible.

My fears were real. Perhaps the horror of what I had just experienced and my disappointment motivated me to keep going to my therapy sessions and to put words to the terror I was experiencing and living with daily. Perhaps the failed ECT treatments were a blessing in disguise. Although I did not look at it this way at the time, looking back, perhaps the horrible reality of those failed treatments opened my eyes to the desperateness of my situation. If I was to recover, I would need to be as aggressive about my treatment as this illness was about trying to destroy me. Fear kept me immobilized most of my life and controlled the poor choices I often made. Now I was given the opportunity to make better choices. Perhaps my fear could be turned into an asset and used for my good, but this would take a great deal of hard work, sacrifice, time, commitment, and patience, along with courage, honesty and love - most of which I did not think I had. I would have to learn what love really meant. I was given the choice to find out the difference between fear controlling my life and love controlling my choices. This was to be quite a journey, but one I needed to take. I was in a desperate place. I became willing to take some risks. Much was at stake.

CHAPTER 5

HIDDEN CONFLICTS

*W*ere there subtle signs and changes early on that I was not aware of? I believe the initial stressor for me was the birth of our first daughter, Emily, two years earlier. I had difficulty handling some of the natural changes that came with pregnancy.

When I was pregnant, I ate healthily and gained the appropriate amount of weight. In the back of my mind, though, each time the nurse weighed me, I thought, what if I gained too much weight? I still thought my worth as a person came from how well I controlled my weight.

I also felt very strongly about the kind of mother I wanted to be and needed to be, both for Emily and myself. Perhaps I was obsessed with it. I read scores of books on child rearing.

Conflicts about parenting styles from my own childhood began slowly stirring inside of me. These buried conflicts were hidden from my consciousness; hidden so deeply I had hoped they were buried forever. I was not yet aware of the influence these memories had upon me. All I knew was that I was committed to being the mother I hoped to be. I took parenting very seriously.

I was in conflict about childrearing with my husband. I had my own ideas as well as ones from the books I had read, and of course, Stephen had his own ideas. I believed I would parent the way I was parented unless I made a conscious effort to do things differently. Stephen and I wanted to learn how to be good parents, and with much effort we managed to develop our own style, which was a mixture of both our parents' influence and our own beliefs, such as giving choices where appropriate, emphasizing the positive, allowing mistakes to occur, allowing for individuality, and teaching right from wrong. Stephen and I spent as much time as possible with Emily, and when she was about four months old I went back to working part-time.

We adjusted slowly to life with Emily, along with all the new joys and fears and feelings of inadequacies that come with being new parents, along with juggling new schedules and sleepless nights. Neither Stephen nor I were big photographers, and this too changed as we started snapping photo after photo of Emily doing this and that for the first time such as trying to capture her first smile or her first step.

We were overjoyed when, a little over a year later, we learned that I was pregnant with our second child. Once Sarah was born my memory of events became sketchy and my mood took a drastic turn for the worse.

Can I pinpoint the exact moment? No, I cannot, because the entire year after Sarah was born is essentially grayed out to me. That is the only way I can describe it. All the emotional conflicts that stirred up in me with raising Emily were magnified with a second child. My fear of not being good enough returned to haunt me with a vengeance. I felt insecure as a mother, even though Sarah was our second child and I had some experience as a mother. I felt inadequate at handling Emily as a toddler, and I had a great deal of difficulty saying no to her. Each time I did I felt guilty, thinking I was a bad person.

I began to have trouble sleeping as my mind raced from anxieties about handling daily activities; I had difficulty interacting with my husband and making decisions with him because I was afraid of making mistakes with our daughters. We seemed to be in constant conflict. I seemed to have lost all the confidence and self-respect I had developed since becoming sober. I began to doubt my decisions, and started to feel uncomfortable with myself again; a feeling I remembered having most of my life.

Even though I was so happy to have Sarah and I loved her dearly, I think my fears and insecurities were too much. I now had a two-year-old daughter and a newborn. I had all these inner conflicts stirring inside of me. I never recovered from Sarah's birth. I went into the hospital one woman and came out a changed woman. How had this happened? I believe things were changing on many different levels. I think it was a combination of physical, emotional, and possibly spiritual factors. Chemical levels in the brain added to my postpartum depression as well as a possible genetic predisposition. I believe my emotional background also contributed. One thing is certain, if it did not contribute to the depression, it definitely complicated it and my recovery.

Despite my best efforts and intentions, I could not control my depression. I was suffering from a serious illness. I loved my family, but suddenly and without warning, my world came crashing down not only upon me, but upon my family.

Nothing on the outside appeared to have changed, yet everything on the inside changed for me. How did I survive that time? What got me through those endless black days and even darker nights? I had no idea at that time. Looking back now, I can see the hand of God was on me each and every moment, although I didn't know it and I certainly couldn't feel Him. How could I? I seemed to be incapable of feeling anything but the darkest emotions including despair, hopelessness, loneliness, and confusion. I was isolated in my own world where I had no dreams, no hope, and the worst for me - at times I had no desire to keep on living.

As hard as it is to write these words, I must, because it is my truth. I tried to end my life numerous times. In my mind and in my heart, I saw no reason to go on. Yes, I could rationalize I had two young daughters and a husband who not only needed me but loved me. I knew deep in my heart and soul that I loved them, but I truly felt incapable of being loved. I can't explain it, but even though people would say the words "I love you" to me they rolled off me. They were unable to penetrate my mind, never coming close to my heart. I genuinely felt and believed that I was unlovable. This was my major struggle; my heart allowed me to take a step forward but then my fear stepped in and told me to pull back. "What do you think you are doing, no one can love you, you are unlovable."

I wasn't capable of accepting love. I could accept it superficially, but when love penetrated into a deeper level something blocked me. I pushed people away, especially the very ones I loved and who loved me. This needed to change. I was incapable of accepting much in my life that was good. Now I was severely depressed at this most blessed time in my life. I didn't want this to be, yet here I am with all of these dark feelings stirring up inside of me and I found myself unable to control them. They are in control of me. Despite this, I can see my adorable daughters who are just babies and hear them say "I love you mommy," and something is different in me when they say those words to me. Something inside of me won't allow me to ignore their words of love for me. I love them too much. Their voices penetrate my heart, and so I let them in. A slight crack in the wall protecting my heart begins to appear. It is as if their voices soften the edges of my heart each time they speak or call out to me, "Read us a bedtime story." Their voices hold a special key to my heart. They enter in where no one else has gone. They are safe. I call it the mother/daughter bond of love. I am their mother and I want to be there for them, yet I remain submerged in the deep undercurrent of the ocean that stays with me wherever I go. How can I possibly break through it? I want to, but I do not have the strength. Many times I do not even feel like I can do it. Yet there must be some way.

I hear my babies' voices. I hold them and look into their blue eyes. I love them so much, yet this darkness is holding me back, refusing to let go. I am willing to try. I am willing to walk. I hear them crying in the night for their mom. I get out of bed and hold them. I comfort and feed them until they go back to sleep. I can't fall back asleep but that is okay. I look at them sleeping. They are so peaceful. I sing them a lullaby as I try to remember back to a time when I felt peaceful and safe, but I cannot. I sit for hours and watch them sleep. I am here for them in case they cry or need to eat during the night or have a nightmare. I try to imagine what they dream about. My dream was to be the best mother I could be to Emily and Sarah. Was that just a dream? Could it be more; could it be a hope? I sit with this thought in my mind. What will happen to our daughters? What will happen to my husband, our marriage, and ultimately, our life?

It is almost as if my daughters are able to love me from the inside out, they are able to enter into a special place in my heart where no one else has been. Others try to love me from the outside in. It is as if my children are looking at me with different eyes; eyes from their heart, innocent eyes, and they see me differently then I see myself. They see me as their mom, not seeing the mistakes I have made or my fears or insecurities; all they see is the love I have for them. They see how much I want to protect them and provide for them. They feel my heart that beat against them when they were in my womb. They know me intimately from the food they were fed. When they drank from my breast we shared a tender and intimate time. We are connected in a most intimate way. Our love for one another is as pure as love can be. They are untarnished by this world even though I am so depressed. My little daughters love me just as I am. What a gift and blessing. I crave the time I spend with them. Even though I often crawl through the day, I try my best to be there for them. I may not have showered and my hair may be a mess, but I feed and bathe my daughters. My husband and I put them to bed. I sing to them. Their dad and I read them bedtime stories. I take both girls for walks, pushing them in a double stroller; and sometimes Stephen and I take them to a park. I want Sarah to have the best food possible so I spend time pumping breast milk so she can have it during the times when we are not together, the same as I did for Emily.

I seem to do things as if I am in a daze, but somehow I manage to do them. Unconsciously I knew my daughters needed me, and this helped me do all that I could for them. Despite everything else that was happening with me emotionally, a part of me connected with Emily and Sarah. The love we had for one another was a vital connection; a source of motivation and strength for me. As they grew, my hopes began to grow with them, not only for them, but eventually for myself. Without realizing the precious gift they gave me, my daughters urged me to recover simply by their presence and unconditional love for me. By their ability to live life they were teaching me how to live life again, with them alongside of me.

I did not know how I would get through this time or what would happen to my family, but I knew that I must not give up.

I couldn't lay in bed all day. I wasn't the mother I hoped to be to our daughters, or the wife I once was to Stephen, but I was not going to let this disease rob me without a fight. Wasn't their love worth so much more than whatever has overtaken me? Taking me was one thing, but taking my daughters was something else entirely. I was a mother. The connection that formed between each daughter and myself, beginning with conception and growing stronger each day as they grew in my womb, was an essential bond; mother to child; child to mother; and it was this basic unconditional love connection that began motivating me to push through my darkness.

The moment each daughter was born had been such a miracle for Stephen and me. An extension of our love yet so much more. These infants were so beautiful; so precious and pure, untouched by life, yet with much opportunity for life and love. So full of love and willing to trust and to be loved, to be held. Dependent on us for their every need and to keep them safe; to protect them from the harshness of life for as long as possible. I heard and replayed their cry when they were born in my mind and I thought of it as a call proclaiming their arrival into this world and into our family; a shout of joy that their time of incubation in my womb was over. They were ready for life. They were eager. They hoped life was ready for them! Sometimes I had not been able to remember clearly in my mind why I mustn't give in to my illness, but I think that the piece of my heart that was connected remembered.

I place my daughters' voices in my mind, hoping I will be able to remember them when I need to. There is something extremely precious and loving and special about their voices. They are beginning their lives and we have the opportunity to love them and teach them about life, love and themselves. A gift too precious to take lightly. I am afraid to make mistakes with them, instead look at what has already happened. I can no longer allow my fear to get in my way. I will continue to put one foot in front of the other. That is all I can do. I cannot let my fear of making mistakes keep me from trying to get better or from letting me try to be the mother I want to be. I am no longer alone. I now have help. It is up to me to take it. I was thrown a life preserver when the storm overtook me. I felt I was drowning out at sea, but my husband knew something was wrong with me. It was my choice to take the help offered. All I had was the moment; thank goodness, as the moment was all I could handle. One step at a time, one fear at a time. If I looked too far ahead all I could see was the endless ocean with worry and unending sadness; and if I dared look behind me, I saw all sorts of regrets and poor choices and missed opportunities and fear. So I tried to stay in the moment, hanging on to the life preserver that was thrown to me. What I realized, however, was that once I grabbed onto it and utilized it, it buoyed me up to a form of safety.

My treatment team consisted of my psychiatrist and psychotherapist. I needed both medication and therapy. My depression was complicated and severe. My illness did not respond positively to the series of ECT treatments. I had been discouraged.

CHAPTER 6

BUILDING A TRUST RELATIONSHIP

*P*erhaps the biggest fear I carried throughout my life was, "Am I unlovable?" I had been too scared to find out the answer because if I was, what did that mean about me? What would I do about it? Could I do anything? I had been asking myself these questions for a long time in different ways, but I never realized or admitted it. As far back as I could remember, I believed I was unlovable. I never felt good enough. I felt like there was no one I could trust. I felt like I was born with a hole in my soul. Was this possible? Was I born so defective that anything and everything I tried would never be enough to fill that hole? Was it possible that my parents, who loved me since birth, never told me what was wrong with me? What IS really wrong with me? Where did these thoughts and feelings come from? Am I so defective and unlovable that I cannot be fixed, and even worse, never be loved?

I never wanted to face the answer to these questions because I believed I knew the answer, and that because I thought and felt a certain way, these things were true. I never came out of hiding long enough to discover the answers to my questions. My fear was too strong. I was too afraid what I thought and felt would be true - my fears would be facts. How could I live with that? Instead, I chose to live with my secret fears rather than risk exposure to my truth, which I feared would be far worse. Little did I know the damage my secret fears were doing to me all of my life. By choosing to stay in my self-imposed prison of fear and secrecy, I was traveling down a dark road of poor choices such as unrealized dreams, unfulfilled relationships, and often loneliness; a deep sense of inadequacy at my profession or anything else I tried to achieve, a cycle of empty addictions to try to fill the void in my heart, mind, and soul, and a deep sense of longing for fulfillment and connection I could never seem to find, regardless of where I looked.

This brought me to my present journey of truth. My world became so dark with deep, desperate depression that my eyes couldn't see where my right foot ended and my left foot began. Even worse, at times I couldn't see where I began and my daughters started. My darkness threatened to overtake me and my new life. It was at these moments fear like I had never experienced entered my heart. I was now connected to my daughters as only a mother and child can be. The blurring of that line started to terrify me. As a mother, I knew I could not afford to take my daughters with me into the depths of this horrendous disease that wanted me dead. In the grips of my disease, it constantly lied to me. I believed my disease was counting on me to withdraw. Fortunately, I connected with my therapist, Dr. Donald McNeil, who was also a psychologist. A friend Stephen and I knew recommended him to us. He became like a lifeline to me, a safe port in the storm, a light in the darkness; the grace of God working mightily through this ordinary yet special man.

Fear motivated me to reach out. Deep down I knew that my daughters needed to be apart from me. We were connected by a very special bond but we were also separate people. My boundaries were difficult to discern at times. I had a strong sense, even before Emily was born, that each child needed to be nurtured and encouraged to be themselves. I needed to nurture them but I could not afford to pass on to them the horrible feeling of not being good enough that tormented me most of my life. I wanted so much more for my daughters. My desire, or dare I call it, love for them, mobilized me to pick up my feet and move through my painful darkness, to do what I could never do before in my life. Just as I was able to bear the pain of childbirth, knowing it would one day end, I knew I needed to get through my fear of reaching out to others. At this point it was important for me to be willing to try.

My fear shouted out to me, "It is not safe to trust! BE CAREFUL! What will people think of you? What if this therapist doesn't keep your confidence?" Thoughts similar to these ran through my mind all throughout my life, but they intensified now and came at me in a relentless wave like a creeping artillery barrage. My mother's voice echoed loudly in my mind, "What happens in this house stays in this house." How could I ignore her voice? The time had come for me to make some choices. This time it would be MY choice as I was now the mother and not the child. I was the wife and not the adolescent, I was a 38-year-old sober, depressed woman, no longer the 12-year-old frightened child hiding her lunches in the bedroom closet. I was responsible for my choices, not my parents; not even my husband, although I needed his advice many times. Others could help but I needed to walk through each painful and lonely dark moment alone. Only I could do what was needed. I desperately needed help but I always refused it. That had been one of my major mistakes in life. I made poor choices when it came to trusting others. Would I repeat that mistake now at this crucial time? I had an appointment with Dr. McNeil later today. Would I keep this appointment? Or would I run away, as I had done in the past?

I showed up at my therapist's office with my husband. I was frightened yet determined to meet my therapist. I wasn't sure what I had to say, or perhaps I was afraid of what I would say. I almost didn't care. I was desperate. The torment I was living was too much for me to endure any longer.

Although some of my earliest therapy sessions were blurred due to my memory loss from my ECT treatments, these are the earliest ones I remember. There were sessions when I was so distraught that Stephen needed to drive me home.

Stephen and I sat in the waiting room. I was confused as I scanned this room. The walls were painted a moss green, causing my fears to stir and rise up inside of me. I began to feel like the walls were closing in on me. I thought to myself, "Oh no, this is the same color as the living room and dining room walls at my house growing up. I hated this color." It was almost as if the walls were taunting me, which caused me to feel a nearly uncontrollable urge to jump up and run out the door.

The memories began flooding back to the forefront of my mind. I recalled the times I asked my mother if we could change the color of the walls and her consistent no response. I recalled how I thought things would never change. I had learned not to talk back to my mother for there was no changing her mind once it was made up. If I started to voice my opinion, I would go too far and start to argue my point, causing me to pay the price. I had paid once too often, and I could feel the sting of my mother's hand across my face and see the red imprint of her hand spreading across my cheek. Her words echoed in my mind, "You will do what I say. You don't talk back to your mother." I learned to superficially submit to my mother out of fear. I began to keep much hidden. My fear reawakened as I sat in this waiting room.

Before the walls could capture me, Dr. McNeil came out of his office and extended his hand in greeting. I felt stuck, with nowhere to go but his office. The one-way sign from those dreadful ECT treatments flashed in my mind like a neon sign. Despite my misgivings, I followed Dr. McNeil into his office and ignored my churning stomach. Once in his office I again focused on my surroundings. I could barely concentrate on the conversation, being preoccupied with looking at the sparsely decorated office. I looked at the comfortable green chair and a quilted wall hanging behind Dr. McNeil's desk. I noticed he did not sit behind his desk but off to the side. Interesting, I thought to myself. No dividers. But it was the plants which caught my attention. They seemed to be everywhere. They looked healthy, and what caught my eye was the variety of green colors, deep forest green, springtime leaf green, clover green, and mint green, which reminded me of mint chocolate chip ice-cream, which I ate in a cone in the summertime at the beach. As I focused on the plants, their vibrant colors seemed to come to life! It was as if they said to me:

"There is hope in this room. What you say here is important. You need to change and grow, and not be stagnant like those oppressive walls in the waiting room. You have become like those walls, blocking out the sunlight of your spirit because of your fear and what you have experienced in life. It is time for you to grow and trust again. It is time for your heart to expand. You can do that with this therapist. He is willing to help you. Are you willing to open yourself and your life and let him help you? You like to travel alone, but it won't work this time. Come here so you can become the woman and mother you want to be."

I tried to take in these words and absorb their meaning; but before I could, I felt a horrifying sensation go through my mind and body. The oppressive green walls of the waiting room triggered something in me. Today I believe that day God broke through the defenses of my darkness and shattered my heart and soul, exposing it to the world. He brought me to a place I needed to go.

My mind and emotions rewound. I returned back to my childhood days.

Isolated scenes flashed before my eyes as I tightly shut them. I saw myself swimming at the beach with my sisters, when suddenly it felt like I was drowning as my head sunk underwater. I opened my mouth, "Someone please help me, I'm drowning!" I cried as the salt water rushed in and gagged me. Then I instantly switched to another memory; this one involved an ice ball hitting my face while I waited for the school bus one winter morning while in grammar school. I pretended it didn't hurt while I cried silently to myself all day in school. Now I'm pulling up to the local donut shop drive-thru window after work. "I'd like one dozen donuts no chocolate ones, please, nothing to drink, thank you, boxed to go." I then drove into a corner of the parking lot where I ripped off the cover and devoured all the donuts in half an hour before rushing home to vomit as my anorexia had turned to bulimia in my attempt to stuff my emerging emotions. This collage of memories was too much for me to handle. I opened my eyes and the walls swirled before me in a kaleidoscope of greens. I barely heard Dr. McNeil's voice in the background, "Marcia, can you hear me?"

He must be speaking to Stephen, I thought. I did not respond. Instead, I broke down, and cried, but not before an image of my dad and me at a cottage I didn't recognize flashed before my eyes. Our faces were distorted. A haze began enveloping my body as FEAR overtook me.

"NO! NO! NO!" I shouted out loud to myself.

In the distant background I heard again, "Marcia, can you hear me? It's Dr. McNeil." Another voice interrupted this distant voice, "I'm sorry, Marcia."

Where did this voice come from?

I felt someone put their arms around me. It must have been Stephen. "Get away from me!" I shouted as I pushed him away. "Leave me alone, just leave me alone!"

I became uncontrollable and uncommunicative. I had lost touch with reality. I SNAPPED. I had no idea what happened.

I floated in and out of this state for several years. I was trapped in my own inner world, constantly reliving a darkness I dared not speak of. This added to my severe depression.

I went home a severely emotionally shattered woman. Another treatment for my depression which was supposed to help me seemed to harm me instead, just like all the others. Was I moving in the wrong direction? I had no idea what had happened to me. I seemed incapable of putting anything I thought or felt into words.

The waves continued to crash around me and over me, attempting to force me to the bottom. Before we left his office, Stephen scheduled another appointment for me. Despite what had happened, both of us sensed I needed to continue what we started. Perhaps both of us were scared and had no idea where else to turn.

CHAPTER 7

A LIFELINE

I continued to meet with Dr. McNeil. We had connected. He looked like an ordinary man. He had blond hair, green eyes. He usually wore a plaid sports coat, a pink or pale green buttoned down shirt and tan pants. I asked him, "Why don't you ever wear black pants?"

"My father was a minister and he always wore black. I am tired of that color so I choose to wear other colors."

I thought, *I'm tired of black too,* not referring to my clothes specifically. His word "choose" caught my attention. I did not feel like I had many choices in my life, especially now, but I was interested in what he had to offer. He wrote with a fountain pen and only used green ink. I was intrigued by both this therapist and his pen! "Green ink," I thought to myself? I hated red ink. It reminded me of all those corrected papers from grammar school bearing those awful stamps at the top, "You can do better, you know you can." Why these memories remained in my mind for all these years I had no idea, but I remembered them as if I just saw them yesterday. Whenever I thought long enough, I remembered the other papers I received with silver or gold colored stars, but these dimmed compared to the other more glaring messages. Apparently I did not carry the stars with me in the same way.

Dr. McNeil loved to read almost as much as I once used to. We hadn't read the same books, but I noticed his office had bookshelves filled with well-read books. I had not noticed these at first. We began to meet three times a week, at the same day and time as much as possible. This added structure and consistency to my unpredictable life. Although I was initially uncomfortable going to therapy, I found myself drawn to his office. I sensed good would come from my time here.

Dr. McNeil had been predictable at a time when I felt my life was unpredictable. I discovered that Dr. McNeil was not controlling, but instead interested in what I thought and how I felt. He asked questions and patiently waited for me to respond, honestly. He wasn't upset by anything I said. He was gentle and caring, and helped me in any way he could.

I remembered his kindness. I did not have a babysitter for Sarah during those early years. Emily went to a preschool for a few days during the week. Many times I brought Sarah with me to therapy where she sat on my lap and slept. As she grew, she stayed in the waiting room and colored, drew, read, and at times did somersaults. Dr. McNeil was never bothered by this young girl turning his waiting room into a playground. Instead, he smiled and took a sincere interest in her. "Sarah, what did you draw today? Can you tell me about your pretty picture? Where are you in the picture? Where is your mom?" he asked as Sarah proudly offered her drawing to him. His caring extended to my family as well as to me.

I wasn't too aware of what I shared during the first several years of therapy. I was severely impaired emotionally after the ECT treatments and the partial flashbacks I experienced that first therapy session. I don't think much of what I said made sense. However, something more important happened during this time. Dr. McNeil was getting to know me and I was getting to know a little about him. I learned he was a safe person and his office was a safe place for me, like a port in the midst of a storm. I didn't learn much about his life but I learned who he was. I learned he was gentle, caring, and was interested in my recovery. I learned he was passionate about life and love and healing. I discovered he was understanding and open. I learned all this and more about him because he revealed himself to me through our relationship. And by doing this I learned quite a bit about myself; one step at a time.

I came to learn I could trust him. I trusted him with my thoughts and feelings, and eventually with my heart and innermost secrets. My therapist became an extremely important person to me. Dr. McNeil was my therapist the entire time I was depressed. Many times, he knew me better than I knew myself. He heard and understood me, but more importantly, he was capable of going with me into the dark places my emotions had taken me. Although he went with me, he also knew how to leave. That was the important piece. He did not get stuck in those dark places, even though I was. He could go there with me but he could leave when he needed to. Our time together taught me coping skills and life skills, but most importantly, I believe Donald, as he eventually had me call him, taught me the value of relationships. The value of a true connection, true communication, and true exposure of self without fear of judgment.

Over sixteen years, we met many times and covered a great deal of territory; some over and over as I was a slow learner. He was patient. He was a comfort. He was the parent I was looking to become for my daughters. Perhaps he became the parent I had looked for all my life. I knew he gave freely and believed in my recovery. He was a skilled psychotherapist who frequently went beyond what he was required to do. I had been grateful for this. He allowed me to phone him whenever I needed, despite the time. I believe I am alive today because of the grace and caring of this man. He did not let other people's opinions stand in his way. He taught me much so that I could become the woman I am today. He taught me that love was more important than other people's opinions, and that love was more important than fear. He taught me to celebrate life and who I was. This lesson took me years to learn.

My feeling of being unlovable haunted me throughout my years in therapy. Dr. McNeil would ask, "What have you done that was so terrible? Tell me one thing."

I replied, "When I was in the sixth grade and sold snacks for recess I stole potato chips because I wanted them. I didn't have the money. I brought my snack from home."

Donald replied, "That happened years ago. Why do you think you can't let go of that guilt and that memory?"

"Because I was bad and no one ever found out. But I know what I did was wrong."

"You were eleven or twelve years old. Don't you think you could forgive yourself for doing that now? You did something which was wrong, but you aren't a bad person because you did that."

"I don't know how to forgive myself. I have no idea what you are talking about."

He said, "If Emily stole a quarter from your purse would you forgive her?"

"Of course I would forgive her," I said.

"Well," he said, "Think of forgiveness for yourself in the same way. Think of what you did when you were eleven or twelve. You are sorry. Forgive yourself. Let it go. It is taking up too much space in your mind and too much energy."

We started with simple things and went from there.

I began talking about my daily life with Donald, and my frustrations and fears. How would I cope? This was a start. Donald told me, "You are good enough." He repeated this to me almost every time I met with him throughout the years. I heard the words, but I looked at him blankly. He smiled kindly. I attempted a smile but a tear came out instead.

Could I relate to him or could he relate to me? Did it matter? I was drawn to him and his easy manner and contentment with life. His voice was quiet, reminding me of a calm ocean; a peaceful place I wanted to be. I was attracted to his manner and gentleness and overall love for life. I felt anxious and seemed to worry about everything. He nurtured me at a time when I needed to be nurtured. I had my own family to nurture. Diapers to change, breast milk to pump, snacks and meals to prepare, clothes to wash and fold, more clothes to wash and fold, dishes to wash, bedtime care, story time, snack time, bath time, nap time, feeding time, walk time, playtime. "What happened to our time, honey," Stephen asked as I distractedly searched for Emily's misplaced favorite striped white, blue and pink blanket as I walked around burping Sarah after feeding her. "You know my mom is willing to watch the girls tonight," Stephen continued, while I was not interested in going out with him or anyone, anywhere. I was too tired and distraught. All I could manage was to cry and cry some more. "How could he even *think about going* out? What was the matter with him?"

I discussed how difficult it was for me to handle these everyday demands of life for an inexperienced mother. I broke down and cried. I spoke about how I wanted to hide myself in the mound of dirty clothes I was staring at instead of putting them in the washing machine. That took too much effort, and energy I didn't have. I felt like a washed-out dish rag. Wrung out. My daughters' needs seemed to be constant, and so did my husband's at times. I was exhausted, but when I laid down I couldn't sleep. The negative thoughts in my head didn't stop. They cycled around like a storm, gathering intensity. l screamed, attempting to wake myself up, but to my horror I was awake. My reality was a living nightmare. I saw my daughters growing before my eyes. Sarah crawled, then took her first steps. Before I knew it, we celebrated her first birthday. "Make a wish Sarah and blow out the candles!" Emily soon began kindergarten. We celebrated the girls' birthdays together as they were three days apart. It seemed easier for all and especially for me to handle. One year my sister-in-law offered to make the cake as I was especially ill. Cookie Monster was the cake decoration that year. I didn't know if our daughters remembered that birthday but I did. My heart and soul felt like they ripped through my body as I was unable to make my own daughters their birthday cake. Perhaps they were too young to notice or care, but I felt devastated. It felt like one more loss or nail in my coffin; the coffin my disease tried to build for me.

Being able to put words to these feelings and thoughts was what tore down the walls of this coffin my depression was building to kill me. My disease wanted me to isolate. It wanted me to despair. It wanted me to ruminate in my negative thoughts and feelings. It did not want me to discuss them with someone else. Donald was a skilled psychologist who was familiar with the challenges of this disease. Still, this disease was relentless.

God's plan was to work through people, and he specifically worked through my therapist. When a session ended, he would say, "I will see you in three days. I'm looking forward to seeing you again."

I sensed he meant that. I felt like Donald understood me, and when he didn't, he made an effort to understand me. I felt like he was sitting beside me even though he sat across from me in his chair. I knew I could talk about anything with him, there were no topics or feelings which were off limits.

I began to see the world differently. I began to focus on shades of green. I began to see that much of my life was not black and white. What was inside of me was making me feel physically and emotionally ill that first day. I viewed the color green the way I saw it for a reason, a valid reason, although I did not know why. I needed to be gently nurtured for many years before I could look at the reasons. The flash that first day in therapy felt like a shark that had risen out of the deep ocean and threatened to attack me. I was terrified. I had already suffered severe postpartum depression. I could not handle the shark attack. I emotionally shut down for at least three years. I had periods of much distress and severe crying.

Donald seemed to ground me. Like the earth, and a tree with roots in the ground; he was connected to what was good and strong and living. He seemed stable and reliable while my world was upside down. I wanted what he had. I was attracted to what he offered without expectations and judgement. Yes, he expected me to show up to therapy and to try, but beyond that it seemed like he just wanted me to get better. The longer I knew him the more firmly grounded he seemed to be. As we shared, I learned I needed to be open and share what was on my heart and mind to create an open connection, a system through which communication and love and emotions could flow. Otherwise not much could be transferred. For this to happen I needed to start trusting Donald. I was afraid but I slowly opened up. His gentleness and openness allowed me to expose myself to someone else. Communication needed to freely flow both ways. This was vital for me and for my recovery. I needed to learn how to be in a healthy relationship, and he provided the tools for me to do it.

As I continued to meet with Donald, I felt like my life preserver had become a raft. Although I was still adrift in the deep ocean, I sensed I was no longer a lone castaway in my journey. Was this because I shared my life with my therapist, or perhaps the inner light burning within compelled me to push forward? Perhaps it was both, and they were interconnected. Although I was often unable to sense the presence of this light, I believed it was there. I needed to believe something was there besides this deep depression and darkness. How could I not? I was staring at my beautiful daughters who seemed so far away from me at times, yet other times I held them in my arms and sang to them. The contrast between darkness and light was so stark. I was confused. I felt desperate many times because I could not seem to bridge the distance between the two, at least not with any consistency. As time passed I clung to Donald and this inner spark for strength, courage, and eventually for direction and hope…

I was still out at sea, but at least now I was able to ride the waves and storms a little bit easier when they came. The raft could more easily remain afloat. It was more difficult to sink the raft than it was to sink the life preserver. I knew many times I hung on for dear life, but there were other times when I could let go and relax and allow the tide to take me where I needed to go. But I could not go to these places alone; they were too dangerous. I was not equipped. I never had been, and I still wasn't. With the help of my therapist, perhaps I would finally develop the tools I needed. The problem was, my fear and depression stood in the way. So I picked up my oar and began to row, one stroke at a time.

I rowed awkwardly at first, but I was willing to at least try. My arms tired easily, and I wanted to quit but Donald gently told me, "It's okay to stop and rest. Your family needs you. We'll continue next time." He treated me with the compassion I was unable to show myself. He said, "Marcia, stop beating yourself up. No one will treat you as badly as you treat yourself."

The relationship and security I felt with Donald was unlike anything I had ever experienced in my life. I craved it. Just like the dry ground soaks up the rain after a drought; my parched soul was soaking up the kindness and warmth that Donald offered me. It was as if I could not get enough at times. In some ways, I had been in my own forty-year drought. My heart had been closed by a fear of letting anyone get close to me. I initially let my husband in, but when I became depressed it became difficult for me to interact with Stephen. I felt different. My mood was too difficult to understand or explain. I no longer understood who I was. I wanted to think I was the same person I was when we met, but was I? I had no idea. I was too afraid to ask Stephen, so I withdrew even farther.

I needed to trust my therapist because there was no one else close to me I felt I could trust. I felt lost. Donald seemed like he would never hurt me if he could possibly help it. This was a wonderful comfort to me because I was dreadfully afraid of getting hurt again. When and how was I hurt in the first place? I couldn't seem to remember, but I sensed it was horrible. I didn't trust people, which caused me to withdraw into myself. At least with Donald I had a chance to establish a human connection and a chance to share what was going on in my mind and in my world. The fact that I had no idea what was happening didn't stop me from trying to interact with him. This showed how desperate I was to connect on the most basic level. He had something very precious to offer me, and I wanted it desperately. If I was honest with myself, I would have admitted that I needed it. I felt like I was scraping the bottom of the ocean floor, looking at the blackest of the earth's dirt. This was how ominous my whole mood became when I had the brightest of the sun's rays to hold in my arms; my newborn daughter and my two-year old daughter. What was the matter with me? I could not understand what was happening to me.

I felt drawn to Donald and to his office. At the time, I did not realize how important this would be for me. I was willing to go to therapy despite how difficult it was for me. My mother's words often echoed in my mind, but my own emotional storm spoke even louder to me. I was gradually able to hear Donald over the din of my mother's words, and my own voice finally started to emerge. Donald helped me to discern the voices of my disease from the rest. This was a process, and one that took time, years actually. But Donald was gentle, persistent, and patient, even when I was not. Being with him helped me to learn how important those qualities were. His gentleness helped break through the darkness of my disease like a light in a dark tunnel. At a time when life seemed so harsh and cruel to me; when I felt utterly defeated by life; when it seemed like all my hopes or dreams of being a good mother to my daughters were shattered; Donald was one of the gentlest and kindest men I had ever met. I remember his gentleness amidst the blackness and terror of my new world, and I recall his calm and steady voice against the noisy background that was the confusion of my own mind and turbulent emotions.

"You are a good mother to Emily and Sarah. They are fortunate to have you," he would say over and over. I desperately wanted to believe him, yet I had difficulty accepting love. Something life giving happened during our therapy sessions, despite the fact that I remained depressed and emotionally ill. His office became that safe harbor, lighting the way to safety when my world became so confusing and I felt defeated. I was able to see the light burning in his office and knew I would be welcome. Whenever I became desperate and lost hope, as I did numerous times, I remembered Donald and his caring and open invitation. His words, "It is good to see you" echoed in my mind, along with "You are not a bad person."

When I was distraught at home or had a particularly difficult time, I would close my eyes and try to focus on my breathing, slowly inhaling through my nose and exhaling through pursed lips. Sometimes this would bring my thoughts back to Sarah's delivery and my anxiety would increase rather than decrease. I would attempt to change my thoughts to the scene in Donald's office, picturing him sitting and relaxed across from me, listening intently as if I were the only person on his schedule for the day. What was more important for me than the image I could pull into my mind, were the feelings it evoked. I would feel a sense of comfort and safety, along with a sense that I was accepted and loved. These feelings, sometimes just weak embers, were enough to keep me focused for the moment or for the day. They gradually grew in intensity as our relationship strengthened, but at times my illness sought to destroy them.

That day I had a partial flashback I felt as if a shark had bitten me. The reality is that shark bit me a long time ago. The problem was I had not felt the depth of the sting and the pain of the bite until now because I was too busy running away from the pain and hurt. I was unaware of the damage that had been done and how the infection had spread. I also didn't realize I was responsible for taking care of the wound that required more than a simple band-aid. The damage was too great. I needed to see that my injury was a serious wound rather than just a moral issue. I was sick. I was not a bad person, and neither were many others in my life. My body, mind, spirit, heart, and soul had been infected by this wound. I needed treatment and care so I could look at life differently. Cleansing the wound would take much time, patience, pain, care, willingness, and LOVE.

Donald knew what we needed to do. Though he was a trained, skilled psychotherapist, he was also a compassionate human being. I suffered from severe depression and was a broken human being. I had no idea what Donald initially saw when he looked at me. All I knew was he treated me with respect, love and compassion. He taught me to treat myself and others the same way, as a priceless gift; a parent to a child, a friend to another friend, one human being to another; I was a child in many ways, and I found I needed to be, for I had much to learn about life and love and relationships.

Perhaps being a child wouldn't be so bad the second time around. I had been given the rare opportunity to have another chance. I didn't necessarily want to do this, but I sensed I had been allowed to travel this path for a reason. I had no idea what this reason was other than I wanted to love my daughters more fully.

I kept going to therapy and taking my medication; crying and getting out of bed in the morning to do the best I could, which didn't seem like much. I had no idea what my disease had in store for me, but I'm not sure I ever really knew what life had in store for me. I did know what my addictions had in store. When I was honest with myself I had to admit I didn't know how to live life. I had been full of fear. I was willing and desperate for help. I had much to live for despite my dark inner feelings that made my bright outer world seem so grey.

Donald listened even when I thought I had nothing to say. He had the wisdom to sit through all the silence, waiting for me to speak. Looking back, it was usually at those times that I had the most to say, but I was too afraid to put words to the pain I felt. Many times he would ask me some nonthreatening question, like "How were the girls this morning before you left?"

I would usually answer with my one-word response, "Fine," followed by "I have to go, I have nothing to say today."

Despite this scene being repeated over and over, something began to happen during these times. I knew I could leave but he simply said, "Are you sure you want to go, we have more time left." And nearly every time that was enough for me to stay. I felt like he actually wanted me there and I began to realize I wanted to be there too! Donald was not threatening to abandon me like so many others in my life had done. I was the one choosing to run. I gradually realized how strong my fear of abandonment was. Donald was not going anywhere. Feeling safe with him was perhaps the best feeling of all!

The process was exactly that, a process, and it wasn't easy by any means. We both worked at it. Sometimes it seemed like there was no progress at all. Or worse, it seemed as if I was moving backwards. As I looked back, despite my darkest thoughts and behaviors during this time that were counterproductive to life, I was getting out of bed each morning and caring for my family as best I could. I was meeting regularly with Donald for weeks, then months, then years. Our time together became much less silent. I began to share my true thoughts and feelings. I started with little things. He also taught me to begin trusting my own feelings in the sense that it is all right for me to have and experience them. Denying that I have feelings does not make them go away, it only suppresses them, forcing me to deal with them at some other, often inconvenient time. In the meantime, they still influence my thoughts and behavior in ways I am probably not even aware of. I also denied my feelings because I thought they made me a "bad" person or a "good" person to feel a certain way. I came to learn that this was not true. I also learned that my feelings are not facts and that my feelings can change, sometimes quickly. I needed to learn a lot about identifying and experiencing my feelings and then choosing whether or not to act upon them.

I began to realize how little I knew, other than experiencing the paralyzing effects or the destructiveness of my fear. The idea of having a choice in how I responded to my feelings was new to me, and I wanted to learn more about this. I didn't know if I understood this yet, but I was definitely interested.

My feelings help me feel alive and to experience the joys, sorrows, and pleasures of life. I learned this from my own experiences. But now I had come to a place where I was overcome by a cycle of the darkest emotions imaginable. It was as if my mind and heart refused to accept anything except the darkest and blackest feelings of despair and hopelessness, anxiety and fear. These thoughts and feelings went with me wherever I went. When I awoke in the morning and lifted my head off the pillow there was my depressed thinking, *"Oh no, how will I ever get through another day feeling like this? God please help me."* When I struggled to help my daughters get dressed for school and helped them brush their hair, my insecurities and fears were right there in front of me as I looked at them and thought, *"I wish I knew how to fix their hair better, Emily keeps asking me to put her hair in a French braid, but no matter how hard I try, it never comes out well. Do their clothes match? I hope they look alright. I think they look wonderful, but what do I know? I am only their mother and look at me."*

But they seemed happy and I let them pick out their outfits. I allowed them to pick what they wanted to wear. It's not as if they're wearing pajamas. They were wearing appropriate clothes. And we kissed each other goodbye.

When I attempted to do the grocery shopping for our family, the dark thoughts were there, as if they were staring back at me through the frozen food case, knowing every detail of my depressed life. While I was waiting in the checkout line my anxiety and fear of what people thought of me and of how I was going to get home without having a panic attack stood right there with me. When my daughters came home from school, eager to share their day, my anxieties and fear were there; when we were sitting at the dinner table, eating grilled cheese sandwiches for the third time in a week because this was Emily's favorite meal, they were eating with us; when I was reading to Emily and Sarah before bed, they stared at me through the pages of I'll Love You To The Moon and Back. When Stephen and I were trying to talk about our day like a typical married couple, despite both of us knowing in our hearts we were not, they sat down beside us; when I laid my head down on my pillow at the end of the day, eighteen hours after I had gotten up that morning, knowing I will be unable to fall asleep again, these same dark and anxious feelings were my constant companions.

It was as if they had become my new identity, having slipped over my old one. I found myself wearing them like a costume to a Halloween party, except the party was over months ago and my costume seemed painted on me with permanent paint. There was no way for me to remove the overwhelming feelings of extreme sadness, anxiety and panic that had brought me to despair at times. They seemed to have grown over my skin and become like a new layer covering me in a cocoon. I didn't like and I didn't want these feelings, but I was stuck with them. Like it or not, I was an adult now and I was responsible to make better decisions in my life. I did not have to like the circumstances but I did have to deal with them. I discussed these issues with Donald. He told me, "You have choices and are responsible for the choices you make in your life. You are no longer a child."

Asking people for help opened up a huge door for me. I was still uncomfortable with this option, but the more I did it the easier it became. Sometimes it wasn't easy to access help, but at other times, when I needed help, I received loving responses that touched my heart and soul. Donald often asked me, "What do you need?" I would be extremely confused. He taught me to identify my needs, which made it easier to ask for help. Donald became like a life teacher to me. I practiced the skills I was learning about relationships and living life with him, and I practiced these in my life. Donald's office became like a classroom for me with room to experiment, practice and take risks, because there was acceptance, encouragement and nurturance. I was encouraged to grow despite mistakes and setbacks. This took much time and care. Patience. LOVE. As our daughters grew, I often asked them as I cooked a meal, "Can you taste the secret ingredient in this recipe?" My answer to them consistently was "the secret ingredient is the LOVE in it."

When I looked at myself in the mirror, I saw a shell of a person. I saw a woman who sometimes cared enough to shower; my hair was often unwashed, unbrushed, and disheveled. I got dressed but didn't care what I wore. My eyes bothered me the most; although they were green in color, they looked black to me, and when I looked long and hard enough they appeared to go nowhere. It was as if I was looking into an empty person, whose insides were a bottomless black pit. Unfortunately, that was an accurate description of how I felt during this time in my life. I felt empty; as if there was a huge void inside of me where I should have been emotionally and spiritually present. I felt like I had no identity. I felt like I was wandering around in a horrible abyss, searching for direction, searching for love, and searching to connect, because my biggest fears were materializing. For as long as I could remember, I felt like I had a hole in my soul. Now this hole had opened up and threatened to swallow me up. And not just me; it also threatened to swallow my husband and daughters.

I had enough awareness to realize that what I did affected them. I did not want to destroy their lives, but I did not know what to do. All I really knew deep in my heart was that I must get better.

One day at a time, that was all I could handle. Projecting into the future did not help me. It was important for me to try to live in the present moment. We practiced focusing thoughts on the present moment in therapy. This was difficult for me for several reasons. I realized that my fear often prevented me from trying new things like learning a new skill. I would read about things and think they were great ideas, but they remained ideas because I was too afraid to try them. What if I tried and I failed? What would that mean about me? Would it mean I was a mistake? Would it mean I wasn't perfect? What would people think about me? What would people do when they knew I wasn't perfect? Worse, what would I do if others realized I wasn't perfect? I focused on these thoughts so long that instead of taking any risks I settled for reading about other people who took risks and accomplished things I would have liked to do.

Perhaps the most tragic part of all was that I lost the desire to even want to try anything; to want to risk, to dream for myself, to have any hopes for myself in life. I stopped believing there was even a possibility for love, or joy, or fun in my life. I had given up on myself a very long time ago. I had given up on God, on faith, on people, and the reality of goodness in this world. My fears were controlling my life and I was living isolated in them. I was in an extremely lonely place. Once I became sober, I started to change. I recognized some of my fears and began to see the impact they had on my life, but this was only a beginning. I still had far to go, but at least I was heading in the right direction. I was sure of this. I knew I was on the right road. When my depression seemed to paralyze me, I knew I could not ignore this. If I did, I risked not just returning to drinking, but I would risk losing my family and everything I had gained in sobriety. I sensed my depression was much bigger than I was and it was something I needed to face. I could run, but that would be an extremely poor choice. I had learned that from my recovery group. I trusted them and had begun to trust God. I had turned a corner but suddenly I was sinking. I must act on what little faith I had. I was drowning in my feelings. Perhaps my faith was not based on my feelings. What was it based on? Did I have any faith right now?

Did I risk and trust my therapist, and continue to share my innermost thoughts and feelings, as raw and painful as they were? Whom did I trust? Donald seemed to be the best option I had; perhaps the only option. I trusted the inner spark within me. I knew I believed in God, who kept me sober one day at a time. I sensed I was on the right road with Donald, he seemed to connect me with much that was life giving. I was ready to trust him. I wanted what he had and what he offered. He was at peace with himself. I was ready to jump in and get my face wet. I had too much to live for. Donald was willing, and for once in my life, so was I.

CHAPTER 8

THE DISEASE OF DEPRESSION

*D*epression is as much a disease as any physical ailment. Clinical depression is not a way to avoid living. It affected my life and my body, emotionally, cognitively, physically and spiritually. Depression took away my desire to live, affecting the life of my family. Depression was not a moral issue and it did not make me a bad person. It made me a sick person.

There was nothing simple about my depression. There were multiple symptoms that affected my personality, and my mood varied greatly from day to day. I realized this disease was powerful, and I had no idea how to handle it or how to live with it. I felt powerless, and pushed beyond my limit of what I could handle. Perhaps that was a blessing right there. I had no idea what had happened to me or how I was going to recover. I felt like I was overcome by an F5 tornado that blew through my life, overtook me, and pushed me underground so that I could no longer look at life from the same perspective as others. It was as if I now looked at life from beneath the earth and everything was colored grey. I could no longer recognize the world or people in the same way. Although I could identity who they were, the way I perceived them and the way I could relate to them was altered. Just as importantly, the way they saw and related to me had changed. I lived in the same house, I wore the same clothes, and my body still had the same shape physically; but when I looked in the mirror I looked different because I viewed myself through this grey film.I felt different, much different— I felt like I lived in a world by myself where no one heard or understood me or felt like I felt - because of what I had just experienced. I couldn't explain it but I knew it had happened. I knew it was real. This new mood affected my body and feelings. I could not shake them off or wish them away like some people thought. This mood was a part of me and affected everything I attempted to do; how I interacted with my daughters and husband, and how I did things for myself. I could no longer do things that were once a routine part of my day. Instead, I found myself spending a lot of time *thinking* about doing things that required a lot of time and effort and energy. I did not care about many of them. How could I begin to explain to others how I felt and how my world had changed so drastically when I didn't even understand what was happening. If I wasn't crying I was anxious and worried; obsessing about things that I needed to do and about what might happen. My life and I had become unrecognizable overnight.

I felt ashamed that I was depressed. As I walked through my path and learned about myself and this disease, I discovered I did nothing to cause my illness. I learned that I did not need to be ashamed any more than a person having the flu would. I suffered from a mental illness, and I needed to accept it. I needed to take responsibility for my illness by taking my medication regularly just as I would for any other sickness. Pretending I didn't have an illness or keeping silent about it for fear of what people thought about me was not a good choice. Suffering from clinical depression was real and painful. Clinical depression was powerful and devastating. It was unspeakable at times; at least it was for me. Suffering from the effects of the disease was difficult enough without adding the effects of shame or guilt. I learned I had no control over the fact that I became depressed. I also came to understand that I had no control over how people reacted when they learned about my condition. I could not afford to let their attitude stop me from reaching out for the help I desperately needed and deserved.

I accepted that I was the one who was sick and needed treatment. I was responsible for getting the treatment I needed to recover. My illness and my fear wanted me to remain quiet. I did this most of my life and this was the exact thing I could not afford now. Isolation was not a choice at all. For me to isolate myself was to say that I was giving up. I would be conceding that I was not willing to try to get better. In essence, I would be saying that I was not willing to fight for my daughters because I would surely lose them. I would become so self-centered that I focused on what I thought I needed and wanted. I would stop trying to live because life became too hard. I depended on professionals who knew what they were doing. I could not allow my fear of people stop me or permit my fear of what others would think of my illness to get in my way.

So I chose to ask for help, from God, a therapist, and from a psychiatrist. In choosing to do this, I made a commitment to my recovery. I was also committing to my daughters, to my husband, and to my love for them and to life, that I would strive to overcome this problem within me. I had made a recommitment to my recovery that began the day I got sober. A spark was lit inside of me that day, and it was that ember that grew and continued to burn inside of me, even though I felt so defeated and lost at times. It was that spark, which I now call the light or care of God, that continued to guide me and motivated me to get up each day and continue on, even when at times I felt it was useless.

I was unaware of the magnitude of the commitment I made, but I was willing to try and that was enough. It seemed enough for me to keep on going, one step at a time; for I was walking in love and for love, even though many times I was unable to feel this. I believed in it, and as I was to learn, my beliefs became more important than my feelings. They would become something I could stand firm upon. My beliefs would become firm like the rocks I saw in the ocean, not like the sand on the shore that gets washed out to sea with the incoming tide. At least I hoped I could stand firm. I couldn't in my past but this was not my past; this was the present moment, which I was learning was all I had.

CHAPTER 9

A PRIMARY CONNECTION

*7*he day came when I realized that Donald could and would disappoint me. Like all people, he was capable of making mistakes. He was able to admit this.

This was difficult for me to accept at first. I vividly recall my disappointment upon first hearing the news. I said to Donald, "I was here yesterday for our scheduled appointment but you weren't here."

He replied, "I thought I told you I had another appointment this week and I needed to cancel our appointment."

I felt abandoned as the tears began rising to my face. I looked away, feeling embarrassed that I was about to cry. I didn't want Donald to see me crying about something so trivial. But this wasn't trivial to me, and he knew it.

I continued, "I don't remember you telling me you were rescheduling our appointment."

Donald opened his calendar. As he looked, he realized that he hadn't erased our appointment. In my mind I thought he was erasing me. He stated, "I'm so sorry, I made a mistake. I thought I told you I had a meeting. I guess I forgot. We will make the appointment up another time. I'm sorry about that. I know how much you count on me being here for you, and how much you count on consistency. I just could not be here yesterday."

I continued to stare at him, almost glaring through my now red-rimmed eyes. I thought he was dismissing me and his mistake too easily. I was taking it extremely seriously, like my life depended upon it. In a way it did, but I had a lot to learn. This was part of the process, a huge part. I needed to allow Donald to be a human being. If I could accept this, I would also eventually be able to accept it was okay for me to make mistakes. My fear was at work in me again. My fear that I or others could not be perfect. I could not afford to run away just because Donald made a mistake. I didn't know what else to do. I didn't know how to stay. I felt abandoned. Yet here was Donald, sitting in front of me. How could I feel abandoned? He admitted he made a mistake. I was not familiar with someone doing this. In the past, whenever I felt abandoned, I ran.

Becoming disappointed in Donald and working through this was important. As we sat in the silence, he looked at me while I stared down at my hands that were clenched together in my lap. I sat through my uncomfortable feelings. Donald eventually initiated the conversation.

"What were you afraid of when I didn't come yesterday?"

I stared down at my hands for a long time until I could say, "I was afraid you moved away without telling me you were leaving. I was afraid you didn't leave a forwarding address. I was afraid you got tired of me and left. My mother did that with my father. She left in the middle of the night after they argued. They thought we were asleep but I heard every word. I heard the garage door open. I heard the car leave, and my mother was in it. I fell asleep before she came home. I never knew if she would be home to meet me the next morning. The worst part was, I didn't know if I wanted her to come home. I needed her and I loved her, but the fighting was so hard to hear. I felt sorry for my father. I was so confused. I felt lost, but I couldn't talk to anyone about it. I hid my face in my pillow and tried to block out the noise and the fighting, but I remember it all. It haunts me to this day. I guess that's why I became afraid when you weren't here."

I was surprised at my words, yet I was relieved. It was as if a lifetime of hurt and fear were suddenly released. I felt my raft inch closer to the shore.

Being disappointed with myself was another hurdle I needed to face. I was often disappointed in myself because I had unrealistic expectations. I learned that I thought I needed to be perfect, and many of my food addiction issues revolved around this need.

Whom or what did I look to that wouldn't disappoint me? That was a difficult question to answer. Food, alcohol, people? Myself? I knew any and all of these things did or would eventually disappoint me. When it happened, where would I turn. Even my husband disappointed me. I disappointed him. Life disappointed me, and I had disappointed others, many times. Was there anything at all to hold onto in this world? If so, what was it? My thoughts turned to my own daughters; were they disappointed in me? Had life disappointed them so early in their young lives? Would they be permanently scarred from me and my illness? If I allowed myself to continue with these thoughts I would bring on a panic attack, causing my thoughts to career out of control. I needed to release them, but how and to whom? As I looked back on my life, I couldn't see anything that stood out. I was disappointed by the people and things I trusted since I was a child. That's a scary thought. My parents and teachers, along with my friends disappointed me. The fairy tales I read disappointed me. Worst of all, I disappointed myself and didn't know what to do with all of this disappointment. I didn't trust anyone, so I ran and hid that disappointment, and I have been hiding ever since. I was frightened as a child when people disappointed me. I was afraid that they would abandon me, so I ran. I stopped the day I put down the drink.

I knew deep down in my heart and soul that I could not remain sober without God and my recovery group. I was willing to let God into my life, but only so far. Although I believed God kept me sober one day at a time, my fear did not allow me to believe that He loved me. I wanted to trust this God of love but I had a huge trust issue. Whenever I became depressed, the trust I had wavered. Would I allow this fear to stand in my way? Would I come to a place where I could trust someone or something despite this unrelenting darkness that surrounded me wherever I went? What and whom would that be? How would I get there? Did it even exist? I believed it did, as I needed something to hold onto as I tried to move forward. I held onto the growing trust I had in my therapist, in the God that was keeping me sober, and in Stephen's love for me. I held more firmly onto the love I felt for my daughters and their love for me — the mother/daughter bond I believed was calling me to become the best mother I could be.

I looked up at the night sky and saw the stars and the moon. They shone so brightly. Just as they illuminated the ocean they illuminated our backyard. Surely the God who made these stars and the moon cared for me. I reached out my arms, attempting to touch the stars and I thought to myself, "If only I could touch one of these stars I could touch the God who made them. Perhaps then I could connect with the God who made me." My desire to connect with my creator increased the longer I was depressed. Even though there were people in my life, a part of me felt cut off from the rest of the world. My pain went so deep it felt like it seared my soul. I began to think that perhaps only God, who created me, could truly understand what I felt like. I felt alone many times despite my time with Donald and my times with our daughters and Stephen. As our daughters grew, I spent many lonely hours by myself. I did not have many interests or the desire to participate in life. My illness stole these from me. I focused and directed my thoughts and energy on our daughters, and when they were at school I waited for them to return home. The years were passing, yet my illness continued to steal precious time. I attended therapy and took medication and went to more appointments and saw more specialists. There were small periods of breakthroughs but no continuous recovery.

One sleepless night, as I looked out the bedroom window, God spoke gently to my heart. "You are like one of these stars to me. I wish you could see yourself the way I see you. When you spend time with your daughters, know that I love you and am with you. Feel their warm touch; hear their gentle voices and see their joy filled faces. See how they love to spend time with you. See how they enjoy life. This is my Love for you."

I let these words touch my heart. I let them soothe my broken spirit. I allowed them to lead me closer to a living God that loves me.

CHAPTER 10

FAMILY LIFE

*I*nitially it seemed like a tidal wave had overtaken our little home. What had become of mom? Overnight it seemed like I had become a different person. I no longer resembled the functioning mother of an infant and toddler. Decisions had to be made and they needed to be made quickly, not only for our children but for my care as well. Doctor's appointments, assistance for our children, and my husband maintaining his work schedule were all priorities.

Our whole life was turned upside down and this was just the beginning. So much more was to follow. Initial medication attempts failed as did the ECT treatments. By this time, I had already been admitted as an inpatient in a mental hospital in an attempt to treat my severe depression.

My illness quickly affected our entire family. My husband had to take on many more childcare responsibilities and household chores. He essentially became both "mom and dad" for our daughters during these early days. In addition, as I was not able to return to my part-time job after Sarah was born, Stephen had to take on the entire financial responsibility for our family.

Day to day living was not easy, but we eventually developed a routine that worked for us. Although it took enormous effort to take care of myself, I was able to take care of Emily and Sarah more easily. It took a great deal of effort to prepare their food and feed them, to wash their clothes and bathe, dress, and diaper them; to read and sing to them and walk them. Despite this effort, there was something about being with Emily and Sarah and caring for them that brought out the best in me during one of the worst periods of my life. Caring for them became an act of love that I could not extend to myself.

As they grew, I continued to drag myself out of bed each morning to make them breakfast and prepare their school lunches; their clothes were washed; and I helped with their homework as I was able. I tried to attend school functions as best I could, even though I was not the most talkative mother or the best dressed. Consistency was a problem, especially when I had episodes where I would spiral downward, and then Stephen and I needed to get assistance from family members or day care as the girls' needs had to come first.

It was hard for Stephen and me to make some of these decisions but we were parents first, despite my illness. Our daughters' safety and well-being were our main priority. Looking back, isn't that what a parent needs to do anyway? Our situation was complicated by my emotional illness. We needed to learn as we went how to address everyone's needs, but our daughters needed to be safe and supported, and raised in a loving environment. We were their parents and they were dependent upon us. We took on that responsibility when we chose to have them. As their parents, we needed to honor that commitment to Emily and Sarah and to each other. As difficult as it was, we made sure that the girls were not in any danger from me. During this time, I was closely monitored by several professionals and took psychotropic medications that were closely monitored. Even when the medications were not working I was careful to take them as prescribed. Many of these medications were strong and had multiple side effects. When the time came to stop taking them, I needed to be weaned off of them. There were times I had difficulty following the medication schedule but Stephen helped me. It was not easy but I did my best to follow the professional advice and recommendations given to me.

Stephen and I tried our best to make good decisions for our daughters and keep them involved with what was happening to me as they got older. We explained to them, "Your mom is so sad and cries so much because she is sick. She has an illness called depression. Your friends' mothers do not cry so easily or so often because they do not have this illness." We felt strongly that they should know what depression was and that I was sick. We wanted to be as open and honest as possible without causing them worry. We thought they had a right and a need to know why I behaved the way I did.

Stephen and I had to make difficult decisions at times. A difficult one Emily and Sarah still talk about was our decision to have them attend daycare three mornings in the summer when they were quite young. Emily and Sarah never understood this no matter how many times we attempted to explain the need for this. "Why can't we stay home all day mama? We don't want to go to that daycare. You will be home. It's summer. We want to be home with you. Please, let us stay home." What they didn't realize was that these three hours in the morning provided me the respite I needed, which enabled me to more effectively care for them when they were with me. Without those few hours of relief I would not have been able to mother my daughters in the best way possible. Thinking I could take care of them full time that summer would not have been a responsible or loving decision for anyone in our family. I found that loving decisions were not always the easiest ones.

I believe love kept our family together. Although I was often self-destructive during these years, I acted lovingly towards my daughters. The mother/daughter bond that formed at conception was a bond of love flowing both ways. Fortunately, even at this darkest of times, I remained connected with my daughters and respected them. Sarah's birth triggered my postpartum depression, but the bond formed with my daughters triggered something far greater and deeper; causing me to look beyond self. My daughters stirred something in me that I hadn't felt in a very long time. Did I even recognize it? Whenever I was with them or thought about them, someplace deep inside of me felt different. I was drawn to this place and to my daughters. It felt so good to hold Sarah, to feed her, and to read to Emily before she went to sleep. Stephen and I read *Good Night Moon* over and over to both girls as it was one of our favorites. I took both girls for a walk, pushing Sarah in the stroller and holding Emily's little hand. I wanted to reach out and give more to both girls. I had to continue. The spark burning inside me was spreading. I felt it at those moments.

For several reasons, when Emily was four and Sarah was two we decided to move to the country. Stephen and I decided to do this before I became ill. Stephen tells me we looked at several houses before deciding on the home we moved into. Due to my memory loss, I have no memory of any of the moving process. One day I opened my eyes and I was in a new bedroom and new kitchen with all of our belongings. I had no memory of packing or looking for a house, or being able to account for the time lapse! I said, "Why are we in this house?" Stephen said, "This is where we live now honey. Don't you remember? We moved here months ago." I was shocked. I had to walk around the house for days. I felt like my old life had been stolen from me, and in a way it had been. Our daughters were more comfortable and aware of our new surroundings and home than I was. There wasn't much I could do about it. Honestly, there wasn't anything I could do about it. This was the result of my memory loss from the ECT treatments and the cognitive haze I suffered. I needed to accept it and move on, the best I could.

There were things I remembered which brought me great joy. I vividly remember combing Sarah's beautiful blonde hair for hours to remove the tangles as she squirmed on my lap. Or Emily laying out her choice of clothes for school the next day on her bedroom floor each night. One day, both girls wrote on their bedroom walls with markers. Neither my husband nor I were too happy about it, although I seemed to be a bit more tolerant than Stephen, probably because it happened while I was with our daughters!

I remember Emily being a bumblebee for Halloween when she was three years old. I remembered being so happy that Emily and I were able to make her costume without sewing. Sewing was not one of my better skills! I came up with the idea of using black duct tape for the stripes and Emily and I had great fun sticking each other and her yellow shirt with the tape. She won the award at her school party. Her picture was in the local newspaper and Stephen and I displayed that bumblebee picture in a frame in our home for many years. I cherished that photo and I know where it is for anyone who wishes to see it at a moment's notice! Sarah was Baby Bop one year and Emily was a witch that Halloween.

One Christmas the girls received American Girl dolls. Samantha was Emily's favorite that year and Sarah loved Itty Bitty Baby which she unfortunately lost at the playground. Itty Bitty was soon replaced. We made numerous trips to that and other playgrounds. I can remember pushing both girls on the swings at the same time until I thought my arms would fall off!

"Push us higher, mama, higher, we want to go higher!" The girls loved the playground. They ran from one swing to the next with complete abandon. I would watch them and envy their freedom and joy. I was happy for them but I was unable to experience these feelings for myself or connect with them deep inside. Yet, a part of me knew these feelings must exist. How could they not? I was looking at the joy on the faces of my daughters. I didn't feel this way right now but did this mean I would never feel this way again? Did this mean I never experienced them when I was a child like Emily and Sarah? I could not seem to remember very many happy times in my life. I did not know if this was because of the mental state I was in or if those times truly did not exist. Sometimes I walked around feeling like I was carrying a physical weight. This added weight seemed to intensify the effort I needed to perform activities I once took for granted. Even automatic activities such as lifting my head off the pillow in the morning, turning to get out of bed, brushing my teeth or lifting a fork to eat dinner now required extreme effort, if I could do them at all.

As difficult as daytime was for me, the evenings were even worse. It wasn't like I had nightmares while I slept because my whole life had become a living nightmare. I was unable to fall asleep most nights. I would sit alone in my arm chair until 2:00 or 3:00 A.M. I was exhausted, yet unable to fall asleep despite medication and attempted relaxation techniques, herbal tea, quiet music, and numerous other attempts to quiet my anxious body and mind.

Sometimes I would be extremely withdrawn verbally. Other times I would cry excessively, and still others I would be overly anxious. My mood remained depressed but the level fluctuated throughout the years. My family came to fully expect to find me emotionally upset when they returned home from school or work. That was how mom was. Although they knew I was sick, they also knew that I was there and able to care for them.

I was depressed but I also thought depressing thoughts. As time progressed, I learned to move these thoughts to the background and focus on my daughters. This required enormous energy. The thoughts in my mind were relentless. I tried to listen to the love from my heart instead of the thoughts in my mind. I focused on my daughters when I was with them. I concentrated on looking into their faces and into their blue eyes while thinking of the present moment. This was exhausting but it worked. Many times I talked myself through what I needed to do for Emily and Sarah. This helped me focus and be present for them one activity at a time. I wasn't always successful, but I was able to be present as best I could be. When my daughters were at preschool, daycare, and eventually grammar school, and I was alone, I would replenish myself and get the care I needed. That is when I slept, went to therapy, my doctor appointments, wrote in my journal, or went to my alcoholic recovery meetings. At times, I just stared at the walls and cried until I thought I couldn't shed another tear. I soon realized I was in over my head. This disease was powerful, but I had something extremely precious calling me forward.

Stephen and I loved to camp and we wanted to share this experience with our new family. Yearly summer camping trips became part of our family life right away. We found that playpens and baby swings were portable and quite adaptable for camp life; as were we!

Once we found our campsite, Emily and Sarah would say, "How about this place for the tent. This seems level and there aren't too many rocks."

Stephen and I would check out the terrain and usually agree after quickly kicking some of the larger rocks away from the site.

We managed to set down our tarp and set up the tent without much trouble. We had a screen house that seemed to cause us such distress every year that as the girls got older we voted to see if we wanted to bother putting it up. We were willing to take our chances getting soaked in the rain rather than having to deal with the hassle of that screen house.

In the evenings we built campfires; Stephen and I walked through the woods, each carrying one girl on our backs for many years. We ate dripping ice cream cones and hot dogs "burnt" right over the campfire. On each trip we ate our share of our famous toasted marshmallows along with our favorite popcorn. We usually played a game of finger puppets on the ceiling of our tent with our flashlights before going to sleep.

The girls would say, "You're a bunny again, mom. Try to think of a different animal next time." The girls were so much more imaginative than I was! No camping trip was complete without some rainy days. Trying to stay dry while tent camping was quite a challenge, although we creatively took it on! Cooking dinner was difficult in the pouring rain. The girls loved it when Stephen and I gave in at times and we all went to a restaurant as a special treat. The days we cooked in the rain we ended up completely soaked along with our dinner; but we managed to eat it anyway. Then we cleaned up in record time, went into our tent early and told stories, spending time with each other until we fell asleep listening to the rain fall against our tent; praying that when we woke up the next morning our tent would be as dry as it was when we went to sleep - or that we wouldn't be swept along with the rain and washed downhill onto another campsite. I think all four of us have fond memories of those times camping. Stephen and I had camped since we met one another. Even when I was eight months pregnant with Emily, we went camping. Once Emily and Sarah were born we continued our camping tradition. It was important for both Stephen and me to spend that time camping with our daughters. We were trying our best to live within the confines of my illness and to hold onto a piece of what we had from the life we knew before I became sick. I believe we were trying to hold onto hope in some tangible way, or reality as we had known it. While Stephen and I did not want my illness to define our life, there was no escaping the fact that the severity and the length of my depression had become an overwhelming presence in our home; but so was the presence of love. Although I had to confront my own darkness and my own feelings, I was not traveling alone. This fact made a huge difference in my recovery.

Camping was within our budget and enabled us to be together away from the stress and strain of home. It allowed us the flexibility to change plans without much advance planning. Being able to sit by the campfire at night, to relax and look up at the stars; waking up early in the morning and seeing the sun rise over the lake; seeing the geese and ducks and birds and moose and bear roaming free; smelling the pine trees and seeing the fields of flowers. Nature seemed to know how to heal what was broken for each one in our family. I relaxed in a way that I could not at home. I loved to be outdoors and found myself drawn to the smells and the sights. These things soothed me and I was much less anxious. I fell asleep each night without lying awake for hours. It was a relief and a gift! Medicine that didn't come in a bottle! This alone would have been reason enough to go camping nightly! Equally important, Stephen and Emily and Sarah had fun on our camping trips. Because I was so much more relaxed, they were too. As the girls grew they became more actively involved. They loved to swim and ride their bikes through the woods and help make the campfires. We hiked together, and they made friends with other campers. We would sit by the fire at night, toast marshmallows, talk and laugh and just be silly. We were a family on vacation. We had fun.

In a sense, it seemed like for a brief two weeks, we escaped the reality of our life and enjoyed this place where laughter, relaxation and ease in our daily routine were the norm, and the darkness and my horrible mood swings were the fantasy. Although we knew this was not the case, we were able to leave our burdens behind. When we returned home, it was with heavy hearts, but renewed spirits to face the reality of our family life as only we knew it. One thing we all agreed on each and every year; even though we loved to camp, we did not like the mosquitoes or the black flies. Whoever was in charge of packing the bug repellant had the most important job of all!

My love of reading was something I wanted to share with our daughters, and some of my fondest memories with both Emily and Sarah since infancy were my reading to them, especially at bedtime; cuddling with them in bed or in a rocking chair, smelling their freshly washed hair, reading and rereading our favorite stories until we almost had them memorized. The girls had their favorite stories as the years passed and Stephen and I had ours. Our family joke was that dad loved to pick the board books with the most pictures and the fewest words. As the girls grew, our roles changed and our daughters began reading those board books to us! How the years passed and changed.

I tried my best and we tried as a family, but my recovery was limited. Despite the professionals' best efforts, I was not responding to the antidepressant medications. I was on this seemingly endless journey of sleepless nights with severe depression, anxiety and mood swings that included suicidal thoughts and attempts, and subsequent hospitalizations and feelings of hopelessness. The months became years, and our daughters began growing up. They were no longer toddlers or in preschool. We planned birthday parties the best we could. Photographs not taken. Family functions not attended.

The only consistency in our home was that mom was going to be depressed and tired, and that I would be going to doctor's appointments and therapy. Our whole family life revolved around my depression. This disease was powerful. Too many times I struggled to stay alive. This disease wanted all of me. I felt so defeated by this disease that when I was at my lowest points I could see no reason to go on. My mind was racing and thoughts like these or similar ones raced back and forth in my mind. "You are such a failure, you will never amount to anything. There is no point in trying any more, everyone will be better off without you. It's all your fault, it's always your fault."

I thought it was a good idea to act on these thoughts at the time. I believe it was at those very lowest points that my precious daughters reached out in love and touched my heart as only they could. It was this bond that interrupted my self-destructive behavior each and every time I didn't want to go on living. I thought of myself as a shell of a person. I felt like I was a huge disappointment to my family. I also knew that my severely depressed mood was affecting the atmosphere in our home.

I knew that Emily and Sarah deserved a happier environment, a mother who was more spontaneous and could handle life's responsibilities more easily. A part of me believed my daughters would be better off without me, but this was my illness speaking to me. My depressed thinking told me that "my family will just forget me and will one day get a new mother, a better mother." Did I ever truly believe my daughters would be better off without me? My depression wanted me to believe that, but I did not really believe that in my heart. I may have thought they would be better off with a different mother but that was because I was focusing on the darkness. My old familiar feelings of insecurity and inferiority were overtaking me once again. I needed to keep putting one foot in front of the other and stay on the path I was walking. I needed to trust the part of me that wanted to live more than the part of me that wanted to die. I needed to keep reaching out and accept the love and kindness being offered to me. My old thoughts and feelings would destroy not only me but my family if my depression did not improve. This was exactly opposite to the commitment I had made as a mother. Destroying myself was one thing, but hurting my family was not acceptable to me. This was what a mother's love was all about. I needed to continue to struggle on my journey no matter how difficult and painful it became. I finally started to understand this is what love is about — love involves pain and sacrifice at times. More importantly, love calls me to look beyond myself. I cannot truly love without feeling pain. The spark inside reminds me that my commitment and connection to God and my family continues to burn.

This gave me the strength to keep going and a reason to hold on. And what did I hold onto?

I held onto being as present as I could be with Emily as I dropped her off at preschool and while helping her learn to draw and print her first letters; I held onto holding Sarah in my lap as she drank her chocolate milk while we watched some of her favorite videos together before nap time; I held onto kissing both girls before bedtime each night and tucking them into their beds. I held onto waking them up each morning and helping them get ready for school. I held onto all of those memories and more. I held onto their hearts and they held onto mine.

Despite whatever memories the ECT treatments may have erased from me, they could never erase the memories from my heart. These are the ones I carried with me wherever my depression took me, even to the point of suicide attempts and mental hospitals time and time again. These are the very ones that called to me above all the rest to keep on the path to recovery, to keep Emily's and Sarah's faces in sight, to keep their voices in my head and keep their love in my hearts. What a gift they were giving me. The least I could do was to keep walking for them, for all of us in love. Our family was worth it.

Our family had its own routines and Stephen and I tried our best to provide our daughters with the best family life we could, given our circumstances. We loved them through our pain. We were as open and honest as possible with them as they grew. We were able to cry together, be disappointed together, and were sad together. Because of this, I believe when we laughed together we truly laughed and enjoyed the happy moments more fully. We knew they wouldn't last but when they came we savored them and tried to hold onto them as long as possible, for just as the sun would set at the end of each day, bringing in the darkness of night, we all knew that my depression would return, sometimes worse than before it had briefly lifted. Unfortunately, the only question was when it would come, not if. Looking back, I did not have much faith that I would recover but I did have enough faith to keep going.

CHAPTER 11

ISOLATION

$\mathcal{M}$ost of my life I thought it was good to isolate myself. My depression called me further into isolation and was sucking what little life I had out of me. Despite my tendency to push people away or my inability to respond to them, it was crucial for me to be around life giving people.

I found isolation to be part of the illness. There is nothing social about depression. As painful as it was for me to be alone, it was more difficult to be with people. When I was, I felt I needed to fit in and be like others; but I was emotionally in agony. I needed to connect with people. This created a constant tension between isolating and reaching out to people. The battle lines were drawn. Throughout the years, I reached out to connect and then pulled back out of fear. It was a process. The longer I was left to myself out in the cold dark ocean, the more I was motivated to risk a relationship, and the less power my fear held over me. I began to let go of what people might think of me or how much I might get hurt; replacing it with what others had that I needed. This seemed selfish to me at first, but I realized that I needed to have something before I could give things away. Other people were filled with life and joy while I was emotionally ill and I needed to be in a relationship with them. My illness magnified my isolation. The very thing I was afraid of for many years I now needed to help me recover; so I tentatively reached out and tested the waters. I made some mistakes, but I also had some successes. It was risky for me, but not as risky as staying stagnant in the water I was in.

While I was depressed I had a difficult time expressing how I felt to others. I did not understand it myself. It is easier for me now, looking back, to have some perspective on that time that I didn't have then. I also had a difficult time understanding other people's often mixed responses to me. Often those closest to me said things that were the most painful to hear.

"Stop feeling sorry for yourself!"

"Do you know how many people are depressed but still go to work and live life? What is wrong with you anyway?"

"You can be as happy as you decide to be."

"If you just kept your mind busy you would forget about being depressed."

"If I had your life, I wouldn't be depressed. Just pull yourself up by your bootstraps."

I found that staying busy had no correlation to my level of depression. Severe depression was not about feeling sorry for myself. It was about an extremely altered mood and way of seeing myself and my world. Unfortunately, I was unable to accurately or adequately put words to my emotional state while I was depressed. My sense of aloneness increased.

As my depression worsened, so did my involvement with my extended family, friends, and the world in general. Part of the reason I became so isolated from my parents and sisters was my inability to describe what I was experiencing mentally, physically, and cognitively. I wished I could describe how my world had become so dark and hopeless that I found myself in a place where

I wanted to end my life. I didn't know how to explain feelings like this to the people I had shared my first twenty years of life with. I was also afraid of how they would respond. My world had become very different from my family's world. I needed to talk about my feelings in order to talk about my depression. The few times I ventured into this area with them it was like I was speaking a foreign language. I felt rejected, like I should not be having these conversations with them. My fear of abandonment and of not fitting in spoke loudly to me when it came to my sisters and parents. I had too much to lose by trying to be myself, but honestly, I had even more to lose by trying to be someone different. I had come to the place where I was beaten by my disease. A part of me was longing to reach out to my sisters and parents for help to describe what I was living through, but the words would not come. I wanted them to, but I could not find them. Was this because I was afraid of how they would respond to me or was it because at the time there were no words to describe the living torment I was living through?

I eventually came to the place where I realized that I needed to be myself, despite what others thought about me or how others responded. My fear was not my best advocate. It never had been and never would be. Being isolated was not good for me when I was depressed. My dark thoughts and feelings seemed to become magnified whenever I was cut off from others. What I did find, was that the smallest light in the dark seemed to shine brightly and was needed the most when I felt so cut off from others. I needed light all the time but I needed it the most during these times. No matter how small, no matter from whom, it made a difference. When I saw the light I was able to respond. That light was like a beacon to me, like a lighthouse beckoning to my raft during the terrible storm. The light led me to the next phase. I could not provide the light for myself.

I was afraid others would hurt me. I desperately needed to let some people in or my illness would consume me. I started with my therapist and slowly widened my circle from there. My time with him was refreshing, like cool water in a lake on a hot summer afternoon. I would wade for quite a while, but I would not go underwater. I was too fearful of getting my face wet. What if I couldn't breathe underwater? My trust was slowly growing. My young daughters learned how to swim when they were two years old and were better swimmers than I was. Because I am not a good swimmer, I do not enjoy water sports and I do not swim underwater. I am too afraid, for good reason I think.

It is the same thing with my ability to trust others. I did not understand why, but I had a reason; so I took my time learning to trust my therapist. He did not rush me. I gradually swam out farther, allowing other people into my life. Sometimes I pulled back or pushed them away, but I was trying. They were patient, that was what mattered. Many times, I was close to drowning. Looking back, having someone with me to share the painful times as well as the more pleasant ones was the better choice. I found it was easier to find something to laugh about and to cry with someone alongside me. It helped put things in perspective or for someone to honestly say, "I don't understand how you feel but I am here with you." Gradually I learned to trust and believe them. In time I wasn't so afraid to express similar words to others.

It was very difficult to stay connected with those who did not live close to me. Some days I couldn't pick up the phone. My disease told me to stay home and draw the curtains, so I could lay in the dark by myself. I did not feel better doing this, I just cried more; but my disease was in control. Fortunately, I had a therapy appointment to go to and then I needed to stop at the grocery store to get the ingredients to make Rice Krispie Treats for the girls before they came home from school. That is what my heart told me to do.

My inability to attend family functions also added to my isolation and the growing tension within my family. As I began progressing through my journey, things did not get easier. I was extremely fragile emotionally and in a precarious situation. I had to stop trying to please other people. I had to start making decisions that would be good ones for me and our family. This terrified me. I had tried to be a people pleaser most of my life. "Avoid conflict at all cost" was one of my mottos, along with "Just try to make other people happy."

I began to see how futile this approach to living was for me. I was now in a position where I could no longer afford to just go along and do what others expected me to do. Many times, going to extended family functions was too stressful for me. I simply could not go. I agonized over these decisions because I was afraid of what my family would think of me; but my emotional health depended on me making better decisions.

It was time I started to make some difficult decisions out of love for myself and my own family. Although this has gotten easier, I still worry at times about what others will think about my choices. I know now from my own experience that it is more important to be true to my heart of love, and that I must take care of myself at times; even when others do not understand or accept this. Although it was necessary, I feel like this distanced us further from my extended family. I was not avoiding them. I was protecting my emotional state. I needed to put my emotional healing first. I often felt rejected, abandoned or hurt during these years by my family, but I could not tell them how I felt. We seemed to be growing farther apart during this time instead of drawing closer together. Our relationships grew strained. Many extended family members did not even know that I was emotionally ill at that time. I could not tell them. We weren't close emotionally, or perhaps I was ashamed or fearful of how they would respond. At this time in my life, I could not handle any more rejection. I was struggling to stay alive and keep my daughters healthy. This was my priority. I learned to let go of the rest and put the results in God's hands. I cannot control others. Out of necessity I let go.

My mother maintained contact with me during these years. She was one of the few people who called me when I was hospitalized. She ended each phone conversation the same way, "I know you will get better. I pray for you every day." My mom was there for me in the way she could be. Maybe there was something about the mother/daughter bond of love with my own mother that was also motivating me to forge ahead. Were we still motivated by love despite all our differences over these years?

My therapist continued to bring a human element to an almost impenetrable loneliness. I was surrounded by my husband and daughters, yet I felt so alone and cut off from others. I felt like I was in my own world where no one could possibly relate to how I felt or thought. Worse, I did not want to reach out, but through it all Donald encouraged me. "I am looking forward to seeing you on Wednesday. Maybe you can try to write some of your thoughts and feelings in your journal. Things will come into clearer focus."

I needed to be a student. Sometimes Donald asked questions and other times I asked the questions. Sometimes no one had any answers. Little by little I started to learn things about myself. It wasn't easy, but it was necessary for me to grow along the way. No matter how dark the road became, Donald encouraged me to keep going.

I often thought others needed to feel like I felt to understand me. I was wrong about this. Many times I became upset with

Donald, especially when Friday came. Donald would say to me, "I hope you have a nice weekend." I would think to myself, "How am I supposed to have a nice weekend? Doesn't he understand how depressed I am?" Then I would say to Donald, "What are you doing this weekend?" He answered," My wife and I are going to a concert tonight and tomorrow we are going into town for the day." I became upset. I thought that others should stay home like I would. I did not understand that he could empathize with me yet still have his own life. He asked me numerous times, "How will you feel better if I did not live my life?" I did not have an answer but I was still upset. Just as I thought Donald should stay home, I thought others needed to join me in my misery in order to understand how I felt. I was confused and did not have a good sense of boundaries. I did not know where I began and where others started. I was confused about my life and about my own identity. I had lost my sense of identity as I was drifting in the ocean, desperately trying to get safely to shore. The ocean water was covering me, and at times I was immersed under the waves. I was terrified when this happened. Sometimes I felt like I was a child, yet I knew I was my daughter's mother. I am my husband's wife, yet I do not feel attractive and no longer have a desire to physically interact with him. My illness has stolen this from me and from us. Who am I really? Am I a woman or a girl? Am I a mother or a child? A wife or a teenager? My sense of self begins to blend together.

Thankfully, when I go to therapy, Donald begins to ground me. He is consistent and protective, and this helps me feel like I can trust him. As I share my feelings, I realize his roots go deep into the earth. He stands on solid ground and does not flinch when I approach difficult topics. We sit through the silence. He encourages me to be myself and helps me discover my limits. He encourages me to respect them.

Donald became like a parent. He saw the best in me and became my best advocate with my family and helped find other professionals I needed for my care. He would not give up or give in to my disease. He believed recovery was not only possible but probable. His determination and commitment to me and my recovery gave me hope. I grabbed onto this hope and clung to it. Sometimes it was just his hope, but that was enough because he had more than enough for both of us. It worked until my hope could grow.

I came to depend upon Donald's care and professional skill. I needed the mother/daughter bond of love with my own daughters and with my mother. I needed the love of my husband. I needed my recovery group. I needed the spark lit within me which I did not understand. I was often unaware of this spark but it guided me through the dark days and even darker nights. As the days passed, I could not find much relief. Days became months which turned into years. What had become of me and my life? I could not seem to get out of this current that seemed to be taking me back out to the deep sea, despite times of relief when I have brief intervals in the sun with my husband and daughters. How long would they wait for me?

CHAPTER 12

CUTTING

"*D*ear God, I don't know how I ended up here but why am I cutting myself? Why do I like to feel the razor cutting through my skin? Why do I need to see the blood flowing from the cuts on my wrists? Why do I like to feel the pain of the cut?"

Just when I thought I could not feel any worse about myself, I did.

Like my other addictions, I became obsessed with self-cutting. Once I started doing it, if I wasn't cutting, I was thinking of cutting and the relief it would provide. I was thinking of where, when, and how I would do it. Before I knew it, the entire process was out of control. Self-cutting owned me. It had become a burden instead of providing the relief I thought it promised. It had betrayed me. I could not trust it. I would make up excuses to my husband and my growing children, but I knew they did not believe me. I knew they were disappointed in me. Again.

Feeling their disappointment was horrible for me. I felt it in the pit of my stomach. Disappointment was not a feeling I handled well. It brought up bad memories for me - my parents, grammar school, boys, disappointing others and being disappointed - I didn't know which was worse for me. I knew that I didn't like either. A part of me wanted to continue, even though it no longer worked. I could not deal with disappointing my family. I was harming myself and in harming myself, I was harming them. This was not loving. I realized I could not stop by myself. I have no ability to stop self-cutting just as I have no ability to stop drinking a day at a time by myself. I am powerless.

The responsible choice was to admit I needed help and ask for it. I did not stop immediately, but I got the help I needed. I started to realize I was a broken person in many ways. I began thinking my issues stemmed from an issue similar to branches breaking off the trunk of a tree. I started to think that my core was rotten and that was why so many branches experienced poor growth. How will I get to the core issues? I thought back to my high school days and college. My room was full of books. I loved to read. My favorite childhood memory was going to the local library every Saturday morning to get new books for the week. Reading was a refuge for me; an escape. When I read, I could lose myself in what I was reading. I would become the characters in the book. I would let my mind take me to places that I could only go in my imagination. I would dream of living with other families or living in different countries. I would imagine myself being a concert pianist or a talented artist. I had aspirations of making a difference in life and doing something with my life when I grew up.

This changed drastically by my teenage years when I became obsessed with reading self-help books. I couldn't find enough of them. I was searching for an answer to why I felt so fearful, insecure, and alone. Even though I began to think I had every problem I read about, I was unable to change the way I felt or thought, or my behavior. I also had religious books but I could not connect with the concepts of God I read about.

Once I started to drink, I was on a different path entirely. I no longer desired any self-help or religious books. Instead, I sought oblivion and isolation. That became my new way of dealing with my painful and difficult feelings. I worked hard at avoiding the issues that existed, when in reality they were staring me in the face each time I dared to look in the mirror each morning when I got out of bed and promised myself that today would be different; that today I would not drink, but a few hours later, I was already planning my next drink because I could not go a day without it.

Broken promises. I knew all about those and how they felt. I made them to myself too many times to count. I remember the disappointment and shame I felt. I did not drink with others. I drank by myself in my apartment. Just me and my bottle, and the feelings I was desperately trying to avoid. I was not enjoying this but I had to drink. I could not stop. My feelings of despair, shame, and guilt over how I was living my life were piling up. I knew I was a disappointment to my parents. I was not raised to live like this. I kept my life hidden from others, another secret to add to the others. The longer I kept it hidden, the worse I became. None of this changed until I was able to share my truth with another person. I had to be honest with myself and share my feelings with another person to get the relief I needed.

I don't understand what it is about me that seems to love to hide. There is a part of me that is afraid to tell my truth to others. What IS this real truth I am referring to? This has been haunting me for a while. There is something deep inside of me, at least I have begun to suspect there is. I am beginning to think that I have not shared it because I have been too afraid that others will not believe me. Perhaps I am afraid of how others will respond; that they will reject me, or worse, abandon me similarly to when I was afraid my mother would leave my father and therefore leave me. Perhaps I am afraid that others will not be pleased with me and won't welcome me into their group, as in grammar school when I was the last person picked for the basketball team in gym because I was not very good at sports. Perhaps I am afraid that I will say the wrong thing and no one will understand me, just as when I was growing up and no one in my family seemed to understand what I was talking about; or perhaps I am afraid that I will say my truth and I will hear my voice loud and clear, and I will know in my heart and soul that it is true but I am afraid it will destroy me, and that I will be unable to bear it.

Instead, I remain silent, saying nothing, and carry my truth deep within; it follows me like a shadow wherever I go. But just as a shadow grows longer as the sun fades, so does the heaviness on my heart until it becomes too much for me to carry. It threatens to overtake me, and swallow me whole. Perhaps this is part of the horrible darkness that I cannot seem to escape.

When I cut myself with the razor I never cut too deeply into my body tissue. I always stopped before I hurt myself too badly. I never knew, however, when I started if this might be the time I wouldn't stop soon enough, if this was the time I would sever an artery. Maybe this would be the time the blood would keep coming.

The hurt and the disappointment, the shame and the guilt, the sense of loss and the disillusionment in goodness and in love and in life itself; this pain resided deep within me. And if, like making that first superficial cut on my skin with that razor, that inner emotional pain, when awakened, would begin to bleed like that blood from the cut, it might never stop coming.

Perhaps, as my fear told me, if that deep emotional pain was awakened it would never stop hurting and it would be so severe it would flow from my heart and from me. If I allowed myself to feel it, it wouldn't stop until I was left lifeless as the intense pain would burn a hole right through me and take me with it. Part of me feared and believed that all I consisted of was this pain and darkness that set up home in me so very long ago. It was as if this was reawakened and ignited by my depression. My fear and disease were raging inside of me - daring me to engage this deep emotional pain in my heart one minute, while telling me to avoid it at all costs the next.

Just like the razor, when I cut and stopped, there existed more in me then just fear and pain. There were both darkness and light, despair and hope, and it was this combination that stopped my hand from cutting deeper, enabling me to embrace that pain deep within me. It was only by embracing and allowing it to come to light that I could discover that the pain did not exist by itself. I was extremely ashamed. I self-cut as a way to "cope" with my depression. Obviously this had been a poor choice. I had not been coping, I had been falling apart. Despite my attempt to hide my behavior from those closest to me, they knew what I did. My daughters said, "Mom, why do you have on a long-sleeved shirt, it's summer?"

I would answer, "I'm cold today," to which they would say "Are you sick? You were cold yesterday. And why do you have that big band-aid on your wrist? What happened to you now. You didn't cut yourself with a knife while you were washing the dishes again did you?"

I would be secretly horrified, but I lied and said to my daughters, "I did cut myself again." I could not live with the increasing guilt I felt from lying to them and my husband about my cutting. This was like sticking a knife into all of our hearts. I began to see what I was doing to them.

I thought I was seeking attention with this behavior, and I certainly got it; negative attention. I thought people might be able to relate to my physical pain in a way they were unable to relate to my emotional pain. At these times, I felt sorry for myself, discouraged and frustrated, and I was acting out like a child. Although I was asking for attention and help, I did not know how to ask in a responsible way. I was asking in a way that was selfish and worrisome to those who loved me. I had much to learn about love and being a responsible adult.

As I recovered and became a responsible adult, the physical scars left by my self-cutting were not severe. My emotional wounds ran deep but they, too, only gradually stopped bleeding by bringing them into the light. Scar tissue remains from my deep emotional wounds but they are now woven into the fabric of my being and are no longer loose threads, threatening to trip me up and destroy me. How did these loose threads become identified? How did they lose their destructive power? Just as a tapestry is woven of many threads and viewed from different perspectives, I found that the threads of my emotional wounds were not going to change. I was the one who needed to change. How would this happen? In addition to these deep wounds that threatened to come to the surface I remained severely depressed. Were these separate issues or were they intricately woven together? How would this ever get resolved?

As I sat on my bench, I reflected on what I know now. I continued on, moving forward one day at a time. One step at a time. It seemed in the past like all I had was time. Suddenly I felt like I had lost years from my life. I felt like our daughters had turned into young teenagers overnight. Where had all these years gone? I knew I would never get them back. Was there a way to stop me from losing even more of their precious lives?

CHAPTER 13

MY DARKEST MOMENTS

$\mathcal{P}$erhaps anyone who has been severely depressed may be able to identify with the soul wrenching pain and emptiness —not only of self but of life - and the deep sense of hopelessness that tormented me emotionally and spiritually. At times, everywhere and any direction I looked, all I could see and feel was a soul-wrenching sense of doom and blackness, a huge void I was convinced I could never cross or fill. I could see no way through this void. My life had become this empty black hole.

All these darkest emotions led back to the deepest loss of self I had felt since childhood. These ate away at me, finally taking away my desire to live at these times. In my mind and heart, I could not reconcile the beauty and the gifts of my present life with the wretchedness and soul sickness I felt. I could not reconcile my past and my present life. I felt ashamed and guilty for loving these precious children while seeming to carry this darkness and sense of "not being good enough" wherever I went. My growing fear was that I would transfer this to my daughters. I was incapable of seeing any way out. I did not want them to suffer any more than they already had. My body, mind, heart, and soul seem to have turned BLACK like the very night that torments me. "There is no escape" I think to myself. "I must end my life for all of us. They will be better off without me. They will have a new start. I must put an end to this life that seems to have begun in darkness and will end the same way." These were my thoughts. Sad but true.

What brought me to the point of attempting suicide? How did I get to that desperate place? As I think back now it seems almost unthinkable, but it wasn't. I was at this stepping off point not just once or twice, but at least six times that I can recall. Once is tragic enough. What would repeatedly bring me to the point of risking my life and that of my family? I believe what happened was that my fear took over at these moments along with my disease of depression. My old familiar feelings overwhelmed my thinking and controlled my actions. Even though I was in therapy and taking medication, I was severely depressed. Throughout these years I felt like there were two parts inside of me — one fighting to survive — the other attempting to destroy me. My illness made my thinking extremely negative and I believed at times I would feel the way I felt "forever." My disease loved fear because it motivated me to keep silent; my fear told me not to reach out and take risks; my fear lied to me.

My pain from depression, the darkness and the desperateness and the hopelessness helped me lose perspective. Without the input of others, I had only my own thoughts to trust. When my depression became unbearable I lost sight of the fact that there were others I could go to for help, who were willing to share in my pain. More importantly, there were others who loved and cared for me even when I couldn't accept love or care about myself. My disease counted on my ignorance, and my disease won at those moments. Because when I forgot that, and when I forgot the spark within me, I relied on myself. All I could see was a black endless pit. I was falling headfirst into this pit. I was ready to end my life. I had lost perspective.

Instead of reaching out for clarity, I reached out to take my life. I couldn't believe there was another way because of what lay at the root of my feelings. The emotions that had been awakened within me were fierce. I was afraid to bring them to light. I had believed I was unlovable ever since I was a child. This was at the root of my suicide attempts.

The problem was, I had not discussed this with my therapist. I was too afraid of what he would think. I was ashamed of myself and what I believed was my truth. I could not consciously face what I believed to be true about myself. I battled these demons internally until I could speak them aloud to Donald or anyone else. When I finally voiced them aloud and named them, I stopped attempting suicide. I could not accept love from God because I thought I knew my truth. I thought I knew better than God. I needed to come to a place where I could accept God's love for me. When I did, I was able to speak my fear. This took five years of inner torment and repeated suicide attempts.

Now I can see this took time and pain, but love was with me all along. I thought my husband and daughters deserved a better wife and mother. I learned that it is not my place to make this judgement. God placed me in their life. He loves me. I needed to look at myself more clearly and in a different light.

God intervened. Before I stepped out in front of a moving vehicle, before I drove somewhere I should not drive, before I emptied a pill bottle I should not be emptying; I picked up the phone and made the most important phone calls of my life — the phone calls that ultimately saved my life. The connection with another human being who knew what to say to me or whose voice was enough — the connection to my therapist brought me back to what mattered — to the choice I needed to make.

"Donald, are you there?"

"Is this you, Marcia?"

"Yes. I am calling to thank you and to say good bye."

"Where are you?" Donald immediately asked me.

"That's not important. I just called to say goodbye. I need to go."

"Wait!" He firmly stated on the phone! "Do not hang up. Emily and Sarah are waiting for you to come home today. Are you listening to me? They are waiting for you right now. Where are you?"

"I am at the train station."

"Are you in your car?

"No, I am standing on the tracks."

Donald calmly replied, "I want you to walk across the tracks to the other side. I will stay on the phone while you do that. It is important that you do not hang up the phone. It is important that you start walking right now. I am here with you. Emily and Sarah will be home soon and they will be waiting to see you. Are you walking towards the side of the tracks, Marcia?"

"Yes," I replied in a faltering voice.

"Are you by your car yet?"

"Almost there," I said.

"That's great," Donald replied in his gentle voice. "Just keep walking. I know that you can get there. You are a great mother. Your daughters will be so happy to see you."

"I'm at my car," I finally said.

"Can you get in and sit down?"

"I can do that."

"That's great. Can you drive your car away from the tracks?"

"Yes," I replied.

"Where are you?" Donald asked me again.

"The town train station."

He continued to talk to me, asking me in his gentle and calm voice, "Why were you standing on the tracks, Marcia? Did something happen today?"

I said, "I feel like my life is over. I am not the mother my daughters deserve or need. I was never good enough and I never will be. I can't go on like this. I don't want to go on like this. Nothing will ever change. My daughters and husband deserve a better mother and wife."

We kept talking. It seems like once I started the words began flowing out of me. How could it be that moments ago I was ready to take my life and now I was sharing my innermost thoughts and feelings? Was it that I felt a connection with this therapist and sensed that for once in my life someone believed in me? In the closed space of my car, I continued to share my deepest feelings with him. I described how I felt not just now, but most of my life as these feelings seemed to consume me and came to the surface. I began to reveal things about myself I thought only my husband would know.

I told Donald, "I feel like I am worthless, I feel like I was born with a hole in my soul. I feel like my family would be better off with me gone, I do not want to go on like this anymore, I feel like I was a mistake and I never should have been born. I feel like I am the scum of the earth, I feel like I am already dead, I am afraid I will never amount to anything, I don't understand why I am like I am. I don't understand why I wasn't good enough for my mother. I don't understand why I am the only one of my sisters who has anything wrong with her. I feel like I will never be good enough or be the mother I want to be or the mother that my daughters deserve."

When I told Donald these thoughts and feelings he listened. I felt connected.

It seemed like once my mind and heart began to open, I was able to go deeper into the dark and secret places. Donald listened and gently responded. "I understand how lost and alone you must have felt. I understand how desperate you feel at times. It is important to feel your feelings. Feelings change. Feelings are not facts. I am sorry your parents and you were not able to talk about how you felt."

This connection with my therapist was enough to cause me to interrupt my thinking. It was really the grace of God working in my life through this man. I needed to stay connected to the deeper reality. My disease was extremely powerful. It still wanted me dead, but there was one more powerful, God, at work in my life. It was easy to lose sight of my goal when I was filled with shattered dreams. My depression was becoming a way of life. Many times I did not have hope but I allowed others to carry it for me.

I couldn't see where I was going. I started to sharpen my listening ability out of necessity. I could hear my daughters and my husband. I tried to listen to what Donald said. I tried to listen closely at recovery meetings. I tried to listen for God's voice, discerning it from among the rest. I found I needed to be still to hear this quiet voice. I found that God spoke gently and quietly to me. I needed to try to discern His voice from all the other thoughts in my mind. This seemed impossible at first. I found, however, the more I sat and practiced, the easier it got for me. My mind was filled with many anxious and worrisome thoughts. I needed to filter these out and search for the quiet and gentle voice of God. It was there, but it was hidden. The more I searched and the more willing I was to search, the easier it was to hear God's voice and the more noticeable it became to me. Perhaps I became a better listener. Or perhaps I was so tired of hearing myself think and getting nowhere I was finally willing to be open to hearing God's gentle leading. Whatever it was, I was grateful. I was also surprised that His voice was gentle and loving. And quiet.

I had expected His voice to be powerful, loud and commanding, even shouting and condemning. God came to me in the stillness and the quiet. He came as I needed Him to come. Gently, with love and care. That showed me how much He knew me, and wanted to love and help me. How great a love was that? As Donald and I spoke while I sat in my car, I felt a warmth come over me as I shared my innermost feelings. I felt like perhaps God was present among us. Quietly listening, inviting me again to share, inviting me to live, a gentle and calm presence in the conversation between my therapist and myself. My heart slowly opened to this invitation to share my pain and darkness that caused me to attempt to take my life. Someone was interested and cared. Someone understood. Certainly Donald did. Apparently this care and concern and love went deeper. I believed at this point that God cared and loved me. Could I accept His love?

In my self-centeredness and illness, I honestly believed that my daughters and husband would be better off without me. I thought I would be doing them a favor. I can see today what I could not see at the time. Donald spent a great deal of time discussing how suicide is selfish.

By ending my life, I would be inflicting unimaginable pain on my daughters and my husband's lives. But my mind could not or would not go there at those moments of extreme desperation. This was another reason I needed to reach out to someone else. Wasn't this the main reason I was walking through this depression in the first place? For my daughters, so they would have a mother who could love them more fully? Now I was ready to commit that most selfish act I was not able to see at the time. My illness did not want me to see that. I needed others to remind me and to keep breaking down my denial to help me see reality. My mental illness wanted to keep me focused on MY situation, but I needed to look outside of myself and look at others around me, to look at WE. I was focused on falling down into that black void that would swallow me up. These thoughts would convince me that although suicide was perhaps not the right answer, it was the only answer for me.

It is more than sufficient to say that these were the most horrible moments of my life. How could they not be? Only by the grace of God am I alive today. No matter how many times, no matter how ashamed I felt of my behavior, I needed to reach out. I did, even when I didn't think I could, and that saved me. I am so grateful today for the gift of life. Deep inside there was a part of me struggling to live. What mattered was that I was still trying. I received the help I needed each and every time. I was desperate at these times. I thought I needed to act on my desperate thoughts and feelings.

The only thing that saved me was the hand on the other side that reached out, took mine, and helped me across. At times, it seemed liked this unseen hand carried me across. Sometimes it seemed like I was gently pushed across, but it was done with love. That was the key for me. At that point in my life I could not respond to anything else. I was so beaten, tired, and discouraged that I didn't think I could respond to anything but gentleness and love. The love my heart was so afraid of for so many years was the exact thing I needed to heal. I was so sick and desperate that I was ready to risk this "love" I had run from all my life. I didn't think I could trust love, but what did I have to lose?

I was ready to take my own life. I am walking because I love my daughters and I want to recover so I can be there for them. I must reach out to the love being offered to me. As difficult as this is, I must accept it. This seems to be the only option I have at this point if I want to survive. I want to do more than survive. I realize that I want to live.

Suicide is not loving for me. Living is the loving response. It is also the more difficult response. I am called to live. If I listen carefully to my daughters' voices, if I am honest, I know this. It seems too difficult. I am afraid, but this is the choice I must make. This is the loving choice for me. I cannot listen to my disease talking to me. I must take a chance to love and to risk. I may never get this chance again. And I find that I want this chance I had from the day I became sober. My depression seemed to set me back and muddied the waters, but I am still afloat. I am tethered to my God of Love. He won't let me go so easily. It is time for me to hold on more tightly, or perhaps it is time for me to let go. Perhaps it is time for me to just surrender to him and let Him lead me. Perhaps it is time for me to trust Him more fully. Whenever I had suicidal thoughts I seldom acted on them, but during those times I did, I was alone with no one to reach out to. My suicidal thoughts became too powerful for me to resist. When I shared my thoughts and intentions with my therapist, he was able to diffuse them or get me the help I desperately needed. I truly believe this is why I am alive today.

Keeping my thoughts to myself was a death sentence hanging over my head. If I had maintained my silence, it would have killed me; and in killing myself I would have destroyed the very lives I was trying to protect; the very young lives I claimed to love so much. Could I really be so focused on my own pain that I was unable to recognize and accept the love being offered so freely from all of those around me? My husband and daughters are not only walking with me in my heart, they are beside me every day. They love me, and I do my best to reciprocate that love, but it is difficult because I am not sure how to express it. I may not be the ideal mother but I am present. Together we are a family with love and some hope. If I commit suicide, then that love and hope will be destroyed. Is that really what I want to do to them? Do I really want this to be their final memory of me? I know deep inside my answer is NO! This is not love for any of us. This is the very opposite of love. Of life. Of commitment. I need help to continue. I want to live.

My eyes began to open. Life is not just about me. I am a mother, a wife, a daughter, a sister, and a friend. These thoughts about my family are not my disease or my fear talking to me; they are love talking to me. These thoughts are coming from my heart. Could they be coming from God, the spark within me that is growing ever stronger with each step I take, although I am not even aware of it at times? Every once in a while, when I feel so desperate, I wish I could reach out and touch Him. I long to take his hand and have Him walk beside me. Perhaps I would even ask him to carry me. I am getting so tired. I would love to ask Him why this is happening to me. I long to sit down and wait for him to answer. I don't understand. I never did. I realize I stopped talking to Him when I was a child, because I didn't understand what was going on in my family. I felt God abandoned me, yet here I am, looking for Him. I need him. I would like to reconnect.

I know in my heart today that it is only by God's grace that I am alive. Reaching out at those times and making human contact was what I needed. Although God's grace was upon me, I also realize that I could have died.

As Donald and I continued to talk on the phone, I heard the sound of my husband's car drive up and park next to me in the train station parking lot. Stephen got out and wrapped his arms tightly around me. I felt myself collapse into his capable arms. Although frantic, he spoke softly into my ear, "I'm glad you're safe, honey. Donald called me. We will get you the help you need. My mother is coming to wait for the girls to come home from school." I sighed deeply.

I picked up the phone I dropped when Stephen arrived. Donald said, "Marcia, you are stronger than you think. It takes a lot of courage to do what you did today. Choosing to live is the better choice. It is the more difficult choice, but it is the loving one."

"I will talk to you as soon as I can."

CHAPTER 14

A NECESSARY COMMITMENT

I was now on my way to the hospital for my first of what would be six hospital stays.

My interrupted suicide attempts brought me to the locked doors of the hospital. My times there were scary and filled with horror. I quickly learned the routine. As soon as I arrived the attendant would say his memorized lines. "I need to search your belongings to make sure you haven't brought in anything that could be used to hurt yourself or others. Nothing with cords and nothing sharp. There is a pay phone in the hall for calls coming in or going out."

Being suicidal, a member of the staff came by and checked on me at ten minute intervals, twenty-four hours a day to be sure I was safe. If I wanted to dry my hair after showering I needed to ask to use a hair dryer. I think I asked to use it one or two times during my six visits. I could barely shower, never mind care about how my hair looked to others. I certainly didn't care how I looked at this time in my life. The goal of being in the hospital was to keep me safe. Once they determined I was no longer suicidal I was released. As terrifying as these times were, they were necessary. While in the hospital, I would attend some groups and go to some doctor appointments, but I would have a fair amount of time to myself which made for a lonely experience. I couldn't understand how I kept ending up in the same place again and again. As traumatic as these times were for me, they were equally as traumatic for my family. Although I was only gone three or four days each time, my absence was definitely disruptive to our family life.

I was ashamed of my thoughts and behavior. My husband visited me as often as possible, bringing our girls. This encouraged me to heal faster. It also helped our daughters understand where their mom was. My husband and I did not hide my illness from them and we sought professionals to help us share with them as appropriate.

Other than my mother, I had little to no contact from any other family members while I was hospitalized. I didn't know if others in my family were afraid to talk to me or if they just had no idea what to say. Or perhaps, others just could not face the fact that I would attempt to kill myself. Whatever the reasons, what I needed most when I was so broken was human acceptance not judgment. I received this from the most amazing place - my young ones who had such love in their eyes and hearts and from my husband. They were able to love and accept me just as I was. I heard them saying "I love you. We miss you mommy. When are you coming home?" These words touched my heart and gave me hope. This motivated me to live. How could it not?

Now I realize this also gave me the strength and desire to want to come home. The mother/daughter bond of love from birth that was often stretched remained unbroken. If anything, my love for my daughters and husband grew stronger during this time. By sharing my pain, I found that I could also share the love of my family. I was a part of something bigger than myself. I was my daughters' mother and my husband's wife. We were a family where there was love amidst the pain. My illness wanted me to believe my life was hopeless, but I was in the psychiatric hospital, surrounded by the love of my husband and daughters. Deep in my heart I knew I had a reason to go on living when I looked into their precious blue eyes and saw the love they had for me. They wanted me to come home and I wanted to be home with them. My husband and I were their parents. I had given birth to these precious girls. I loved this family as I have never loved before. This was all the reason I needed to keep on living. For Emily. For Sarah. For Stephen and myself both as their parents and for us as husband and wife. I may have felt alone but all I needed to do was look around and see who was by my side each and every day. Stephen, Emily, and Sarah were a part of my daily life. We were living life as a family. What kept us together? How were we surviving? As the months turned into years, the girls were growing. They were becoming beautiful young ladies with personalities of their own. They were talented. They did their school work. They had friends and were loving. Something kept us connected and kept us going. Life was not easy but we sauntered on. My steps grew steadier and stronger at times. I had more to lose the more I walked. My heart grew fuller with love for my family. I had to embrace this darkness. I did not have the strength on my own; I never did, but people were tugging at my heart. Emily and Sarah were connected to me in a very deep way. This connection called me to walk and look at where my journey had taken me. I was now motivated out of love instead of entirely out of fear. What a difference! And that was what kept me going. I started to feel love in my heart, not just hear about it in my mind. While walking through the darkness I had been touched by people's love, but it took time. I began to see that this was what my walk was about. It was a journey into my heart. To be the mother I wanted to be I needed to be able to truly love my daughters. Before I could do that, I had to be able to love myself and God. I needed to look into my own heart, as dark as it was in places, to see what laid there; to see what was keeping me from loving freely. Then, and only then, if I chose to do the work I needed to do, would I be able to walk on a different path. The choice was always mine to make. Love was freeing but I didn't know that. There was so much I didn't know about life and myself, but it was time to learn. I always thought I knew what love wasn't. But what was love really?

My thoughts returned to the present. Stephen would pick me up later today and drive me home. The hospital social worker had looked for a day treatment program for me, but, as with my past hospitalizations, there seemed to be a lack of available programs. Either they were filled or there were no appropriate programs, or if there were, none of them accepted our insurance. The contrast from twenty-four-hour care to being home alone was stark but there were no other options. We would do the best we can. I am sent home with an appointment scheduled with my therapist and my regular medication schedule in place. I was no longer suicidal. Instead I was ready to leave and anxious to be home with my family. I was ready to try again. I tried not to think too much about the future or if I would return to this hospital. When Stephen picked me up I said goodbye and silently hoped it would be my final stay.

So what did I find as I searched my heart during my time alone in that psychiatric hospital? I knew I was a shattered person; I could feel it. It was as if pieces of myself were scattered all over the place, like I was a broken mirror which needed to be put back together or pieces of sand that the wind had dispersed throughout the ocean. But the problem seemed to be bigger than that. Some of the scattered pieces did not seem to belong to me. I realized that I had been looking for myself most of my life. This was a horrifying thought but it was an honest one. I tucked it away for safekeeping. I realized that Donald had been trying to get me to look at this question for a while now, but he did not push me too hard. He had a way of getting me to question myself when I was ready. He did not seem to have a timetable for me or too many expectations. This freed me to approach him, especially during times like these, after I had been hospitalized and tended to think of myself as a failure. Although I saw myself that way, Donald did not. He saw me as an ill person and treated me the same as before I was hospitalized, with respect, care and concern. His kindness was almost too much for me to accept, but it was this very kindness that broke down the barriers I had carried around and still carried at times when my fears surfaced. It seemed that he only wanted me to heal. When I talked with him, I felt like he understood me. I felt like he knew what I was saying and even more, a part of him could feel my pain and mistrust of people, and my insecurity, shame, and brokenness. I felt like he would gladly trade places with me if he could, but we both knew that was not possible. I often cried when I was with him and sometimes I didn't know if these were tears of sadness or relief; tears resulting from the calm assurance I was finally able to be with someone, after all these years of searching in the wrong places, who understood me and was capable of being there for me. Someone who could emphasize with me, who believed me when I described how I felt. He valued my thoughts, but more importantly, he valued me for who I was. He encouraged me to be myself. He was interested in what I had to say and in what I thought. This had quite an effect on me.

This helped me pick up the scattered pieces and start honestly examining what I saw. Once I did, I could identify which pieces belonged to me and which belonged to others that affected my life. I also began discerning which pieces I could discard. I may have carried them for a time, but they were not me or were no longer needed.

As I attempted to place these shattered pieces of myself together, I wondered if they could really be put back together. I felt so broken, as if I had been sheared through so many layers and not cleanly cut. I briefly saw a flash of my father's face. I painfully remembered how I did not have a single card or letter with his signature on it; nothing that said "Dad" or "Love, Dad." This thought was fleeting but it was extremely painful for me. It is one I do not allow myself to remember often, if at all; because it cuts through me like a knife. It opens the window a crack to many painful emotions I would rather not face. My dad has been dead for a few years and I miss him, but the truth is, I have missed my dad my whole life. He was physically present in my life but not emotionally present.

When I think of my parents, I tend to think about my mother, not my dad. My head begins to hurt, trying to make sense out of all this. I file it away, thinking I will bring it up in therapy at some point, secretly knowing I won't because I don't have anything to say. What is there to say except that we did not have a relationship. End of story. Or so I thought. Or so I hoped.

Despite my desire to shut the window on this subject, it has been opened and my thoughts and feelings had begun to resurface. Like bubbles on the surface of the water, I was unaware of where they came from. Perhaps I wasn't in a place where I was ready because this was a huge piece of my shattered self; the piece about my father I am too eager to discard. Perhaps this might have been a warning sign to me but it wasn't. I was too broken and afraid; my familiar companion at work again. Some professionals asked if I remembered any trauma that might have happened to me. "What trauma?" I thought to myself. I had been open about my food addiction and alcoholism, and as horrifying and shameful as it was for me, my suicide attempts. "What else could they possibly be referring to," I thought to myself. I know how helpful sharing these issues and my personal feelings with my therapist has been. But I know there is nothing else because I don't remember anything else. Today I know that I was not ready, and I am grateful for that. I could not have faced some of the more jagged pieces of my inner self until I was in a better place to recover, until I was better prepared to face the reality of the depth of the hurt I carried.

As these thoughts were whirling through my mind, my fear of returning, or worse, of remaining in the mental hospital, tore at my heart and soul. I knew God was keeping me sober each day, despite the darkness and the shame I felt for trying to end my life. I am somehow brought closer to my God during this time. In the silence of my hospital room, in my moment of deep need, I surrendered myself to God's love and care. I could no longer afford to doubt that He loved me. I desperately needed something to hold onto as I lay in that hospital bed. I couldn't leave the hospital that sixth time without something more than the fear I had when I entered. I needed more than knowing that my therapist believed in me; more than knowing my husband loved me; even more than knowing my daughters loved me. When I had some moments of clarity I wondered how I kept ending back in this hospital, despite wanting to live. The part of me that was brutally honest knew that I needed God's help and care. I craved this and was ready to risk more of God's love. I knew all about being afraid of God, but now I was much more afraid of what I could and would do to myself, and ultimately to my family through the destructiveness of my disease. I was ready to risk God's love, so I surrendered the best I knew how. I asked God to help me believe he loved me, and to help me trust His love for me. I continued to be severely depressed, but I stopped debating whether or not God loved me. I continued to put one foot in front of the other and walked through each day, some easier than others.

Today I know that the doors of the mental hospital do not always swing both ways. The hand of God was upon me, guiding me each time I was in there; enabling me to come when I desperately needed a reprieve and enabling me to leave to come home. I was fortunate to have a home to come back to after each hospitalization.

When I accepted God's love this time, my heart opened to allow Him into my life more fully. I was not too sure about trusting this God of love, but I was desperate. I was willing. At least, that is what I thought; but there seemed to be obstacles that kept blocking my path. The initial tsunami that crashed into me never stopped. The waves kept coming through the years. It seemed like any progress I made was demolished by the next powerful wave. I could not seem to get any consistent recovery or perspective on myself or my life.

But I also did not know too much about the ocean. There is a rhythm to the ocean and the tide. The tide comes in and goes out in a predictable manner. Waves, even powerful ones, come in, but when the tide goes out it takes seaweed and sand with it. What I could not see was that the tide in my life was taking the debris out to sea. But just because I was not aware of it did not mean it was not happening. Part of my problem was, I was too focused on the incoming waves that I thought were tsunamis when sometimes they were just the incoming tide. My life also had a rhythm. With each passing hospitalization and with each day of therapy and each surrender to God, I moved closer to the surface. I was moving in the right direction as my emotional debris continued being swept out to sea. I could not comprehend all that was happening. Just as I was unaware of the magnitude of God's love or presence, I was not aware of the recovery happening in my life. I needed to trust. I needed to stay connected. I needed to believe I did not know the answers. I needed to keep going. As I was bridging the gap between the ocean and the ground where my family lived, I was moving closer to living life as an emotionally healthy person. Just one more day to continue on; one step closer.

I needed to believe more fully in the God of love who was keeping me sober, one day at a time, despite the inner darkness I was living in. I needed to believe more fully that recovery was possible and that the inner spark was guiding me. I needed to believe that I could and would one day be that mother and wife for my family. I needed to believe that God loved me and saw me differently than I saw myself. I needed to believe that there was another way of seeing things than my way. I needed to believe in goodness and love and life because this is what I was looking at when I looked at my daughters each and every day. How could I not believe in all of these things? They were present and breathing and loving, and I saw and felt their love. I wanted to believe that this was possible for me to have, so I did. I don't remember the day or the time but I do remember the feeling. I felt hope for myself. I felt lighter. I felt that if I continued to do what I needed to do then one day things would change for me. I hoped it would be sooner rather than later.

CHAPTER 15

IN SICKNESS AND
IN HEALTH

"*J*UST TELL ME WHAT I CAN DO TO HELP YOU FEEL BETTER. I CAN'T HELP YOU UNLESS YOU TELL ME WHAT YOU NEED!"

Stephen repeated these words to me countless times throughout those years. So much, they still echo in my mind today. My reply often was, "There isn't anything you can do to make me feel better. Nothing. Could you hold me instead?" Stephen often held me as I cried. However, he did become frustrated with my response and apparent lack of progress as the years passed.

Our marriage suffered greatly from my illness. Initially, as a new mother, my focus had been on our newborn daughters. As the years passed, I was unable to move some of this focus off of our daughters and onto Stephen. Today I know some of this was my illness and another problem was my fear of intimacy. The result was a rocky thirteen-year relationship with many questions and hurt. Our trust and love for one another had been questioned. We were called to look at our relationship more deeply and challenge one another to grow together and separately so we could stay together and try to have a fulfilling relationship despite the external circumstances. If not, we could choose to go our separate ways. We had more to consider than ourselves. We had two daughters depending on us. We did not want to stay together and provide them a hostile home environment. Providing an honest environment where we were working to correct our problems was difficult enough.

Our marriage had not been an ideal marriage at many points, but when the tough times came, love taught us that LOVE was an action and each of us needed to respond. It wasn't easy and it wasn't comfortable, but it was our reality.

When I met Stephen, my life gradually changed for the better. I knew I had met a person that I could relate to. We shared many things together, including our love for camping, nature and the beach. I ended up sharing things I thought I would never tell another human being. We talked for hours usually while sitting on the beach wall or walking on the beach. I told Stephen how growing up, I often thought that perhaps I was adopted because I seemed to be so different from my sisters. I never felt like I fit in. He shared his own feelings in response, "I know how you feel. I remember feeling different in school. I didn't feel the same as other students in my class because it took me longer to learn something. I felt like I wasn't as good as they were." Exchanges like these became common between us. We grew closer because we were able to share our feelings and our deeper thoughts. I came to deeply love him. We married after knowing one another for four years.

We became emotionally and physically close. We both looked forward to sharing our lives together and raising a family. When I became depressed, no one was more severely affected by my illness than Stephen. He sacrificed many of his own goals for those of his family.

Adding to these stresses, the woman he had known and loved had drastically changed, and none of the professionals could assure him when, or even if, I would recover. With each passing day, I seemed to regress. I seemed to establish a trusting and growing relationship with my therapist while I was growing more silent with him. I found it extremely difficult to communicate my feelings to Stephen. I cried often, yet I could not explain what was wrong. Worse, I could not tell Stephen how he could help me. The tension between us and in our home grew. We attempted to improve our relationship but my emotional state was constantly the priority. I was no longer interested in maintaining a physical relationship with Stephen. My depression and the side effects from the medication removed my desire for sexual intimacy.

I was withdrawn. My attention and limited energy was focused on our daughters. Our conversations were limited to how badly I felt. Any plans we made as a family were usually cancelled as I did not feel well when it was time to go. We eventually made very few plans and Stephen often took the girls to events by himself.

After working all day, Stephen came home to a chaotic household. He never knew what mood I would be in. Certainly I would be depressed, but I might also have been anxious or withdrawn. The girls grew and their needs changed. Stephen needed to address the ones I couldn't. Dinner was whatever I happened to throw together "again." Nothing was usually planned as I was not too interested in food or much else at that point in my life. I was also not interested in going out on a Saturday night for a date with Stephen. Initially, I did not want to leave our daughters and then I became too tired and disinterested in "life" in general.

Our relationship became stressed and strained, almost to the breaking point. I continued to go to therapy; Stephen eventually went to therapy himself to help cope with his own issues of living with me and dealing with my depression. Eventually we both went to a marriage counselor to deal with the overwhelming issues we faced such as lack of physical intimacy, inability to communicate feelings, trust issues, and many misunderstandings. Other people throughout the years had opinions about what Stephen should do about our marriage and our children, but he remained committed to our relationship. Despite the growing tension between us, he believed any decisions were to be our decisions and not influenced by others, unless they were professionals directly involved in my care.

We eventually sought legal advice for a separation prior to obtaining a divorce, however once we went to the lawyer's office, reality took over. Although we were frustrated with one other and with my illness, we realized we still loved each other "for better and for worse," and this was for worse. We were not willing or ready to split up. When we were honest and sat in the stillness we could see the anger we had because our lives had been destroyed by my disease. Our original plans were gone; our hopes and dreams a mere speck of sand on the beach, being blown away by the wind. We needed to express these feelings and thoughts honestly with each other and see what lay underneath the anger, disappointment and hurt. When we did this, I realized something extremely important. Despite all that had happened and all the lost dreams and events, Stephen had been there for me. Yes, I loved him when we got married, but during these past years I had learned to trust him because he was there despite what my disease brought our way. When the despair became too much for me and I found myself on the brink of suicide, Stephen did not turn away from me. He accepted me and loved me in my most vulnerable condition. He loved me just as I was. He loved me through the darkest of times. Even more, he brought our daughters to see me when I was hospitalized. He knew I needed to see them and he knew they needed to see me. One of the biggest gifts he gave our daughters and me had been to show them how to love me when I felt most unlovable.

This was true love. He knew our family was connected in love and acceptance. Our daughters saw me at some of my worst moments growing up. They loved me in spite of that, and their love did for me what I could never do for myself, and what I could never find most of my life. Their love strengthened my connection to them. It grew in my heart and gave me the courage to get out of that hospital and keep going. Despite the lost dreams and our interrupted life, we remained a family. We cared for one another. We had a reason to keep on going when "I" couldn't find one many times by myself. "We" may have lost much, but "we" had much for which to be grateful.

We continued to remain together. Our patience was stretched. We didn't understand one another. We were often frustrated and disappointed. We argued and disagreed and argued some more. We cried together. Stephen was frightened. I was frightened. We were frightened together. He held my hand. I held his hand. And we held our daughters' hands through it all.

I owed a lot to my husband. He was there for me, even when I wanted to push him away. In fact, I tried many times; this was what most of our arguments were about — I did not want to accept love, at least not his love. I could not accept it because deep down I believed I was unlovable. I did not know that then but I know it today. I was afraid of what accepting his love would mean to me. I was very ill emotionally. Many times my fear tried to control my thinking. Fortunately, Stephen stayed. I could not push hard enough. He invited me back. He loved me just as much as I loved him; perhaps more, and he wouldn't let me push him away. There was a part of me that couldn't let him go. I loved Stephen; we had our daughters together, and something inside of me was changing. I didn't want to admit it, but I needed his love and I needed to love him. We were in a special relationship and we had a special family together. We were connected. This was stronger than the illness that was trying its best to destroy me and our marriage.

Our marriage vows were tested time and time again. Fortunately, both Stephen and I went to therapy instead of waiting around for our situation to improve. The harsh truth was our situation was not improving and was not going to improve by itself. Even with much help and prayer, our relationship was tremendously strained during these years due to the constant effects of my illness. We would be deluding ourselves by thinking our marriage was "fine" when we could not communicate most days. My emotional illness had far reaching effects on my marriage. In this way, my depression could be seen as a family illness. Living with me as a severely depressed person for thirteen years could not help but affect those I lived with and loved dearly.

Accepting love wasn't easy for me, but it was necessary. It gave me the strength for my journey. It all came back to my heart. I needed to open it to love; giving and receiving it freely. I needed to risk getting hurt and risk hurting others.

My choice again. Always my choice. What was it going to be? I gradually learned that I would get better at relationships by actually being in them. I would need to walk through my fear a little at a time and risk being hurt, so that I could also risk being known and being loved. But for a long time, being known and being loved was just as scary for me. That needed to change if I was to not only recover but to have any chance of being the mother I wanted to be. And the wife I not only wanted to be but the wife my husband needed and deserved. I came to realize that to become this person I needed to start on another road and make some drastic changes, or I would never arrive. I would always be in the process of becoming that mother and wife and person, so long as I was willing to be open to truth and to love and to life. My fear made sure I was not open to any of these before now. I was in the process of changing. In fact, my fear was part of what was motivating me to change. My fear of not being there for my daughters, my fear of not being the mother they needed, my fear of not protecting them, my fear of breaking that love connection with them.

These fears were healthy fears because they mobilized me to positive action. They motivated me to get out of bed each morning, even when my disease told me to pull the covers over my head and ignore my children's cries for breakfast; they motivated me to keep going to my therapy sessions when I was too exhausted; they motivated me to keep attending my weekly therapy group despite the three hour drive and my reluctance to participate, or my inability to notice any improvement; they motivated me to find a reason to go on when my thoughts and emotions wanted me to give up entirely. When I thought I could not hold on another minute, my fear encouraged me to do something I never thought possible. I needed to relax my hold in my mind and in my heart, and let the memories come flooding back. I needed to relax my control and my fears of getting hurt; I needed to reach out and allow God and others in. Holding on too tightly to some things, out of fear, was standing in my way of progress. I wanted to get to a certain place and my past was getting in my way, but there was a way to handle it. Again, the choice was mine. Holding on and letting go - I began to learn there is a delicate balance between the two in my life, or at least, there needed to be.

CHAPTER 16

SPEAKING THE UNSPEAKABLE

*A*s I continued in therapy, I began to have flashbacks from my past. An especially painful one came to the forefront of my mind from my sophomore year in college.

I had dated my first boyfriend, Tim, for at least one year. I was afraid of boys but I enjoyed being with him. Although I was attracted to Tim, I was not interested in a physical relationship.

One day, as I sat in therapy I heard a voice that sounded like mine shouting:

"NO, STOP LEAVE ME ALONE!" I was startled and horrified! I had no idea how long I was screaming. I heard Donald saying, "You are safe Marcia, I am right here beside you. You are in my office. That happened a long time ago. Take my hands." I opened my eyes and saw I was holding Donald's hands. Memories came flooding back to me:

Tim had raped me at college on a Friday night in March. We had been to a campus party. While we were walking back to my dorm we stopped to talk on a bench. Before I knew it, Tim was kissing me. I pulled away but then he started to touch me. I screamed for him to stop. It was the same screaming I heard right now. I pushed him away. It didn't seem to matter what I said or did because he didn't stop. I finally ran to my dorm room as fast as I could, feeling ripped apart inside and out. I rushed to take a shower, tearing my clothes off and throwing them away in the trash can. I stood in the shower for what seemed like hours. No matter how hard I scrubbed or how much soap I used I could not remove the dirt or the shame I felt inside of me. I couldn't understand how this had happened. I thought Tim and I loved each other. At least that is what we told each other. This is what I wanted to believe. I wanted so much for this time to be different. But what did I mean by "this time" I thought to myself? Tim was my first boyfriend. Is this what love looked like? Is this how love felt? Thinking back, I knew there was a reason I didn't trust people. I should not have trusted Tim in the first place. I should have known better. Why did I let my guard down? "This is my own fault," I told myself. There was no one I could tell. Surely not my mother. She would tell me it was my own fault. I already knew that. I would have to deal with this on my own like I did with everything else.

The problem was I did not deal with being raped. I didn't tell anyone, instead I pushed my thoughts and feelings away. I went on with my life as best I could. Tim came to see me the next day. "I'm so sorry for what happened last night. I think I had too much to drink. I didn't mean for that to happen. I wanted to stop but I couldn't help myself. I'm sorry. I know I hurt you. I am not the same person I was when we met. I am leaving college and moving out of state."

I stared at him blankly before I started to cry. He attempted to hold me but I pushed him away. "I'm sorry too, Tim," I said. "I wish none of this happened. I guess you should just go."

I never saw or heard from him again. Several months later I received word that he attempted suicide. I didn't want to believe it. I couldn't deal with being raped and I definitely couldn't handle the fact that my former boyfriend tried to commit suicide. My world was spiraling out of control, and I was going down with it, or so I feared. How would I go on? Did I even want to?

The shame and guilt I felt were overwhelming. Worse, my fear told me there was no one I could possibly trust with my feelings and with the truth. So I moved on with my life the best I could, my mind repressing the feelings and memories, enabling me to survive. And that is what I did; I survived. I got through each day the best I could. I felt dirty, violated, and used. I was confused. I felt sorry for Tim. I felt I was responsible for being raped. That belief haunted me. It connected with something deep inside of me. Something I could not understand then and couldn't understand now thirty years later. Something resonated deep inside of me. I thought, "How could I think I was lovable in the first place?" I didn't know why I carried this feeling inside me. I started to see that I believed I deserved to have bad things happen to me. This was one reason drinking was useful to me. My drinking hid these haunting feelings for periods of time, but as the years passed my drinking needed to increase to continue making sure these thoughts and feelings would stay hidden. Now, as I remembered this incident, the feelings came hurling through with hurricane force, catching me off guard.

These memories overpowered me as they returned. I felt a release when I shared them. I relived the trauma with support. I would not be destroyed and devastated as I was when it happened. I cried and experienced the anger, confusion, hurt, disappointment, shame, guilt, and fear I had been avoiding all this time. It wasn't easy but Donald knew how to help me through it. It took time to resolve these issues, and some of them I am still working through.

I felt emotionally depleted and exhausted at times, but I also felt lighter, as if an anchor had been lifted. It took me some time to share the details of my rape with my husband. When I did, Stephen held me and told me he loved me. I wrote furiously in my journal until I eventually felt peace and relief.

Worse than feeling guilt over being raped, I felt like I was responsible in some way for Tim's tragic life. I needed to process that part for much longer before I could come to a place of acceptance, peace and understanding. I learned in my own case that attempting suicide was an extremely lonely and tragic attempt to end a seemingly hopeless state. I do not know what it was for Tim, but I do know that when I attempted to reach out to others, I did not try to kill myself. I may have thought about it, but I did not try to act on it. Something about my connection with others kept me safe and the feelings and thoughts passed.

Although I shared this part of my past with Donald, Stephen, and my doctors, I chose not to share it with anyone else before now. It was too raw and personal for me. I choose to share it now to show the destructive power my secrets had over me and to show the wonderful hope that recovery is possible. The rape happened when I was twenty years old, and I carried that burden around in private, unconsciously for at least twenty-five years before sharing it with another soul. Releasing it was like the day my mother opened the door to my bedroom closet and found my uneaten lunches. At first I was scared of what would happen when she found them, but secretly I was incredibly relieved that my secret was known. I could breathe easier. Although I continued to hide my lunches, I no longer felt like I was deceiving my parents and perhaps, in some way, myself. It took me many years to be able to seek help for my eating disorder, but as Donald told me, in some way it was a coping mechanism for me. Surely it was not healthy, but it was needed at that time. I needed help. My world continued to spiral out of control for quite a while.

When food no longer worked, I turned to alcohol. My world was not necessarily better, I just appeared to function better to other people. That was what I cared about. What others thought of me was of utmost importance because I knew how little I thought of myself. I lived in almost constant fear, insecurity, loneliness, and mistrust. I wanted to be anyone but me, I thought to myself. I'll be anyone you want me to be. That was how I lived my life. As I worked through my feelings and issues from being raped, the thought began to bother me about why I felt so responsible, why it felt so familiar, like it had happened to me before in my life. Those thoughts began to nag me like a horsefly at the beach when you are trying to rest on a beach towel but end up having to swat that nagging horsefly that just won't go away. These thoughts would not leave me alone and began to torture me, day and night. I was no closer to identifying their source but I could no longer pretend they weren't there. I knew deep in my heart and soul there was something to them.

I could no longer afford to be afraid of what I would find. I was tired and frustrated from being depressed for so long. I desperately wanted relief for myself, my daughters and my husband. I was trying to face my reality instead of running from it. This was quite a switch for me! This was a part of me I did not know. I dislike confrontation of any kind, but the cost of avoidance is too high for me now. I have paid dearly. The cost includes not just me, but my daughters and my husband as well. This must be what love is about. Thinking about others and what is good for them, I continue to put one foot in front of the other. My heart knows what I am holding and I know it is priceless. If I lose my daughters and husband, I will be lost. I don't know if I can bear that. I will keep going. I cannot think beyond today, just take one more step, right foot, left foot, right foot, left foot.

CHAPTER 17

A DAY AT THE BEACH?

*O*ne day I sat outside in our backyard by our pool, waiting for the girls to come home from school. They were older now and would come home on the bus after staying late for after school activities. I sat in a lounge chair, staring at the water. Because of the pool liner and the angle of the afternoon sun in April, the water looked an aqua shade of blue. I stared as if I was mesmerized by the water. I saw and heard the children next door playing in their yard. Memories of another day and time came flooding back into my mind as if they were happening in this moment: My sisters and I were swinging on the swing set at the beach. I saw the white and blue ice cream truck pulling away from the beach. My sisters and I were running after it yelling, "Wait, come back for us, we want ice cream today. Come back, PLEASE!!" But this faded into the background and all I saw was me with my father. We were at the summer cottage. I was crying but I could not tell if these tears were real or if they were from another time. I was confused at first. The picture came into clearer focus, much clearer as if I was there.

Memories began to flood my mind. I didn't want them to, but once they began to come, I couldn't stop them. Something deep inside me told me to allow them. "I am with you," goes through my mind. "You are loved." I saw myself as a young girl. My dad and I were alone in the cottage.

The memories came rushing back and threatened to overwhelm me. As they came, a sense of relief overtook me deep inside, along with a rush of overwhelming emotions; fear, shame, guilt, horror, terror, confusion, embarrassment, anger.

As the repressed memories surfaced, I went back in time. I relived those moments. I was a child again. It was like watching a movie but it was a living nightmare. The images were clear, the colors vivid, the characters too familiar. I sobbed. I was so young, just a child really, seven or eight, not much younger than Emily and Sarah were now. My dad and I were in the bedroom. I didn't understand why he was undressing me and throwing my favorite pink bathing suit on the floor. I usually got ready for bed myself. If I needed help, my mother would help me. Come to think of it, where was my mother? I looked around the bedroom for my pajamas but I didn't see them. Before I knew what happened my dad was touching me. I asked, "Dad, what are you doing? Please stop." It seemed like he didn't hear me. He kept going. I started to cry. He didn't seem to see me crying either. I began to panic and thought something was wrong. I began to yell "STOP! You are hurting me!" But he didn't stop. Could it be he didn't hear me, or was it he didn't care he was hurting me? I didn't know because when he finally stopped we were both crying. I knew he saw my tears then. My father wrapped me in the blanket from the bed. He held me and said, "I'm sorry. Please don't tell anyone." He looked like he couldn't believe what had just happened. I heard myself say "I'm sorry" back to him. I went on to say those two words throughout my life. It was as if those words were burned into my mind and came from my mouth automatically.

I tried to pretend this horror was a fairy tale but it was more like a nightmare. I was confused and frightened; terrified really. I tried to forget it but I could never forget my dad molesting me. I could never forget the sound of my voice begging him to stop. My heart was broken for both of us. A part of me felt like I failed to take away his pain and loneliness. I thought my father molested me in order to feel better. That was the worst part of the secret I carried with me all this time. In my childlike mind, I thought I was responsible for what happened. Why else would my father do these terrible things to me? My seven-year-old mind could not make sense of what happened. I could not bear to think that my father would hurt me. Instead, I told myself I failed in some way and did something wrong. I knew what happened was wrong.

There was no one I could go to with my "secret" besides I promised my dad I wouldn't tell anyone. Who would believe me anyway? Certainly not my mother and definitely not the nuns in school. Why would I want to tell anyone if I was the one who was responsible? What would happen to me? After the initial trauma, it seemed like the memories were erased from my memory. But I was left feeling like I was different. I felt like I had lost my childhood. I felt like I had lost myself, and in a way I had. I spent the next forty years hiding from myself, the world, and God. I was too afraid to face who I had become and what I had lost.

Could it be that my real work all these years, and perhaps now, was to find myself in this darkness? I had spent years of my life lost since that day and I was still lost. The difference was that I was now in my forties and emotionally in the dark. How lost and low can a person go I thought to myself? When was enough enough? Maybe by acknowledging this pain I would begin to find myself. The truth may not be what I wanted, but it might be what I needed to see.

Part of me was relieved. A part of me began to rise to the surface of the water and I began to breathe deeply from the fresh air. My lungs expanded more fully and I opened my eyes. They initially stung as I shook the salt water from them, but as I did I was able to open them more fully. What I saw was not what I hoped to see, but it was my truth; by seeing it I finally had a chance to begin to break free from the source of the destructive nets that entangled and entwined me and were enmeshed within the fabric of my being. I no longer felt like I was sinking. Confronting my truth released me. The fresh ocean air felt good on my body. I had much work to do. My heart was hurt by the repressed memories I remembered, but I was now free to swim and make progress. I continued to go to therapy. I took deep breaths. I began to swim slowly towards the shoreline that was finally within sight. I was eager to get there, but I was not in a hurry to encounter my inner pain. I was eager to see what lay ahead. I wanted to share more fully in my daughters' and my husband's lives.

I went around saying I'm sorry and feeling sorry for all types of things most of my life. In reality, I had taken on things I had no control over or power to fix. In my child's mind I didn't know this. I only wanted my dad to be happy. He looked so sad. So did my mom. I thought I could fix both of them, or worse, that I was the cause of their unhappiness. I knew now that neither of these were true, but I couldn't risk talking to either my mother or father. My life depended on them. Instead of growing up secure in love, I grew up afraid of it. I had it mixed up because of circumstances. I was full of fear. I couldn't bear the thought of my parents being in pain or seeing other people unhappy. Perhaps I couldn't bear the thought that my parents were not perfect, or perhaps I couldn't bear the thought that I wasn't perfect. Whatever the real reasons, I knew I changed that day.

I lost the ability to trust that those who cared for me and loved me would not hurt me, or that they would not abandon me. I walked around with this horrific secret. I was seven years old. I no longer felt safe around people. Would I ever feel safe again? No one else in my family appeared to view things the way I not only viewed them, but experienced them. This seemed to alienate me further. I began to feel that something was wrong or that things were not as they seemed. I thought of those green walls again in the living room and the dining room at our childhood house. What had they seen? If I could talk to them what else would they tell me? After all, I was the only one who seemed to hate the color. If I could talk to those walls at our home, what would I ask them? Had anyone else in my family been molested? Did my mother know what my dad did to me? If so, why hadn't she done anything about it? Was she protecting my dad? Wasn't she supposed to be protecting me if she knew? Who was protecting me? Why did I try to protect my father? What was really going on here?

My mother did not do anything about my eating disorder, so maybe she chose not to do anything about my father molesting me. "What do you know walls? Were any of my sisters molested? If so, do they remember? If I was the only one, what would they do when they found out? If only these walls could talk."

I realized that the walls could not talk. I realized both my parents had passed on. I realized eventually this was my truth and my path, and my darkness to embrace. I chose not to share this with my sisters for several reasons. The primary reason was that they were living their lives and we were not connected on that level when my memories came back to me. I had been depressed for eleven years by that time, and the emotional void between us was huge. I felt it best to heal. I trusted that God would direct and guide me as time passed with how best to share this experience, if I did. Healing was to be in God's time, not mine as I learned. My recovery continues as I live life daily.

I began to feel like I did not fit into my family. I felt different, not good enough. Being told to keep it a secret began to grow in the dark, and the lies it began to tell me took on a life all its own. They eventually came to influence my thoughts and behavior for the next thirty to forty years of my life.

I began to withdraw from my family and friends. I was outwardly present but absent emotionally. I couldn't be present because the truth I carried was too much of a burden. I believe my mind buried those memories to protect me at that very young and vulnerable age so I could survive. And that is what I began to do. I began to survive and protect myself.

Life lost something at that moment. Without being aware of it I lost the childlike faith I once had in my parents, in the world, and in God. I lost the faith I had in myself and life. From that moment on I could no longer trust love. I couldn't trust that people cared for me or cared about me. Worse, I began to believe that I was unlovable. A common thought in my mind was "if you really knew me you wouldn't like me." This is how I kept myself distant from people as I grew. I was afraid to take risks, and when I did, I was afraid of rejection or betrayal. I had a few close friends but my goal was to hide. I did that well by building up protective layers around my heart.

As these memories came flooding back, I realized that this is where my feelings and sense of being unlovable initially came from.

As I became conscious of these memories, I became aware of much more. I realized my core identity of being unlovable was birthed that night. I thought my father did not love me because I failed to take away his pain when he molested me. I longed to hear him say "I love you" all my life. Truthfully, I was still waiting to hear those words. Perhaps he never could. I did not know. All I knew was that I was devastated by this. I had no way to handle my disappointment and loss. It was more than disappointment for me. I felt as if my identity depended upon it. As the years passed, it became apparent that my dad and I were never going to have a close relationship. Instead, I had that false close relationship with food, alcohol, and even compulsive shopping.

The cottage that once represented safety and fun was no longer either. I stopped enjoying the beach in the summertime. Although I still went to the beach, I began to see it differently. Instead of relaxing and enjoying the sand and ocean, I saw the beach as a dangerous place. I became a bystander instead of participating in activities. At times I wanted to learn to become a better swimmer or to canoe, but whenever friends asked, I used my usual excuse "I'm afraid." I could not move beyond my fear. For a while I wanted to, but then I stopped having any desire to enjoy water activities. I associated the ocean with what happened to me at the cottage but I didn't understand why. The ocean came to represent danger for me, not fun, freedom and opportunity. My childlike spirit was crushed that summer. My desire to live life was taken from me. I began to seek what I thought were safer, more narrow roads instead of the wide-open ocean of life. These were rather poor choices, but it was the best I could do under the circumstances. The longer I allowed my fear to control me, the more difficult it became for me to break out of that pattern of my destructive choices.

In the stillness of my heart I trusted these memories. The feelings and memories were real. I couldn't handle them before and I knew I couldn't handle them now. I had a lot more to lose now than just myself. What I did and the decisions I made affected my family as well as me. Wasn't that what being a responsible mother was all about? So this time I made a better choice. I made another much-needed phone call to my therapist. "Donald, can we meet? I need to talk with you about something very important?"

We met and talked but it wasn't easy. It took me quite a while to share all that I remembered after forty years. I didn't know that the trauma I suffered and repressed during childhood could influence me throughout my life. The secrets needed to come out. The lies I believed needed to be seen for what they were. I needed to embrace my darkness in order to get out. I thought this would break my heart, but the opposite occurred. My heart had already been broken for years. I hadn't realized it or allowed myself to feel it. The moment the light broke through the darkness of my memories my heart began to heal. My heart hurt badly, but it was a healing hurt.

I had a lot of work to do, but the light made the rest of my journey easier. At least now I could see where my feet were. I was finally walking on the ground. I was still walking to recover from my depression, but the additional contributing issues were finally identified. I was relieved. There had been a huge change inside of me. I was now ready to face these issues. I now knew I suffered from post traumatic stress disorder. Deep down, as painful as all this was for me, I knew I had reached my truth. Something finally felt right. In fact, I had finally connected with myself in a way I had never done before. The pieces began to make sense to me. Some were jagged and cut deeply, but they belonged to me. They were part of my childhood and I knew it. I could not and I would not deny it. Whatever else happened and whatever else I had been thinking about wouldn't fit if I ignored the framework or border of my puzzle. I found myself trying to jam other pieces in and make them fit. More importantly, I knew I needed to look at this so that this trauma no longer defined who I was. My identity did not come from what happened to me as a child or from other experiences. My true identity came from God. I needed to process what happened or it would continue to haunt me. I had a choice here.

It was time for me to learn how be an adult. I believe God knew that I was not only ready to face my truths, but that He had put the right supports in place.

I was on a journey of love, and God not only revealed His heart to me during this time, He touched my heart. I needed His love now more than ever as I looked at these painful wounds I had carried for years. I would need His guidance and compassion and comfort as I worked through not only the memories, but the feelings associated with those childhood memories. I found that God was interested in what was on my mind and in my heart. He wanted me to be honest about what I thought and how I felt. I found there was a lifetime of healing needed here. My life perspective had been affected. I needed to honestly question my beliefs about myself, life, the world, and God. My journey continued. The bonds between my daughters, my husband, and me became stronger. I connected with my therapist, and I began to connect with others in the world. The spark within me began to ignite. I moved forward as if I was on fire.

My perspective needed to change. I felt like I was finally walking on the ground, even though I was stumbling to find my way. But at least I no longer felt like I was in the deep ocean. I saw the earth as dirty. Certainly the ground is dirty, or is it myself I see this way? What has happened to me?

These memories were a vital piece of my darkness. It took many years into my depression for me to remember them. As I grappled with how they would integrate into my new forming sense of self, as a person, woman, wife, mother, sister, friend, daughter, my heart and mind continued to open to the Hope I desperately sought to recover from this relentless depression - first as a mother for fear of losing my daughters, but eventually for myself, as a person, loved for being the person I never wanted to be, MYSELF.

CHAPTER 18

OUR EXPANDING FAMILY

*W*hen the girls were quite young, Stephen and our girls came home one Saturday afternoon with a surprise for me; one I would never have imagined.

"Look mom," Emily and Sarah said. "Isn't she the most adorable puppy you have ever seen? And she's ours now. Isn't that great? Come pet her. Where will she sleep? Where will we put her bed? Where will we put her food and water bowls? Do you like the ones we bought her? What should we name her?"

When the girls walked into our kitchen with their dad, Emily was carrying a little black and grey furry German Shepherd puppy in her little hands. I was speechless. Stephen knew I was afraid of puppies. He also knew I would not want one. That's why he went on this puppy mission without me! She wasn't particularly cute because I was afraid of her even though I towered over her. I thought she would bite me. Stephen and our daughters seemed to know how to hold her and play with her, but I never had any pets growing up. I didn't know how to care for a dog, but apparently we now had one of our own. Stephen and the girls were so excited. I couldn't say no. We could use a little cheering up in our household and this little furry dog, now named Duchess by unanimous vote, seemed to be doing just that.

So I joined in, slowly and apprehensively; petting Duchess as we welcomed her into our family. Duchess seemed to grow remarkably quickly that first year. She was a beautiful dog. There were many staring contests with Sarah, and to her chagrin Duchess usually won. During the week I took Duchess for her morning walks. It was good for me. We both seemed to need our daily walks. Duchess loved to walk, rain or shine. Before long, I enjoyed my time with Duchess. I had connected with her and looked forward to watching her instead of thinking about myself, especially when I was home alone.

Two years later, we decided Duchess needed a sibling. This time we went together and welcomed an eleven-week-old black Labrador Retriever into our growing family. We attempted to bring him home in a shoebox but he refused to stay in the box; an early sign he would not be contained or travel well in the car! We quickly named our new puppy Buddy. He was a very special puppy. His heart was as big as the great outdoors where he loved to run and swim even more. Buddy loved life and people, and people seemed to love Buddy. I knew he was mine. I quickly thought of Buddy as one of my best friends.

Buddy came into a wounded family that needed healing. Anyone who came close to him couldn't help but catch his love for life. Buddy was a generous dog who loved to give of himself. He seemed to intuitively know what people needed. I knew this because Buddy and I spent a lot of time together. Buddy sensed what I needed before I seemed to know it myself. Whenever I was upset or crying, Buddy was close to give me a special puppy hug. When I needed some time alone, Buddy would lay in the same room but not bother me. When I went into another room and Buddy thought I was gone too long, he came to find me to make sure I was okay. Buddy loved affection and was affectionate. Buddy loved to follow all of us. I would often find Buddy lying beside Stephen as he worked on a car in the garage. Other times, he would be lying underneath the truck, catching some shade during the heat of the summer. Buddy had no qualms about climbing the basement stairs to find Stephen while he repaired the washing machine, or running up the first level staircase to jump onto Emily or Sarah's bed while they prepared to get ready for soccer practice. Buddy's favorite time was swimming time. Whether pool or lake or ocean, he loved to swim or dive in and retrieve a toy. "Jump, Buddy, Jump! Get your toy" was often heard by the pool. He was adorable, inside and out. Oh, I almost forgot, he liked to chase the ducks on the ponds. He never caught up with them, but he sure did have fun trying. Almost as much fun as we had watching him.

One week, Buddy earned himself the nickname "Bagel Buddy!" Without knowing the entire story, Buddy escaped from our yard three days in a row and returned each day with an unopened bag of bagels. What a surprise. No, we did not eat them for breakfast. And neither did Buddy! To his chagrin.

Buddy communicated without words. Everyone in our family had a relationship with him.

Buddy was adorable inside and out. He taught me much about living life. He brought much joy to our family. He was a true friend, a true buddy to all who knew him.

We lost Buddy two years ago. He became ill very quickly. We decided to let Buddy go in peace before he suffered too much. That was our gift back to him. As difficult a decision as that was for us to make, we knew in our hearts it was the right one. Buddy gave his all to our family. It was our time to give a special gift of love back to him.

Buddy added joy to my life from the moment I saw him. I started to think, despite how depressed I was, that maybe there was one thing I could enjoy or think about each day that I was grateful for in my life. This helped me get through some rough moments, even if it didn't heal my depression.

Both Duchess and Buddy added much needed life, laughter, and joy to our family. They also added a much-needed diversion and dimension our family lacked. They provided a sense of normalcy. Although I was hesitant at first to keep Duchess, my heart opened to her once she was in our home. Now, I can't imagine our family and home without a dog.

Our daughters wanted a puppy, as did Stephen. This was something we could provide them. All of our lives expanded by having a puppy. We were able to take our dogs with us on our camping vacations. We were able to take walks and explore with them while the girls learned how to take care of them. We all loved and enjoyed them, and our hearts were broken when they were taken out of our lives. Our puppies became like members of our families at a time when our lives seemed so sad. We were able to love them and they loved us back unconditionally. They allowed us to open our hearts and home, and see that despite what sadness was in our days, there was also joy, light and love for the taking; and more importantly for the giving.

When Duchess was about seven years old, we unfortunately had to give her away. We lived in the country and Duchess had gotten into our neighbor's yard one too many times. Our neighbor was not too tolerant of Duchess. Although we lost Duchess, she went to a caretaker who loved German Shepherds. So our life continued with just Buddy to spoil for several years before we decided he needed a playmate! This time we decided to adopt a "Little Great Pyrenees," our dog Dakota who now lives with us. Dakota was five months old when we welcomed her into our family. Although the initial transition was noisy as Dakota loves to bark and can be quite stubborn, her gorgeous long white fur, beautiful eyes and love for the outdoors and play has won all of us over, including Buddy before he sadly left us. Now Dakota thinks she is the queen of the family. Many times she is! The longer she is with us the dearer she becomes. No walk is complete when someone does not notice her. We often hear "What kind of dog is she?" or "How do you keep her so white?" She often brings a smile to a person's face. Little children can be heard saying "Look at that puppy dad, it is so big!" Dakota is a big dog in size but her cuteness and personality make up for the time it takes to clean up from her white fur. I like to say, "I can't go anywhere without taking Dakota with me" as her fur sheds just about everywhere!

Dakota was a small, young, scared puppy when we adopted her at five months old. Today she is comfortable and plays and runs and even hugs us. We consider her one of our family. We do not know how she was abused in her early months of life, but she has grown and flourished in her time with our family due to consistent gentle love and care. It took time, patience and love. Her young life has turned around. We are blessed to enjoy her and to care for her. To love her and share her with those she meets.

CHAPTER 19

MOST TROUBLED RELATIONSHIPS

*M*y relationships with my three surviving sisters were complicated even before I became depressed. We were close in age, with only five years separating the four of us. We grew up in the same house with the same parents, went to the same grammar school, high school, and church. We had the same extended family. We watched the same television shows and went on the same family vacations. But that was where our similarities ended. My experiences growing up were different from theirs. I now realize that our perspectives were different. I was extremely sensitive, and often hid my emotions. I was born after my oldest sister, Mary Ann, died at fourteen. I was the one striving for perfection, thinking I was her replacement. As I grew older, I became an alcoholic and became anorexic. These two illnesses complicated our relationships. I wanted to be closer to each of my sisters. Many times I wanted to be like them as they often seemed more confident, smarter, and prettier than me, but despite my best efforts and desires, a wedge grew between us. I was

afraid my sisters would find my hidden school lunches, but there was much more.

The true wedge was my unconscious fear that my sisters would find out I was different from them in a way too difficult to even contemplate, never mind speak about. What would happen if they ever found out the secret I was unconsciously carrying deep in my heart? Would they still love and accept me? Would they believe me? Or would they reject and abandon me?

I wanted to be myself growing up, but I couldn't do this in my family any more then I could be myself with anyone else. How could I be since I had no idea who I was? I was full of fear, which consumed me. It forced me to focus on how people looked instead of focusing on how they felt. I was unable to relate to my sisters when I was depressed, just as I was unable to relate to them when I was a child. I continued to look at how perfect their lives looked. I do not know how they felt because we never communicated our feelings. Perhaps they were dealing with their own emotional pain, I do not know. I was unable to put into words how I felt during those years. I was afraid to risk my true self for fear my sisters would reject me, or that I would be misunderstood. That seemed to happen anyway. Not sharing my feelings, I unintentionally blocked my sisters out of my life. Eventually there was such a distance between us it seemed like we would never be close again. Worse, by distancing myself from my sisters, my daughters were distanced from more intimate relationships with their aunts, uncles, and cousins. It didn't help that we didn't live geographically close.

My perspective is different today than it was when I was so severely depressed. Depression has much more to do with my feelings and thinking than with my external circumstances. I had many of the things I wanted and longed for, yet I could not appreciate or enjoy them. I was despondent and despairing, ready to end my life at times. I felt hopeless. I felt empty as a person at a time when my life was at its fullest. My illness was not about "Look at my life," but LOOK AT THE INSIDE OF ME AND SEE WHAT I FEEL LIKE. That was what the disease of severe depression was about for me. Ultimately, this was what I needed to learn and accept, whether or not others understood me. My depression was about my inner darkness which affected how I experienced my outer world.

When I became depressed, my sisters initially offered to assist me with taking care of our daughters. They lived out of state, which would have meant taking our daughters away from my husband and me, so we decided against this. This decision proved to be an extremely wise one for us. Not only did it enable us to remain together as a family unit, having our daughters gave me the motivation I needed to keep going. While I was extremely depressed, I was able to care for my daughters and was able to reach out and connect to the love I had for them. The times when we needed help, we got it either from extended family or we hired someone. I was in danger from myself, but our daughters were safe and well cared for. If I was a threat to our daughters or Stephen, the professionals involved in my care would have intervened. Somehow the love present in our home overpowered the negative forces of my illness when it came to our daughters.

Initially my sisters and I remained in contact by phone, but as time went on that frequency decreased. There was a big discrepancy between their lives and mine. Our lives were taking extremely different paths. Although we were different people, we grew up in a home where emotions were seldom discussed, if at all, and personal problems were never discussed with anyone outside of the family. I needed therapy and my ability to talk about how I felt with my sisters was limited. I didn't feel comfortable sharing with them and they were not comfortable listening to my feelings. As the severity of my issues increased, their ability to handle my darker emotions decreased. I came to realize that I needed to respect them and that I had a therapist for my issues. The barrier between us seemed to grow even wider.

Today, when my sisters and I talk, it is as if those years in my life never happened. I accept this today. I was not easy to reach emotionally while I was depressed because that was part of the illness. Trying to break through the hard shell that surrounded me was frustrating for people. Words might have appeared to fail as I did not readily respond, but I believe I often heard them. Reading a letter or a card someone sent would touch a special place in my heart. The gift of a card was that I could carry it with me and reread it whenever I wanted. I did not receive too many letters or cards, but the ones I did receive helped me tremendously, and I still have them. Any attempts people made, however brief and unsuccessful they may have seemed at the time, were life giving to me during that time when my illness called me deeper and deeper into isolation, loneliness, and despair. My disease wanted me dead. I needed and craved life and human connection and light. These were life giving and life sustaining to me. I had enough darkness. So, any attempts made out of love to me, even when I was only able to cry or say nothing in response, were not futile, because they reached me. I may have needed time to respond and seemed to be unreachable by words or certain medications, but I believe that love broke down the ultimate barriers of my disease. My darkness was so intense, I believe it took time and the effort of all involved to reach me. I was so deeply entrenched in the darkness that I needed a great deal of help and time to respond. Love reached me when nothing else could. Or more accurately, when my heart responded to love and I was able to begin embracing what lay in my darkness, the other multiple pieces of my treatment began to work much more effectively.

As I continued to walk, I would come to learn that it was not so important *who* reached out to me, but that they risked to reach out and they did it in love — perhaps it wasn't who I wanted or expected, but as long as I was open, love was all that could really heal my wounds. Love needed to come first and bind my brokenness before anything else could be added. For this I am grateful, and to all who reached out to me I say, Thank You from the bottom of my heart.

Another big part of depression is that it focuses on self. Being depressed for so long, my sisters' lives progressed and they needed to live their own lives. Whether they understood my depression or not, they had lives and families of their own. It would be self-centered of me to expect them to be invested in my well-being for that amount of time. I was hurt because I felt misunderstood. At times I felt rejected. I felt like life was passing me by, and again, I was the one who didn't fit in and wasn't good enough. It took me years to come to a place of peace and acceptance that these were my insecurities and the reality of my life journey. They were my feelings and not facts.

I love my sisters today as much as I ever have - perhaps more; enough to know that love sometimes means facing difficult truths. As we have each lived our separate lives, none of us has been left untouched by the pain of reality. Equally true, none of us has been untouched by God's blessings, each in our own way. Accepting that each of us is on our own journey and allowing everyone the freedom to be on that journey is not easy, but necessary. It is risky. I need to trust that our love and relationships are strong enough to withstand the distance and the unknown and the differences. Each of us is still loved. Freedom to risk, trust, and love, not to control.

I need to allow my sisters, as I allow myself, the freedom to be who they are. I tried to fit in by being someone I was not.

I now realize I can only fit in by being myself. I try to accept this, and when I do I am at peace. When I don't, I have a more difficult day. I am learning that my life is not about fitting in so that I can be accepted, it is about being myself so I can accept the love freely offered me so that I can freely offer it in return. When I do this, I am never quite sure where this will bring me, but I know it will lead to a more joy-filled and lighter place.

As I came to a place of love and acceptance of myself, the question is how did I ever get to that place that always seemed so unreachable and unattainable? I would have to endure more heartache and honest self-scrutiny, but that alone would not bring me to a place of self-acceptance and the love I desperately needed. What changed me so drastically? It had a lot to do with the gradual surrender I began to make to God. If I was to have any hope for recovery and to change as drastically as I needed to change, at the heart level, I knew I needed more than human assistance.

My emotions were ill but so were my spirit and soul. I was gradually coming to rely on a God who cared for me, but I still had difficulty trusting that He loved me. I came to the place where I realized that I needed to trust God with all of myself and turn myself over to His love and care just as I was, even though I didn't understand what that meant. I needed God more than I needed to understand Him. I began to hold onto the fact that He loved me as I was.

With one hand holding onto this truth, I began to surrender my fears to God each day. My other hand continued to reach out to my therapist and family, and I continued to walk as I realized I was learning something new. I was in unchartered waters; I thought it was best for me to trust God and follow those He had put in my life. They knew how to swim. They knew how to handle life situations better than I did. Afraid or not, my life and my family's depended on my willingness to learn. I didn't have to like it, I just had to do it.

My willingness at this point became stronger than my reluctance and fear. I realized I needed to be grounded on a new foundation so that when waves came my way, I would not be constantly overwhelmed or washed ashore or thrown backwards. I would not permit the waves to impede my progress. I needed something to stand upon that was firm, despite the rocky condition I was in. Slowly, I began to realize that this could be and was God's love for me. I could stand firm on that love if I chose. I was ready to take that step of faith and stand on that Love. "What did I have to lose?" I asked myself. He was keeping me sober and I was still alive. The love that connected me with my daughters and husband, and the connection with my therapist is imperative, but that is not enough. More is needed for my recovery and I know it. I reach out, tentatively, with an open hand as I see the next wave coming on the horizon. I know I do not have the strength on my own to withstand its force. I take God's hand and plunge into the wave with Him.

I said, "I trust you and your love for me."

God said to me. "I love you so much that I sent my son Jesus to die for you and for your sins."

CHAPTER 20

THE ELUSIVE MEDICATION ROAD

*F*inding an effective treatment for my depression was extremely frustrating and overwhelming, not only for me but for my husband as well. Ever since I became severely depressed, medication was tried. After the series of ECT treatments were finished, the psychiatrists I saw continued to try different psychotropic medications in various combinations to treat my depression.

Besides being severely depressed, I was anxious, unable to concentrate, and exhausted due to many sleepless nights. My mind would race and I suffered from panic attacks. I also suffered from horrible mood swings. Some of these symptoms were from the depression but others were side effects from the medication. Some of these included weight gain, sleepiness, inability to concentrate, and loss of sexual interest.

Adjusting the medication took time and patience, and at times I was not that patient. Sometimes weeks or months would pass before the medication would kick in. When I did respond to a particular medication, it was usually for a brief period and then it stopped working. As the years passed, I began to detach myself from these changes in medication or medication adjustments. As much as I wanted them to work, I could no longer afford the disappointment I felt when the medication failed again.

Some of the side effects were terrible. At times I gained fifty pounds and my face was bloated. I could not recognize myself. Looking at pictures I would ask my daughters, "Who is this person with you at your birthday party in our backyard?" They would reply, "That's you mom. What's the matter, don't you recognize yourself in that picture? We always laughed when you wore those pants. We thought they were funny but you liked them." I wasn't focusing on the pants, I was trying to recognize my face. And yes, I had to agree with my now older daughters that my taste in clothes had been a bit strange. At least I was dressed, I consoled myself, and had not been in pajamas. It could be worse! That would truly be a picture I would not want to see!

I changed psychiatrists during the years but I had one at a time. The medications I took were strong. I was careful to follow the doctor's recommendations. The medications had safety caps and we kept them in a safe place. They were closely monitored and whenever my antidepressant was changed we discarded the old medication. Because of my suicidal history, and for general safety, there was no reason to keep excess pills in the house. Since my depression was so severe, my medication had been and still is prescribed by a mental health professional and not my primary care physician. Many of the medications were potent, and there were times, especially when the dosages were adjusted, when I was over medicated. I needed to work closely with my psychiatrist. Medication adjustment seemed to me to be a constant struggle.

When my depression lessoned a bit, it was for a short duration and this challenged not only me, but my doctors, to persevere.

As the years passed, the doctors exhausted the categories of medications to try. I realized that treating severe depression was not easy, and some psychiatrists were more sympathetic and open than others. Some were also more willing to try less conventional dosages or medications. Fortunately, my therapist encouraged me to search for psychiatrists at different hospitals, and I was never without one who was willing to be involved in my care.

One psychiatrist refused to treat me because he did not want to be bothered with suicidal calls during the night. At first I was appalled by this, but then I was grateful he was honest because it enabled me to find the appropriate person for my care. I had to be willing to look. Sometimes it took time. I wasn't always willing to be patient, but I learned I needed to look out for myself. There were better fits than others with medication prescribers and therapists.

At times I felt intimidated by a psychiatrist when a medication did not work. I felt like a failure or disappointment. I thought, "After all, he wouldn't have prescribed this for me in the first place if it didn't work." I needed to discuss this with my therapist. Whenever I was with my psychiatrist, it was important to be honest about how I felt with the medication prescribed. This was my life at stake here. I could not afford to be a people pleaser. I was anxious about my appointment and it would be brief, usually 15 minutes; so I needed to get to the point. My therapist, again, helped me with this. My husband went to some appointments with me but most of the time his work schedule did not allow it. I needed to learn to be my own advocate. I felt awkward many times with the psychiatrist but I had to keep going. It eventually got easier, but I still go because I need this aspect of treatment. I also could not receive psychotropic medications without being in therapy.

As the years passed, different professionals began to think perhaps I had other emotional illnesses in addition to severe depression. They recommended different medications to more effectively treat my depression. I had different diagnostic labels including borderline personality disorder and bipolar disorder. I thought the only advantage to the label was it aided in finding the correct medication.

Today (2019) I have a better understanding of how important a proper mental health illness diagnosis is both for more effective medication management and to understand the illness itself. I learned the professionals were correct. I do have another emotional illness. I have post traumatic stress disorder as a direct result from the sexual abuse I suffered during my childhood and teenage years. Knowing I have this illness makes a huge difference in the effective management of my illness and in the management of the symptoms. My PTSD is currently managed by some medication and with trauma therapy geared to help me live a more healthy life with the symptoms I experience from my illness. The current goals of therapy are to also help teach me better coping skills and to address the root causes of my trauma which have turned out to be much more complex and widespread than the first repressed memories revealed.

No matter what my diagnosis, however, I am a person first and I believe I need to be seen and treated like one, not as a label or diagnosis. This happened when I was hospitalized, especially with doctors presenting case studies and interns learning for medical purposes. I would be presented as "a 42-year-old woman with repeated hospitalizations for severe medicine resistant depression with a history of repeated suicide attempts. We suspect possible ..." I would be sitting in front of the room of medical professionals and they would discuss my case as if I was invisible and did not have feelings. I agreed to the case presentation in order to be helpful, but by the time it was done I felt like a guinea pig that was dissected, exposed, and left there for all to see. Worse, no attempts were made to put me back together again.

Today, I know that I am a human being who suffers from a mental illness. I am not my label any more than I am my illness.

I found that people reacted to me in a wide variety of ways while I was depressed. Like any other illness, my illness needed to be treated. I needed to seek out professionals who were trained in this area, and I needed to follow their recommendations. I cannot begin to think what my life would have been like if I had not done so. Expecting others to understand me was unrealistic at times. I wanted them to, but I often couldn't even understand myself. It was my responsibility to get treatment and learn about my illness. If others wanted to learn that was helpful, but ultimately I needed to take responsibility for my illness. All my life I wanted people to understand and accept me, but how could they when I couldn't understand or accept myself? I was learning the valuable lesson that this was my journey and my life path, and I needed to walk it despite what others thought or understood.

Despite all the complications and frustrations of the medication routine, some of it worked. It was important that Stephen and I believed in recovery and kept searching. Hope became as simple as perhaps today, when I woke up, I might feel a little pleasure I did not feel the day before. As the years began to pass, my husband and I were no longer expecting a huge improvement; instead, we became content with small changes. I began to learn more about depression and realized that treatment was not an exact science and was influenced by many factors. While there were medications for depression, the way each one affected someone varied from person to person - much like medications for physical illness. My emotions were severely involved and other factors, including my past life experiences, also played a role. Medication was only a piece of the treatment, which was why I was involved in therapy on a consistent basis. It is important to repeat the professionals were correct. I did have additional underlying emotional trauma which complicated my depression. It took time for that to come to the surface. When it did, I needed treatment and much love. Not necessarily in that order.

In the beginning, my husband and I would get our hopes up, especially when a psychiatrist would say, "I've had great success in the past with this medication." I had long since been given the diagnosis "severe medicine resistant clinical depression." Despite long years of therapy and trials of medications I did not seem to be much farther along than when I started.

After ten years, our hopes were beginning to fade. We were hoping that I would stabilize and stop having these extreme mood swings so that we as a family could have a more stable life. Our daughters were no longer toddlers or even young children. They were now in junior high school and high school. I felt like life was passing me by and I was still a broken woman, struggling to pick up the pieces of myself. Despite how I felt, our daughters were becoming more sure of themselves. They were able to function in this world and branch out and grow — I realized some healing had taken place inside me. My soul was filled with love for my daughters. I knew they could feel and see that love at work in our home and life. I could not yet fully see that love because I was still looking at myself through the grey lens of depression that colored my view of myself and the world. I seemed to have a clear spot when it came to my daughters. Where they were concerned,

I seemed to be able to see more clearly, and I saw them as lovely, precious and worth living for.

I saw them as lovable and good and I believed in them. I saw in them all the things I could not see for myself or that I could not seem to believe in for myself. I believed they had a future in this world and there was hope for them. I believed they would make a difference. I wanted to support and protect them. I wanted to do all that I possibly could for them. I was their mother, and I would give my life for them if I could. Wait, I thought to myself, that is what I had to do here. I must give up this old life I am carrying around day to day. Whatever is preventing me from living my life as the mother I am meant to be to these daughters, I am ready to give it up. I give up trying to figure all this out. Despite how much I try, I cannot make any sense of these thoughts. They don't connect. I don't even know where they come from. In the silence of my heart I surrender again. I don't give in to my disease, but I give up fighting my own diseased and extremely negative thinking. I give up control and ask God for help. I ask Him for help with my shattered thoughts. I feel like I will lose my daughters soon if I do not recover. They are growing so quickly, or is it that I am recovering so slowly? Whichever it is, I must do whatever is necessary to recover. I want more for them and for us as a family. I want to be a part of their lives as they graduate from high school and learn to drive, I want to be a part of their lives as they go to college, and eventually get married and have children of their own. My journey seems to be a continuing surrender to God's love.

I ask God to take the shattered pieces that haunt me and do with them as He will. I don't understand them and I never did. They seem to be a broken version of me, but I am tired of navigating my boat and getting nowhere. I just circle around the murky water. I hope God has a clearer view than I have.

This is not living. Carrying this darkness and living in it for so long while being haunted by tormenting thoughts is like being underwater and unable to breathe. I am gasping for air. I want to feel joy and put my face to the sunshine. I want to look up instead of down. I want to see the world in color instead of black and white. I know you can help me Lord. I am ready to jump in. I don't know what I will find but you are in control now. Just remember, I am not a good swimmer. Maybe you could throw me another life preserver or something a little bigger this time? That would be great. Thanks!!

I am counting on You. I think this is what it means to trust. Is this faith or simply being desperate? Whatever it is, I know I cannot do it and I know or Hope you can. I am ready. At least, I think I am, before I think about this any longer.

CHAPTER 21

THE NEVER-ENDING GROUP...

*O*ne of the stops along the way was what I call "the never-ending group."

One of my psychiatrists recommended I attend a weekly outpatient group held at a hospital that was out of the area. I was interviewed by the therapist who facilitated the group. Once I was accepted into the group I was terrified of joining, but decided to attend anyway. I drove ninety minutes each way to get to the hospital. The meetings were ninety minutes long. I did this for six years every Wednesday despite the New England weather. The group was for people with borderline personality disorder. Although I was not diagnosed with this illness, my doctors thought I might benefit from being a part of this group. That was reason enough for me to stay for six years!

Attending the group added structure to my week. It required me to shower and dress properly even when I didn't want to get dressed. Looking back, somehow I made it there and I made it on time. I had made a commitment to the group, to myself, and to my recovery. I did not feel like I fit in, but that was one of the reasons I was there. Part of the group focused on mindfulness, and on being present in the moment. As I think back, that aspect of the group helped me the most. At the time, I was incapable of focusing my thoughts.

I was finally ready to move on. I noticed subtle changes. When I was with my family, I experienced more moments of pleasure with them. I had periods of time when my world felt brighter and lighter, as if someone lifted the shades on the windows and let the sunlight into my otherwise dark mind and emotions. When we ate dinner, Emily and Sarah would talk about their days at school and I would join in the laughter. I would attend Sarah's soccer game, and cheer her on with the other parents when she scored a goal, then hug her when the game was over. I would go to Emily's school concerts and listen to her sing, her voice touching my soul. I would hug her and give her yellow roses after the final curtain came down. I thought of how fortunate I was to be able to attend all these events. This was progress. These were bright spots of color popping up against the bleak backdrop that had become my constant reality. I became attracted to moments like these like a bee to honey. The sweetness of these moments was addictive to me. I wanted more. I was awakening to life. I cherished these moments. They became etched on my heart and in my memory. I had been at school events in the past but I was unable to experience the joy of being there. Now, it seemed that the sensations of the events were heightened - the colors vivid, the voices clear and resounding, and I was present with the other parents, excited to be cheering on my children and our school teams.

I was slowly awakening to the possibilities of life. This brought me joy, yet it came in spurts as if it was a tease. After every brief period of awakening, I seemed to fall back into darkness, only now I didn't fall quite as far down and it didn't take quite as long to come back to the light of day. It was a gradual shift. These seemingly little pleasures were not small things for me, how could they be? I had been able to experience them only briefly with my daughters. These were bright new experiences for us. They were brand new memories we were making, and I was a part of them. This gave me hope to push on. My heart swelled and filled me with a love and sweetness I hadn't felt before. But it pushed against something, it seemed like something was blocking my heart from expanding more fully. Whatever that was, it needed to go. I wanted my heart to fully expand, so that I could soar like a hot air balloon with my daughters and husband, sailing wherever our life and hearts and dreams took us. It was time for us to soar, to be light as a feather, weightless in a sense. The darkness that surrounded me had permeated our home and family and weighed us all down. If I could come through this somehow, we would all be much freer and lighter.

I needed help to see what was weighing me down, what was blocking my heart.

I continued to put one foot in front of the other, one step at a time.

CHAPTER 22

THE ORANGE JUICE TRIP

*N*o one was more surprised than I was! Okay, maybe my husband and daughters were, and maybe you will be too. In the midst of all this darkness, there were happy times and this was one that stands out.

The evening Stephen brought me home from my last hospitalization in 2006 we stood outside our home. The phone rang and I rushed inside to answer. The woman on the other end told me I had won an all-expense paid round-trip for four people to Disney World for five days and four nights. I asked, "How could I win a trip, I haven't entered anything?" She answered "You entered an orange juice contest at the grocery store." I insisted I didn't but she said, "You bought orange juice and you were automatically entered from your grocery receipt." She ended the conversation stating, "Your information will arrive in the mail in a few days." Just as promised, the information arrived in the mail. It was not a hoax, so my family and I enthusiastically made plans for our trip to Disney World that coming July.

What an unexpected gift. If we could not believe our good fortune before we got to Disney World, once we arrived we truly could not believe this happened to us. Here we were, standing in the middle of the Magic Kingdom with Mickey Mouse. How did we end up here for five days? Three months ago I was in the hospital for a suicide attempt and now we are standing as a family in the Magic Kingdom. As I looked around, I realized how blessed I am. I did nothing to earn this trip. It was given to me and my family as a gift the very day, actually within an hour, of my returning home from the hospital.

I realized how fortunate I was to be alive and with my family on a vacation that we could not afford. How did we get here? I knew in my heart this was a gift and one to be enjoyed, and we did! So much so that Emily and Sarah even talked me into going on Space Mountain at least three times despite my disliking roller coasters. I was even in the front seat one time with my daughter! My children couldn't seem to get enough of the rides. As soon as we got off one ride we got in line for another. We realized very quickly that Florida in July is extremely hot, so we ate more than our share of ice cream and popsicles and frozen lemonade and milk shakes. We stayed up late to watch the parade and the fireworks. Stephen would alternately hold each girl on his shoulders so no one would miss a single minute of the fun!

As with most vacations, it seemed like we were on the plane returning home far too quickly. But we had our memories to take home with us along with some huge stuffed animals. Thankfully, they did not require their own plane ticket or seat! We also had many photos of our magic time in Disney World. We were in them along with many of our favorite Disney characters. The time away was wonderful for all of us, and so unexpected. That added much to the excitement and fun of the trip.

When we returned home, Buddy and Duchess were very excited to see us but they were upset with us for several days. As they always came with us on our camping trips, they had a very hard time understanding why they had to stay with a dog sitter this time. We were able to tolerate their sad puppy eyes and long dog faces for a few days because our trip was definitely worth it! Our trip helped relieve the constant tension and seemingly endless dark mood that was over our home. Our time away gave all of us a reprieve. When I came home it was as if I had a renewed energy to continue on that I would not have had without the trip. I had the experience of being able to reconnect with my family after being discharged from the hospital. I felt like being in that magical place reawakened a part of me that had been asleep for years. The joys and the magic and the lightness of Disney World helped part of me feel like a child again - something I had not felt for a long time. So long in fact that I forgot what it felt like. Emily and Sarah were fascinated by the lights and colors and rides and magical places. Being able to see the wonder and excitement in their eyes, I realized I wanted that for myself. When I rode the ride at space mountain, I felt a thrill inside of me that I never felt before, and I liked it. It helped me feel alive. Of all the places God could have chosen to send us He picked Disney World. I wondered what He was trying to tell me? That I needed to became more like a child? That I needed to enjoy life more? That I needed to learn from my children as they played and explored and lived life to the fullest?

As I thought about this, my mind drifted back to my conversation with Him in the hospital a few months ago. Trust Him and His love. Perhaps I am to trust Him like a child trusts. Could this be His message to me I wonder?

CHAPTER 23

BECOMING LIKE A CHILD AGAIN

$\mathcal{P}$erhaps because they were in such sharp contrast to the times when I attempted suicide, these were times when I felt like I was physically fighting the darkness, when I was fighting to stay alive.

I felt at these times like I had to retreat into the center of my being where I thought no one and nothing could reach me. I felt like my world had become so dark I would succumb and drown. The pain felt like it would pierce my soul and destroy me in the process. I felt like there was no way to escape it. At these times I was fighting to live!

I felt like I had become a fetus in the womb, physically and emotionally seeking comfort, protection and warmth. Perhaps that was the only place I ever felt safe. No, I thought to myself, I felt safe with Donald. So I rushed over to his office before my tormenting thoughts and feelings overtook me. I literally hid underneath a chair like a child. Thankfully, I have not returned to the hospital in months now, but at times like these my thoughts and feelings feel like they will overtake me. Hiding under a chair is no solution. I was an adult after all, not a child.

Donald asked me, "What's wrong?" I said, "I feel like my pain is going to kill me. I have nowhere to escape, nowhere to run and hide. It will destroy me. I don't know what to do. I can't take this anymore. I'm not good enough. I never was and I never will be. I am so afraid of what is going to happen to me and to my daughters and Stephen." I cried like a baby with complete abandon.

Now I realize that perhaps I had reached a point that, like a baby, I was ready to trust love, trust life, and trust goodness; to trust my heart that loved my own daughters and husband so much. That, like a baby, I was willing to depend on God, understanding that He meant for me to be alive and to be the mother Emily and Sarah needed, and a wife to Stephen. That I was willing to trust in His love and goodness, to open myself to others, and to begin again. To live a life motivated by love instead of fear. In a sense, in order to become the mother I wanted to be, I had to become like a child in many ways. I had to be open to life again and risk getting hurt, but I had to also risk being loved. To risk loving with all my heart as the mother I wanted to be. But this meant I needed to risk opening my heart to all of life. To do this I had to come out from under the chair. I could not hide any longer. I was ready. I knew that my life without trust and love was too difficult. I was terrified and tired of how black my world had become.

The longer I walked, the more I was learning to depend upon God and His love for me, but I still questioned if God loved me. My faith was growing but my doubts would not disappear. Why would God love me? My mind tormented me at times and I knew that I did not love myself.

The truth be told, I was afraid of love. I was able to love my daughters and my husband but I found it difficult to accept love from others. While I can accept love superficially, a deeper connection terrifies me. At the same time, I crave this deeper connection. My daughters seem to have established this deep bond and I cannot let it go. I must embrace my fear of being loved or risk losing this connection with my daughters and my husband.

I realize at these moments that becoming like a baby and then a child while continuing to grow does not mean I am no longer connected. It means being connected in a new way. Being in a community allows for strengths and weaknesses and sharing. Being in a family is where I learn and teach my daughters these things. Needing help and helping is part of loving. I am connected this way within my family and my alcoholism recovery group. But my fear continually tells me to try to hide my real needs along with my strengths.

Donald told me, "It's time to come out from under that chair. You have nothing to hide from."

I realized that being dependent on God allowed me the freedom to come out from my darkness. I needed to embrace my reality. That spark within me kept growing brighter and stronger, although I did not see it and often didn't feel it. That is belief, that is faith. I felt it at times, and I believe my daughters and husband saw the spark burning inside of me. They felt that warmth and goodness deep within me, the true love I carried for them. That light flickered and grew dim but never went out. In fact, that light helped lead me to face my truth. When I finally did, it reflected who I am because it is the light of Jesus burning in me. The light doesn't exist by itself. That light exists in relationship, in connection and in love.

There was no escaping the reality I carried deep in my soul. I needed more of God's love before I could access it.

I realized it was time to start living. It was my disease that wanted me dead, not me. But I also realized something else; I loved my daughters and husband and God, and they loved me — but love does not exist without pain. I cannot honestly love in this world without being willing to open myself to pain. I certainly can experience pain without being open to love — I only had to look back on my own life experiences to see that. I am at a new place now in my walk, and I am ready, willing, and possibly able to more deeply love and trust.

As I have been walking, I have been developing a trust relationship with Donald. I have been growing to trust God and His love for me. Life and love are important but so is trust. I learned I needed to trust God the way my young daughters trusted me and their dad. They had a childlike trust and this is what God wanted me to have for Him. I thought back to the night He whispered to me to "watch and listen to my children." Perhaps this was what He was referring to. So I began to do more than just watch.

I played alongside my daughters with their colored play dough as they formed make believe figures. I was amazed at their imagination. I slowly began to make things with them. This was an effort for me, but for Emily and Sarah it seemed to flow naturally from their little hands. Their little figures were cute while mine were stiff and formless.

We played hide and seek in our backyard and they would call out, "Come and find us mommy." They were quite clever where they hid. As I started to take my turn to hide and call back to them, "Come and find your mommy," I started to have fun. Learning to play was hard work but it was important that I learned. I wanted to be a part of my daughters' lives. I wanted to play with them and not just watch them, but playing was not a natural part of my world. I needed to learn by playing with my daughters. They were the experts, and I needed to meet them where they were. They were more than willing to meet me where I was. I learned about making mistakes from my young daughters. They forgave and continued to play. They didn't hold on to the hurt. They loved to play and never seemed to get tired of it. I had to plead with them to take a nap. They were full of energy for life, to explore and to learn, to create and to risk — I had much to learn from them.

They seemed to be the opposite of me in many ways. I was filled with a desire to withdraw from life and the world. They seemed to have an indescribable joy and love for life. There didn't seem to be any limit to their love and energy, and desire to explore and create. When I looked at them and then looked at myself there was such a discrepancy. I had to think about this. What happened to my joy and deep sense of love for life? Would it ever return? Did I ever possess it in the first place, or did my fear always own me?

As I think back, thoughts like these surface and the feelings of insecurity and fear of not being good enough or being unloved and abandoned fill me. As time passed, they were sometimes countered with opposing thoughts and feelings of a newfound peace that I did not recognize; feelings with which I was not too familiar.

It seemed as if the love of my daughters had transcended my fear and anxiety. Our love for one another had brought us closer than I could have hoped, but how could this be? As I think about how much I love my daughters and about how much I would be willing to do for them, my thoughts turned to God.

I don't want to be afraid of Him. I have often thought of God as my Father, a concept I had often read about. As I was not close to my own dad, this concept of having a loving and intimate relationship with God had been difficult for me to imagine. As I looked at my daughters, I was certain that God loved them. I began to wonder if God once loved me when I was young like my daughters. Did He stop loving me or did I stop believing that He loved me?

As I played alongside my daughters, some isolated memories from my own childhood started to come to my mind. I found this strange as I did not often think back to those days. As I pushed Emily and Sarah on the swings in our backyard or at the playground, I found myself on my own swing with my dad, forty years ago. I am yelling, "Push me higher daddy, Push me higher!"

I recall playing with my sisters. We always found something to do, especially during summer vacation. We often played pretend games such as dress up or school. Every summer my parents took us somewhere for vacation. When we were younger, it was to the beach, but as we got older we traveled somewhere different along the east coast.

I tried to remember more personal times with my mom and dad, but for some reason I always seemed to focus on my dad. I cannot seem to recall any close personal times. I remember my dad working long hours in a factory to support us. Money was tight but my sisters and I always had enough food and clothes and a warm home. Both my parents grew up during the Depression and they knew what it was like not to have extra or even enough at times. They tried their hardest to provide for us.

One day as I was in the backyard playing with Emily and Sarah, I remembered about my dad fighting in World War II, as had many men from his generation. What was surprising was that I never knew this about him when I was younger. When I was in my late twenties my dad put up a picture of his unit in the basement and I remembered being shocked to see it.

Unfortunately, I never spoke to my dad about his time in the war. It's not that I didn't want to ask him or that I wasn't interested. I wanted to know where he fought and more than that, I wanted to know what it was like for him but I couldn't ask him. I just couldn't get the words out of my mouth. I was too scared to even look closely at the picture. I was horrified to think my dad was there, fighting, and he could have been killed. It was sadder to think that he survived the war and was here with me and neither one of us could talk to one another about anything that mattered. That scared me more. What had become of both of us I wondered? Although I could never remember a time when we were particularly close, I did remember *wanting* to be close to my dad. I remember hoping he would hold me in his lap and read me a story or tuck me into bed, but most of all, I wanted him to tell me that he loved me.

As time went on, I stopped hoping for any of that to happen. Instead, I settled for the push on the swing. Although I told myself he probably loved me, there was a huge part of me that wanted and needed to hear him tell me he did. Without hearing the words and being unable to spend any special time with him, I questioned if I was lovable. I could not begin to think that my dad was not perfect, after all he was my dad. I wanted to be special. Obviously, I wasn't that special and perfect; I told myself. I had failed again. First with my mom and now with my dad. The only difference was that my dad was silent about his disapproval.

Seeing that picture in the basement scared me and reawakened the need and hope I once had of hearing my dad tell me he loved me. More than that, though, I still needed to know that he loved me. But I failed to look at myself all those years, and my own inability to tell my dad that I loved him. Perhaps that was the deeper tragedy for me. I would kiss him a harried good night before running upstairs to bed, but the very words I longed to hear from my dad I failed to say. This became a reality too painful for me to carry each day. My food addiction and alcoholism hid that pain, but now these soul wrenching memories tore at me. How could I have been so selfish? Or was it my fear? Why had I continued to act so childish when I was no longer a child?

This was painful to think about, but I was no longer in a place where I could afford to run and hide. Plus, I had not recalled these memories for many years, if I ever could remember. I need to pay attention to where my mind and heart are leading me but I hesitate. My fear tells me I don't need to go here, but the spark burning within me tells me that these thoughts will consume me if I ignore them.

CHAPTER 24

FINANCES, OR LACK THEREOF

*A*lthough Stephen and I did our best to provide for our daughters, we seemed to constantly struggle financially from the moment our income changed from a two income family to a one income family and the size of our family increased from three to four. We also made some financial mistakes. Our plan was for me to return to work part-time after Sarah was born, as I had once Emily was born. This did not happen, and it would have a significant impact on our financial picture, especially as the girls grew older.

At times, we tried to give our daughters what they wanted instead of what they needed. Some of this was motivated by the guilt I felt over not being the mother they deserved. We did not have an extravagant lifestyle, but at times as parents we could have said no when we said yes. To be honest, I needed to say no to myself more often than to anyone else. I did not, and we paid dearly for my mistakes. Like most families we knew, we struggled to keep up with the needs of our growing children and daily living. New sneakers or new cleats needed for soccer season each fall, musical instruments to rent for band, new school clothes as old ones were outgrown. Fortunately, we had medical insurance but even with insurance, the cost of my constant multiple prescriptions and medical appointments through the years strained our monthly budget.

We eventually had to draw off our savings to meet our monthly expenses, but we managed to get by each month, sometimes just barely. Eventually our savings grew quite slim. The financial stress became too great at times and we needed to seek assistance from my parents for help with unexpected bills.

I do not remember the exact year, but along the way I became a compulsive shopper. The initial distraction and relief this provided disappeared too quickly. Like my previous addictions, it was extremely difficult to stop this behavior once it started. I bought clothes I didn't need, returned them, bought more clothes, returned them, and the cycle continued. The merry-go-round I was on wouldn't stop. Worse, I was headed for destruction.

Shopping became another illusion for me. No matter how hard I tried, no matter what I bought or how expensive, it could not cover up my deep-seated feelings of inadequacy, fear, inferiority, and shame. These were glaring issues staring at me through the mirror. I realized these were anchors that kept dragging me further down each time I attempted to move forward. I did not like to see them because I thought these feelings were essential to who I was, and an integral part of my identity. "What would I be without them?" I thought to myself. My compulsive shopping caused Stephen a lot of concern, frustration, and worry; and rightfully so. I was unable to see the damage I was causing. It took a long time for me to recognize what was happening. The hours I spent shopping robbed my family of time I could have been with them. Clearly I was in the grip of another addiction.

I tried to create a new identity for myself by buying different types of clothes —different styles, colors, and designs from what I usually wore. I was trying to recreate myself into a person who looked beautiful on the outside in order to mask the pain I felt on the inside. My fear was in full control at this time. I was tired of being depressed and feeling like I was unattractive. Even though I was the one not interested in having a physical relationship I wanted to be like others I saw; I wanted to fit in and be happy. I wanted to get dressed in something nice and look pretty and attractive. If I stopped long enough to think about what I was thinking and feeling, I would have recognized these familiar feelings ran deep. I would have realized I couldn't cover them up with a new wardrobe no matter how expensive the clothes or how different the style. I would be putting these clothes over me, and my physical body was not the problem. I could compare my emotional self with how other people looked all I wanted, but that would not change how I saw myself. I was learning in therapy that what mattered was how I felt inside, what I believed and what my values were and what laid in my heart. What mattered was the person I was and how I treated myself and others. When I slowed down enough to think and feel and talk with my therapist I could see this, but I was not yet able to get to the source of these issues. I have a greater awareness of what has troubled me in my life, but they are fragments and I cannot seem to connect them. At least not yet.

I knew this was not how I wanted to be living but I was afraid. It was time to face my truth. I sensed there were deep seated issues inside of me. Despite years of therapy with Donald and meeting with psychiatrists, we often hit a wall. I was unable to accept positive feedback. My mantras in therapy had become

"If you knew me like I knew myself you would not like me either," along with "I was born with a hole in my soul." Donald repeatedly asked me, "What have you done that was so horrible or wrong?" but I had no answer for him. I just knew I did something. I thought I was a mistake. I needed to learn that what I thought and felt was not the truth. I had to look at what I was carrying deep inside my heart and mind. I could no longer depend on what I thought was there. To look required courage and love that I thought I did not have. I knew I had fear, just like when I slipped into compulsive shopping. My fear shouted in my mind, "Keep quiet! Hide what you are doing. No one needs to know. You are not hurting anyone but yourself!" But I knew in my heart and soul that these were lies. I was hurting others as well as myself. Hiding the shopping bags underneath the bed or in the bedroom closest no longer worked. I now had another way to live. I could ask God and others for help.

I was afraid of deeper relationships. But I also loved my husband and daughters and I wanted to move forward in my life. I began trusting God more. It was not easy but I needed to get help for my shopping addiction. It was a huge struggle and we worked through it. Looking back, it was worth it, but as I struggled there were times when I did not think so.

This addiction tries to come back into my life when I am fearful. I am not completely free of it. By God's grace I have a choice, today, and I can ask for help. I need to be honest about it. It is not the glaring issue it was while I was depressed, but I can fall into this destructive behavior when I am faced with difficult emotions or situations in my life. What I cannot afford to do is hide this behavior or look the other way. Even when small amounts of money or time are involved, the important thing is what the behavior is doing to me or what emotions I am trying to avoid.

I had a problem with love because I had a problem with pain. I thought I was capable of taking away someone else's pain, or perhaps I thought I was responsible for making other people happy. I was confused about love and about life and about relationships. I ran because I didn't want to be hurt and did not like to see other people hurt. I said I didn't believe in fairy tales, yet I wanted to deny that pain existed in life. I did not want to accept that pain and brokenness were real, but denying them did not make them go away. I was learning about this from my addictive behaviors. I would soon learn more.

Others who told me I had a problem only helped me to a point. I had to take ownership of my problem. I could not wish it away or think it away. I could not just read about it in books. I needed to do something about it. When I was ready, the choice was always mine. When I reached out for help, many people responded in love. That was the difference for me. I wasn't judged or criticized, I was accepted. I wasn't told I should know better; I was treated with respect. Even though I made poor choices I was learning I was not the mistake. This was a huge step forward for me.

I was initially willing to pay the price for the euphoria I felt from buying clothes then bringing them home and trying them on. Before long this was replaced with the all too familiar shame and guilt. I would have to tell Stephen I shopped again, then put the clothes back in the shopping bags and sort out the multiple receipts. Stephen needed to come with me to return piles of clothes to numerous stores. If I wasn't embarrassed before, I was when I was returning these clothes we couldn't afford. It was a mess. I began to feel like I disappointed Stephen and myself. Here I was again, unable to control something I thought I could control. Sound like a familiar pattern? I also began to feel like I had disappointed my daughters. They are now old enough to realize what I am doing.

When they ask me, "Where are you going mom?"

I answer, "To the store."

They ask, "Again mom?"

The only good answer is the truth so I say, "Again, girls. Mom needs to go to the store again."

When Stephen comes with me to the store our daughters also had to come. This is not a side of me I want our daughters to see, yet I wasn't able to help it. Being depressed is difficult enough, but knowing I am exposing my daughters to my shopping addiction breaks my heart. The truth hits me like a hammer between my eyes when I finally admit what I am doing, not only to myself but to my family.

I struggled to let go of this addiction. Although I was ashamed, my fear told me, "The next time you shop will be different. You will be able to control your spending." My depressed thinking told me I had little else bringing me release and pleasure. When I kept these thoughts to myself I usually went shopping. When I shared them, my perspective often changed and I received strength to make a better choice. For that day. For that moment. I could begin again the next moment if I chose to. The next day was definitely a new chance to begin again. Acceptance, patience, surrender, one thought at a time…

I needed to stop and think— I am an addict and this is what an addict does. I needed to take responsibility for my behavior. There was a way up and out. God did not want me to keep blaming myself. I needed to be responsible and move on, but blaming myself would not allow that. Forgiving myself and taking responsibility to change my behavior would.

I am an addict — now with compulsive shopping. There is something deeper going on with me. I have no ability to discern what is at the core of my issues. I go from one addiction to another. I am trying to rely on God, and by His grace, I am sober. I am still depressed and struggling with life and life issues. I feel like I am a huge disappointment. Am I really a disappointment? I realize this feeling goes deep. Addiction. Alcoholism. Compulsion. Eating disorder. Are they related? Why haven't I ever thought about these together before now? I have gone to different eating disorder programs to try and help recover or manage my eating issues, yet I have never thought about what triggered my anorexia when I was ten. Disappointment, shame, a need for a new identity; thoughts like these start to float around in my mind. I am getting better at recognizing some of the broken pieces of myself that I have carried for so long. As I share these feelings with Donald, he suggests it is time I consider how the actions of others might have affected my actions or my feelings. I am so used to thinking only of myself — addiction is centered on me and so is depression. I need help to look at the bigger picture. Another reason I find Donald's perspective so valuable is often by myself it seems I get tunnel vision. I either see only my perspective or I fail to see that a bigger picture exists. My actions reflect my thoughts and what I carry inside me. The part of me controlled by my fear tells me, "Don't look" but the other part says "It's time, there is something there." My fears keep me from looking, but I am beginning to notice that my behavior affects those around me. If that's the case, then why wouldn't other people's behavior affect me? I believe deep down I knew this when I became a mother. I did not want to pass on my destructive thoughts or behaviors to my children. Some part of me was in touch with my brokenness and my truth and knew that I was wounded. I knew unconsciously I was carrying hurts that needed to be healed or I would wound my own children with them. Most of all, God knew this and He stepped in to help me. He knew I could not fix this by myself. I still do not even know what my truth is. All I know is something is there, although it continues to elude me.

My inability to return to work was another big factor that contributed to our struggling financial picture as the years passed. How could I? I was barely able to take care of myself even though I had a college degree in occupational therapy. Along with my depression and memory loss, I had severe problems with concentration, focusing, panic attacks, and drowsiness. All of these interfered with my ability to work professionally as well as maintain my license each year. Although I briefly worked part-time during these years, it became clear that I needed to let go of my professional license.

The loss of my profession was a difficult one to accept. I thought it was a part of my identity, and that my self-esteem and identity had suffered enough. I felt like I was losing another piece of myself. "What would be left of me?" I thought. I felt like the tide was taking another part of the shoreline out to sea, and all that would remain on the beach would be the seaweed. By now I wanted to be a pretty seashell. Instead I felt like the seaweed that was washed up on the shore after the tide went out, or the broken shells left after a major storm. Worse, I thought, because I was broken and not pretty, people walking along the beach would never pick me up and bring me home to place me in jars or vases to brighten their tables. They only picked up the beautiful shells. When I was honest with myself, I could admit that I had never been the beautiful shell on the beach. I always preferred to be alone, isolated in the sand on the beach. Even though I thought I wanted to be that pretty seashell, picked up and put in the vase, I lived my life isolated from people. Perhaps deep inside, I longed to be that pretty seashell after all. I certainly longed to be picked up and cared for, to be loved and put in a safe place. Instead, I had lived my life like that broken seashell that was washed ashore over and over, never knowing where I was going to end up; hoping for the best, but always seeming to end up in the same lonely place. Despite thinking I didn't want anyone to be close to me, I desperately wanted a close relationship with someone; but instead my relationships were with substances; ones that promised me fulfillment initially, but then turned on me. I was like those broken seashells, and I was starting to wonder if I would ever be a whole seashell. If so, what or whom would I resemble? I was surely lost and beginning to think I had never known who I was. I felt like I had been lost at sea for as far back as I could remember. I just floated along, too afraid to commit to anything that would have me stand up for what I believed in or have me recognize who I was. Depression descended and muddied the waters around me so that it was nearly impossible to discern where I began and the dark, murky water started. So losing my profession, although it was necessary, was difficult. It was just another piece of myself that I felt was gone forever. I didn't know then that I needed to let some things go in order to allow other things to come into my life.

In thinking about those shells, I began to realize that although I was broken, I had a purpose now, as a mother and as a wife, even though I no longer had my profession. Although I longed to be put back together so I could fulfill my purpose more meaningfully and begin to enjoy life, I understood that there were all types of shells with different colors and shapes and different varieties. My purpose at this time in my life was to be a mother and a wife, not to be employed outside of the home. My responsibility was to do the very best I could under the circumstances I was given. I was extremely frustrated and frightened of losing more precious years from our daughters' lives. I began to wonder if I would ever recover. I was holding onto that spark within me. I was trusting God, but frankly, at times like these, my hold seemed tenuous. I continued to ask for help and kept putting one foot in front of the other. I continued to get out of bed each morning. I realized that the possibility of anything good happening only existed if I got out of bed and showed up for life. I took things one at a time. A gift from my recovery program. An approach to life that worked for me, especially during these more difficult times.

When I asked God for help, He expected me to do some work. Whenever thoughts to go shopping entered my mind, I needed to practice sitting with my anxiety and other uncomfortable feelings instead of rushing off to the store. I needed to focus on my thoughts and release them instead of holding onto them and deciding they were a good idea. I needed to practice allowing them to leave. I did not have to act on each one. This was how I healed. I needed to take things one moment at a time.

CHAPTER 25

PEN AND PAPER EVERYWHERE

*M*y diary was probably my best friend while I was growing up and throughout my life until I met Stephen. I loved my dairy. Even today, I respect the power of writing. I would write in my diary in my bedroom that I shared with my closest sister who was one year younger than me. I locked and hid it in one of my dresser drawers. In many ways, my diary was a substitute for the friends I never had in my life.

I was enraged one day when I was about twelve and confronted my mother. "Why have you been in my room and why have you been looking through my dresser drawers?" I continued yelling, not waiting for her response. "Why have you read my diary? That's personal! That's supposed to be private. Give it back to me! It's not yours! It's mine."

My mother stared at me as she held the offending document in her hand, wielding it like a weapon. "I have a right to see anything that is in this house," she said in response to me. "You can have it back but you have no need to hide it or to lock it. There should be nothing you have to write down that you cannot say to me in person."

I was horrified after that incident. Knowing that my mother discovered my diary was bad enough, but the fact that she unlocked and read it was too much for me. I felt violated. I thought if my things were not safe in my house maybe I wasn't safe either. How could I trust my mother? Of course, I never discussed these thoughts with anyone. They remained private thoughts and joined my long list of secret fears.

Writing became important for me early in life, not so much for what I wrote, but because I could express myself freely. I felt oppressed in my home, like my thoughts and feelings were not important to my family, but when I sat down with my pen and paper, I felt a freedom to write whatever came to my mind and let all my heartaches out. I felt like I could be myself on paper. In this way, writing provided a much-needed outlet. It gave me some comfort in a world I found to be frightening and confusing. I found I was able to express my truest thoughts and feelings despite how horrible they sounded even to me. I found myself writing about how I felt like I didn't fit in anywhere; how I felt like I needed to hide from the world and be invisible and silent; how I felt like I needed to become someone, anyone other than who I was, because who I was was too awful; how I felt unlovable; how I felt insecure and afraid of making mistakes; how I felt alone and afraid of sharing my thoughts and feelings with anyone. These were my truest thoughts and feelings, they lay in the recesses of my heart, mind and soul and I had to express them some way to keep from going insane.

As a young teenager, I was aware of these personal demons and I tried to put them down in black and white, pen to paper, and my hand faltered. The words that came from my pen sounded terrifying, even to my own ears, but it was my truth. Why did I even write it? What did it matter? No one would care. It would make no difference. Everyone would ask me what was the matter with me? How could I write such things? What would or could I say? How could I explain myself? I didn't know why I felt this way. This was how I felt. I was only thirteen and I hated myself. There was no one I could possibly tell. No one would believe me or understand me. But as I wrote, I knew this was my private truth. It could go no further than this paper. Then, as the realization that the deepest and most personal hurts that are in the very fabric of my being were no longer permitted to be private, but broadcast for all the world to see, I ripped my journal into tiny pieces. Too bad I cannot tear myself into tiny pieces. At least I had my food; my only true friend. Even when my mother discovered the food hidden in my bedroom closet she didn't ask too many questions. She seemed to have less of a problem with it than with my diary. Why was that? Was it because she didn't care, or because she couldn't bear to hear the truth of why that food was there? Why was she going through my things in the first place? Does she mistrust me? It does not matter because nothing changes when she finds my secrets. Either my parents don't care how I feel or they do not understand, or they understand but choose not to do anything about it. If they don't understand, why don't they just ask me if they are truly concerned about me? Clearly I am troubled, but what is not clear is why I am so troubled. I want to feel good enough. Is that too much for a child or a teenager to ask?

I feel like my mother doesn't trust me. I can't talk to anyone about how I feel. I will have to be good enough at being the thinnest in the family. Maybe someone will notice me then. At least I feel better when I don't eat. Food has become my confidante, my best friend. I am so glad I have something I can trust that will never let me down.

But when food eventually betrayed me, writing remained a loyal friend. I found writing to be very helpful and comforting for me. I was able to write things down that I couldn't seem to say easily to another person. I was able to write down thoughts and feelings I wasn't even aware I had. They just seemed to come out on paper. Maybe my level of fear wasn't the same when I was writing. It was just my pen and paper and me. I would sit and write, and at times I was quite surprised at what I wrote. I never thought or worried about sharing what I wrote. It was a personal time and a private time.

I did not have many friends growing up, and I remember that I loved to read and write. I loved to express myself on paper because I felt like no one would judge me, myself included. I felt like this was a safe way to express myself when talking with other people was too risky. I never knew how others would react or what they would say to me. I decided at a young age not to keep quiet. So writing became one of my closest friends.

Journaling continued to work for me while I was so depressed. This became even more important for me, something I could utilize when so many other options seemed to fail. Since it was so hard for me to interact with people, writing was like a lifeline for me. It didn't seem to matter if I wrote the same things over and over; just the process of writing was healing. It was familiar and comforting, and sometimes I found myself writing things that were helpful to be shared in therapy. In fact, as the years passed I began to use my journaling as a therapy tool to write about specific topics or issues that I then shared in therapy sessions. Writing filled a need for me now like it did when I was a child. It allowed me to release feelings or thoughts I held deep inside of me without fear of being judged. For years I wrote to release these feelings, but now I found that I needed to go one step further. I needed to share these feelings with a trusted person so that I could look at them from a different perspective. Writing about my feelings was no longer enough. I was so emotionally ill from my depression and listening to my negative thinking that I needed the input of others. I desperately needed to continue to connect with the people in my life. The initial life preservers thrown my way, especially by my therapist, would be of no use if I did not continue trusting him. It wasn't easy or without struggles, but as with any rescue from the ocean, it went easier if I relaxed and participated and did my part. If I followed the directions of someone more experienced who knew what to do, I would safely make it to the life raft, but my fear was keeping me from reaching out to grab hold for safety.

There were many times when writing saved me. When I was awake until 3:00 in the morning, unable to fall asleep; I would write in my journal. When I wandered through the house during the day, unable to focus on anything constructive, I wrote. Even if repetitive, I was able to express myself in written words when my voice left me. It was not self-destructive in the way that self-cutting or compulsive shopping was. It was also a way for me to organize my thoughts and feelings at a time when I felt like my world was out of control.

There were times when I needed to write down destructive thoughts. By writing them down it helped get them out of by head. When they were in my mind they were too powerful. They owned me. But by putting them down on paper and seeing them for what they were, which was my illness talking to me, these thoughts lost most of their power over me. They were further diffused when I shared them with a trusted person.

I could write anytime I needed to, but I could not always talk to someone when I needed to. There were also things I could not say to just anyone. I had begun to learn that while I could trust others with parts of myself, I needed to use discretion. So

I tried to carry a journal and a pen with me wherever I went. I began to write what was on my mind and eventually what I felt was on my heart. I needed a way to express myself, so journaling was extremely helpful for me. As time passed, I began to see patterns in my writing.

After thirteen years, I had filled quite a few journals. They had served their purpose. The words I had written had been shared with who they were meant to be shared. They were extremely personal and contained some of the most horrible thoughts and emotions of my life, including some of my most destructive thoughts. I decided the wisest thing to do would be to burn these journals. Having done my work, I did not need to leave them lying around for anyone, especially my daughters, to come across and read someday. There was a lot of heartbreak in them. I felt that my daughters did not need to read or hear any more about my deep pain. They had experienced enough. I felt the most loving thing to do for my family was to let these journals go. Whatever good that could come of them had already been done. I needed to release those journals as a sign that I was willing to release my past. Burning them was a symbol of my willingness to move on and let go.

I try to remember how healing writing is for me, and sometimes for the other person who receives a written letter or card. I am still a person who finds it easier to write than speak with another person, so I try to take some time and reach out by writing to others whenever I can. I try to remember how I felt when I received a card during those years. Or more importantly, when I didn't receive any cards.

I have some special letters I received through the years that have made a profound impact on my life. I still enjoy rereading those letters. I think how the written word has been a special gift that I have unwrapped over and over again through the years. I remember the special moments when a heartfelt word was needed to get me through a difficult day or situation or just bring a smile to my day. Sometimes they remind me of incredible people that have passed through my life and touched me with their love. I treasure these gifts, and I am still unwrapping them. Thank you. These are truly special gifts from special people who have touched my life.

As I recall these moments, I try to remember to reach out today to other people and give a simple gift that they can unwrap in their day. Little gifts, I have found, coming from my heart, can touch a person and help them through their day, knowing that someone is thinking of them. For myself, that connection, that sense of not being alone in my pain and darkness was one of the biggest gifts I received. As I move on, I try to extend my hand, often in writing, because that is my preferred method of reaching out. But I try to be gentle because I remember how fragile I was and I could not have responded to anything else. As this is my story, I can only tell what I know worked for me. Gentleness, kindness, and love.

CHAPTER 26

AN UNEXPECTED BOND

*A*nother very important, yet unexpected bond was the one I developed with my mother-in-law, Audrey. I first met Audrey several years before Stephen and I got married. I liked Audrey and she liked me. It was refreshing, and we had a wonderful relationship throughout all the years I knew her. Unlike the relationship I had with my own mother, Audrey and I were able to speak openly with each other. Audrey accepted me and our family situation as it was. While she could not understand why I was so depressed any more than anyone else in my life, she had the advantage, or perhaps the disadvantage, of living closer to us. This enabled her to see firsthand the day to day chaos we were living through. She saw the confusion and disruption my illness brought to our family life. She also saw the frustrations Stephen had to deal with on a daily basis.

I found that I could count on Audrey to be there for the four of us. She was willing to lend a helping hand any way she could, and Stephen and I called on her many times to babysit Emily and Sarah. She stayed at our home when I was hospitalized. Perhaps the biggest gifts Audrey gave me was not judging me or my illness or the choices Stephen and I made on how to raise our daughters. While she did not agree with some of them, she respected our decisions.

She was compassionate. Audrey would attend school functions with me and drive me to therapy appointments whenever she could. She was not embarrassed to be seen with me and stood by Stephen and me as the years passed.

As supportive as Audrey was to me, I believe she was more supportive to Stephen. Everything seemed to revolve around me; my doctor's appointments, therapy appointments, medications, moods; everything was my, my, my. Although I knew Audrey cared for me, she was Stephen's mother and was able to be there for him as only a mother could be. She provided an outlet for him and a sounding board when he needed one. Sometimes Stephen needed to get away for a few hours, and fortunately his mother was available. I liked to think of her house as "neutral ground." Audrey had a way of listening without judging. She occasionally offered a suggestion, but I thought her strength was the ability to listen to multiple sides and be impartial. She was helpful without being critical, she was patient, and she loved her granddaughters. She even tolerated our German Shepherd, Duchess.

Audrey was there for all four of us. Both my husband and I were able to go to her any time, with any issue, and she was available for us — together or separately. She did not speak negatively about either one of us. During a time when we were trying to find a solution to my illness she provided the listening that was so needed and welcome. She also provided meals at times, especially her American chop suey that we all loved. She brought Sarah her favorite mint patties, Duchess her empty peanut butter containers, and Emily took her chances on whatever nana brought her.

It was sad for our family when my mother-in law and my own mother died two months apart. These were difficult losses for our family. Although neither one of them saw me recover, they knew I was on my way. We miss them greatly.

CHAPTER 27

ARE THESE MY PARENTS?

*W*hen Emily was born, my parents were overjoyed. I remember Stephen calling my mother, father, and mother-in-law minutes after the delivery, telling them that they were grandparents and that their granddaughter's name was Emily. Once I came home from the hospital my mom came to stay with us for two weeks. I welcomed this time but I was also apprehensive due to our past strained relationship. Being a new mom renewed my sense of wanting to connect with my mother in a way I was previously unable to do.

Two years later, I do not remember the phone calls announcing Sarah's arrival into our family nor do I remember my mother coming to stay with us. Stephen assured me my mother did come and we have the photos to prove it. I know that I was never the same emotionally when I came home from the hospital with Sarah and I only got worse. My memory loss is sporadic. In some places years are lost while in others only days or certain events are lost. Stephen would ask me, "Do you remember when we went to…?"

I looked blankly at him and replied, "I never went there with you."

He replied in a sad voice, "Of course you did. We went together about six years ago. I wish you could remember." Talk about needing to trust!

During the next few years, both my mom and dad came to visit Emily and Sarah. I remember being very happy about this because I never had the opportunity to know my own grandparents. Unfortunately, my dad died four years after Sarah was born, but both our daughters have happy memories of their grandparents.

I was amazed watching my parents interact with our daughters. I was particularly taken with my dad as he seemed so happy and talkative with his granddaughters when he held them and played with them. He was holding Emily or Sarah on his lap and would read to them. I remember looking at them and thinking, "Is this my dad?" It was great to see, but I was surprised and confused and hurt. I couldn't recall any memories of sitting on his lap and being read to as a child. I was his daughter, after all, I thought.

As I watched, vivid memories and feelings swelled inside of me similar to a wave gathering strength as it rushes to shore with the incoming tide.

I remembered my dad sitting in the living room, wearing one of his flannel shirts; my favorite, the navy and green checkered one. It always looked so soft. I longed to touch it and wrap my arms around him, to sit on his lap and have my dad wrap his arms around me. But for some reason that I didn't understand, this never happened. If I closed my eyes I can still imagine how soft that flannel shirt would feel against my now adult skin but the only way I ever knew the softness and the warmth of that shirt was from folding the weekly laundry.

I wanted more from my dad than to sit in his lap. I had this deep need to be close to him, to have him read to me, to have him ask me how my day was at school or have him play games with me, to just sit with me and pretend I was his princess or that I was the most important person in the world to him. I wanted him to take me out for an ice cream cone in the summer, to teach me how to ride a bicycle without training wheels or teach me how to ice skate in the winter or take me sledding. I wanted him to take a special interest in me. I not only wanted this, I desperately needed it. What I needed more than spending time with my dad was for him to tell me what I longed to hear since I was a child, not much older than Emily and Sarah are now. I desperately needed my dad to tell me "I love you." I thought these three words would change me and complete me. I thought they would connect me with all that was good and beautiful and safe in myself and in this world. Sadly, I realized I was still waiting to hear them.

As I watched my dad holding my daughters, I wondered where these memories and thoughts came from. I hadn't thought about my dad like this in years. Once I did, a door seemed to open. I began thinking about what was and never had been and perhaps what never would be.

This brought me to a very dark place emotionally. I couldn't handle it. I shut down and retreated deep into myself to a place I go where I think I am safe and no one can reach me, where not even my rawest feelings can touch me. There is no other way to protect myself. I have no place to run. These thoughts torture me. How can I admit, never mind come to accept that my dad does not love me? How can I be unlovable? What did I do? Was I born this way? I feel my disappointment and self-hate rise from my stomach and enter my throat. I feel like I am going to be sick. I am disgusted with myself. My own father doesn't love me.

I tried so hard to deny this for so long, to tell myself it didn't matter, that I didn't care; but of course I care and it definitely matters; it matters a lot to me. How can I go on, knowing that my own father does not love me, his own daughter? I am familiar with this feeling. I have worked hard to keep it disguised and hidden. I hoped it was hidden forever. I hoped my dad was not capable of loving, but look at how he loves my daughters. It must be true that I am the one who is unlovable. This is too horrific for me to handle. This confirms my worst fear. How can I live with myself now that I know this is true?

As I hear my father tell my daughters he loves them my heart splits in two. I want him to love his granddaughters, what kind of mother would I be if I didn't want my dad to love his own granddaughters? At the same time, my heart aches with such jealousy and resentment I don't know if I can put words to my pain. I don't understand why my father never put his arms around me like he hugs Emily and Sarah. Didn't he know I longed for his comfort and love all my life? How could he not know? I am his daughter. For years I had hoped that maybe he wasn't capable of loving, but now I can see that he does love. My worst fears are confirmed. He does not love ME.

As all this sears through my mind, heart, and body, I run to my bedroom, leaving my daughters in their grandparents' capable hands. As sobs wrack through my body, I release tears stored up for years. They flow from me like a dam bursting. I cry out in my despair and desperation to the only God I know but do not understand:

"Dear God, are you there? I feel like my heart is being torn out of my chest. The pain is ripping my body to shreds — it is like the pain of childbirth except I am not giving birth to a precious child here. I am giving birth to an unbearable burden that I cannot begin to comprehend. This seems so twisted. I can't understand it. The truth is I never could. I have run from this all my life. My heart is broken, shattered like a mirror broken into a thousand tiny pieces. How can I go on? I knew all along I was unlovable but I never wanted to admit it. That's why I ran and hid. My fear was right all along. My father looked so sad all his life. I felt sorry for him. I wanted to love him but I was too afraid that he wouldn't return my love. I guess I was right."

If I am so unlovable what am I doing with my daughters? What do I think I am offering them? Am I deceiving myself by thinking I can be a mother that loves and cares and protects her children? Is my depression a punishment? As thoughts like these go through my head, a still quiet voice speaks to my heart. It was not the sound of any voices I remember, not my mother or father or teachers or friends.

A voice I believe to be God said to me gently:

"You're right, you can't do this, but we can. Let me help you. I love you more than you love your own daughters. My love is not like human love. Try to accept my love. Don't try to understand it. I have sent my son, Jesus, to walk with you. Let him. He will never let you go."

I made a choice that day. I whispered, "I want and need your help." I didn't understand, but I wanted to believe there was something greater than me that was willing to love me as I was. This gave me the strength to get up and leave my bedroom and join my parents and daughters, now one and three.

I tucked that conversation into the recesses of my memory. I continued to live through my depression, many times unaware of what was carrying me through each day and the darker endless nights, but I was aware of the spark within me. I often thought that spark was lit the day I became sober, and perhaps it was, but looking back now and remembering that conversation, I believe that spark was reignited that night. I could never carry the terrible thoughts I had become aware of that night. If I had been thinking more clearly or was more emotionally well, I might have seen that God was pouring His love on me freely that night. He was telling me I was indeed lovable, so what I feared and thought I had proven was false. I would need to walk my own road. He loved me too much to have me walk through that pain alone. He joined me that night. He walked with me quietly until my fear allowed me to become conscious of His presence in my life.

I was unable to accept the horror of thinking my worst fear was confirmed. I also could not speak about this; it was too much for me. I shut off that corner of my heart, vowing to keep it to myself. This was another piece that added to my depression and darkness. I did not trust anyone to confine this most horrible and intimate truth about myself.

I could not accept myself. I never could.

This flashback joined the other partial flashbacks that were filed in my dark mind and the dark recesses of my heart. I carried the burden of them with each heavy step I took, unable to consciously share them with another person. I was too afraid that no one would understand me, or worse, that I was unlovable and would be rejected and abandoned. What would that mean? At the same time, I thought I heard God tell me that He loved me and that he sent his Son for me and he would never leave me. What did that mean? How did I reconcile that with the fact that I am unlovable? When others find out that I am unlovable will God still love me? God probably already knows I am unlovable, I think to myself. I think this is too much for me.

No wonder my feet hurt and my way is so dark. No wonder I am emotionally ill and confused. But I am willing.

The day came when I started working on these feelings and this issue, but this took several years. Things were complicated. I believe I needed to come to a place of readiness to handle my truth. Even though I was frustrated with the length of my journey, I see today that many times the steps I took were preparing me for what was to come. I lacked many life and relationship skills. I needed to grow emotionally and spiritually.

I eventually told Donald I felt like I was born with a hole in my soul. That was as close as I could come to the truth of what was in my tormented mind. We went from there but it wasn't easy. We were on the right road. Being in a therapeutic relationship was vital for me. It helped me realize that my perspective of myself was wrong. Donald guided me and helped me navigate through my darkness.

Once we delved into this area, many other issues emerged that affected my life, including feeling disappointed in myself and other people; looking for my identity in others; being full of fear; never feeling good enough. I was full of self-doubt and self-hate. We chipped away at these issues. Even though there didn't seem to be any tangible results for quite a while, I was drawn to therapy. Somewhere deep inside me, it was as if I found a lighthouse while drowning in that deep ocean. I was attracted to that light, my therapist. There were some points in time when perhaps I became too attached to Donald, when I held on for dear life. He allowed me to, for a while, perhaps because he knew how fragile I was, or because he knew how broken I was. Perhaps because he knew how depressed I was, or maybe because he knew how human I was, how lonely and afraid of losing what was left of myself and my daughters and husband to this horrible disease. Whatever the reason, he allowed me to cling for a while because without him I would have drifted further out into the ocean and I would have died. I would have sunk to the ocean floor and I would have stayed there. Donald reached out in love and accepted me as I was, and once the crisis passed, he slowly withdrew and encouraged me to connect with others. As difficult as this was for me, I knew I needed to do it, and I did.

I wasn't consciously aware of where I got the strength to talk about these issues. As the years passed, I started to see my walk as a gradual surrender to God's love. I knew He was keeping me sober. I could see that I was still with my daughters despite my depression. These were definite gifts in my otherwise dark world. Then, one night while at a meeting in church I heard the message directly, similar to the one I had heard once before. I knew this message was for me. I knew I had heard it before. These words or similar ones echoed in my heart, bypassing my mind.

I heard the words God sent HIS SON JESUS TO DIE FOR ME AND FOR MY SINS BECAUSE HE LOVED ME. He did this so that I would be restored to a relationship with God. He sacrificed his son for me — out of LOVE. I went home and cried tears of relief instead of tears of pain or sadness. As a mother, I connected with the concept of the cost of giving up a child. How great a love was this, I thought to myself.

What helped break through my insecure feelings was God stating "All have sinned and fallen short of the glory of God." All my life I thought I was the one who was not perfect, but I now saw that my situation was not unique. Everyone fell short, just as I did with my mother. Yet, the message went on to lift me out of despair for despite God knowing my imperfections, I finally came to understand that He loved me in spite of that. God was offering me His Son, Jesus, out of His great love for ME! I wanted this badly, yet I was struggling to accept this love.

My heart responded. I was ready and able to accept His gift. This had to be love and I wanted and needed it. I knelt down and accepted Jesus into my life. I asked forgiveness for my sins. A peace came over me— as a presence came to live inside of me. I felt like Jesus was with me and from that point on I no longer felt an emptiness inside of me. I was connected to God through Jesus his Son in a real way. This was not in my mind, this was not my fear. God wanted me to be in a relationship with his son for a long time but I was too afraid of his love. But God never gave up. His love was more powerful than my fear. My journey changed that day. My heart continued to open as did my eyes. I began to walk more securely in God's love and in his light. I still had depression issues but I felt more confident, like I was on the right path. I had renewed hope. I knew I needed to continue doing what I had been doing for my illness, going to therapy and taking my medication. I could not give up. I knew more than ever that I needed to keep going. Restoring a relationship spoke volumes to me. Relationships had been absent from my life for an extremely long time. If God wanted so badly to restore my relationship to Him what else was He speaking to me about regarding other relationships in my life? I began to focus on this as I walked forward.

I thought about my fear of being unlovable and how God could love me. All my thoughts and old fears began to stir again in my mind. What would God do when He found out I was unlovable? What would people do?

A gentle, still voice spoke among the loud voices. The still quiet voice got my attention. "Be still and know that I am God" (Psalm 46:10).

As difficult as it was for me, I forced myself to focus my mind on that still quiet voice. Those six years of my therapy group were not wasted. God was speaking to me through the chaos of my own mind.

Be still. Know that He is God.

I focused on this and learned much. I learned that I was not in control. I learned to adjust my expectations. I learned I needed to slow down my thoughts, my breathing, and my anxious mind.

I learned I needed to allow God to lead me.

CHAPTER 28

YOGA

I ended up at a yoga class.

New possibilities opened for me, or perhaps I simply became open to new possibilities. It seemed like I struggled constantly to relax. My body physically hurt from being inactive and from anxiety. I needed more exercise than I was getting from walking our dogs each morning. My posture resembled the defeated woman I felt like; my head down, my shoulders rolled forward, my neck and upper body stooped from looking at the ground. One of my care providers recommended I start doing yoga.

I was afraid to try new things. What if I could not do the postures? What if I was the worst in the class? What if it didn't help?

Stephen said to me, "You have nothing to lose by trying." I found that I was now willing. I found a class and dressed in my baggiest workout outfit. I swallowed my fear and went. I got my mat and joined the others on the floor. As awkward as I felt, I stretched and attempted the poses. I attempted the focused breathing and the relaxation period. I went back to a second class then a third. As I continued going, I improved and reaped the benefits. So did my family.

Although the first classes were challenging, I found that getting down on the mat and stretching was difficult but not impossible. Perhaps, okay definitely, I was not doing the stretches well, but I was trying to do them. It didn't feel good at first but at least I was there. I realized while I was down on my mat that I often avoided trying new things because I thought I would not be good at them, or because I was afraid of what people would think of me. I realized that this didn't matter, or at least it shouldn't matter. Here, lying on my mat, stretching my tight muscles, I realized that I felt a slight release. It felt good! I found that both the instructor and the other members of the class were accepting and encouraging. The instructor emphasized respecting our own bodies and going to our own limit. That was helpful to me. I eventually found myself better able to focus both at class and at home. This gave me a technique I could use at home anytime I wanted or needed. My posture slowly began to improve. Surprisingly, so did my attitude. I felt better about my body, and my mind was a little clearer. I began to see how my mind, body, and spirit were interconnected. The relief and release I felt in my body was incredible after all these years with my muscles so tense. It took months of gradually stretching for my body to assume a new posture but the time and effort were well worth it. The uncomfortable pain I initially wanted to run away from I started to run towards because it produced positive results in me. This was so typical of my choices and behavior in life.

I was able to practice my relaxation breathing wherever I was. This gave me a practical tool I could use and helped me feel like I was doing something concrete to help get better. These things brought about tangible results. It took a little time, but shortly after I started classes I became less anxious. I accepted any improvement at this point. It has been a long time coming. I was excited.

Focused breathing helped me to relax. As my mind slowed down, I found I was able to think different thoughts than I usually did — more positive thoughts; thoughts that helped build me up instead of tearing me down. Yoga also gave me more energy, which helped me stay awake during the day. As I was able to focus I began feeding my mind instead of endlessly drowning in my own negative thoughts. I do not remember the name of the book, but I was overjoyed that I was able to read. I could not sit and read for long periods of time, but I didn't care. I was so relieved and happy that I could finally read and enjoy a book. Other than reading to our daughters when they were young, I had not been able to read for my own pleasure in twelve years! It was similar to being parched on a hike on a ninety-degree summer day. I finally came upon some hikers who had water bottles and were willing to share.

I could not stop after taking that first cold sip. It tasted too good and one sip did not quench my thirst. I was parched. My body craved more water. Once I took the first sip of ice water it was like a dam had been released inside of me. I not only wanted to drink the entire bottle of water, I wanted to pour another one over my head as quickly as possible. I am not in control. I try to accept small steps of progress. A page in my book at a time. Then a chapter.

After all this time, I am truly excited. Relieved. Naturally I want more, but I try to be grateful for any noticeable progress. I still have my spending urge to go out and buy all of the bestsellers from the last ten years. In my spare moments I read instead of napping. I struggle to maintain attention, but the act of reading helps to do this. I take this as a sign of tangible hope. I know that God did this for me at a time when I needed a sign that recovery was possible for me. He knew what was important to me and what would bring me comfort. He knew so much more about me than I ever realized. I was on a different path with Him. I never had a relationship with God. I thought I knew Him but I didn't. My eyes were opening as was my heart. We continued on.

I began to look up instead of looking at the ground. I started to see the sun and the sky instead of a dark, dank hole. I dared to hope that my life, or more precisely, that I could be different, that my mood could change permanently. It seemed that my awareness of positive things both outside and within me was growing. Still slowly, but I was moving in the right direction. My connection with God was becoming more solid. I was finding that the more open I was, the more ways God was able to enter my life. Little ways and little things began making a big difference — sitting outside in the sunshine instead of lying on the couch during the day; reading; laughing spontaneously when I see our dogs playing together; waiting eagerly for my daughters to come home from school so we can go to the park to play.

I felt the warmth after all this time of darkness. I felt like I was connecting to the light and this connection would continue to pull me through. This connection would not break. It was strong and becoming solid. I was broken, but this connection with light and God's love was the source of power I always lacked in my life. By connecting with Him through Jesus His son, I am connected with God's love and His forgiveness and His light and strength. He often worked through people in my life. I needed to be CONNECTED. A part of me still shudders in fear when I think of that word. Because connection to me implies trust and pain and fear. But I know now that being connected is what will save me. Connected to my feelings, to God, to people, and even to my past. I know now there are unresolved issues there.

I still don't know the full extent of what they are, but I know that I must face them if I am ever to make the most important connection I have been walking for all this time — my desire for a more loving connection with my daughters and husband in the present.

In order for that to happen, I soon learn that I need a much better connection with myself. Perhaps that was what this walk was about in the first place; my connection with myself. It was skewed and had been for a very long time. So long in fact that my connection with myself seemed correct to me but it needed to be shattered. I was broken. My world had been torn apart a very long time ago when I was a young child, just a few years younger than Sarah is now. As I grew older, the pieces of that young girl continued to break and fall apart because I had a secret. I didn't choose to hide that secret but I was so ashamed. I felt so guilty, like I had no choice. I was only seven years old. I was destroyed by what happened to me. I was confused and lost. So I ran.

I was in pain but didn't know it, or rather I didn't acknowledge it. How could I? I had repressed the memories but the pain didn't go away. I carried it with me wherever I went. The edges cut into me. They hurt. I bled. The edges were jagged. I was alone since I trusted no one. There was no one to put on a band-aid. The cuts bled and got infected and festered and eventually oozed. They never healed. I continued on the only way I knew. I looked okay to others but my heart and soul were broken. The jagged edges were destroying me. I didn't believe I could ever be put back together. I drank to forget the pain of who I was and who I became.

When I realized I wanted to die at the age of twenty-nine, God entered my life and opened my eyes. I started on a new life journey, and this journey of sobriety helped me begin to heal. But my wounds ran too deep. I couldn't know the depth. I was a shattered person, and I never would have survived on my own. My heart healed enough to be able to love Stephen and to have our daughters; but as I tried to reach deeper into my heart to love more fully there was a barrier. As I reached inward, my hand came up jagged and almost severed from my arm because the cut edges of my heart at the depth where I was reaching for deeper love and trust was broken. My heart at this level was too broken and simply incapable of love.

My options were to heal or to only be able to love my family at the level I was loving them. The choice was mine. At first I did not feel like this was much of a choice, but I realized that I had already made my choice when I decided to marry and have our daughters. I am a mother and wife, and the bond between my family and me has already been formed and was growing. I must walk forward for all of us, in love, and for love. I couldn't do it for myself at first. I didn't understand anything, but I knew I wanted to love my daughters more fully. I wanted to provide for them and protect them. I knew deep inside my heart that I already loved them more fully than I was able to express. Something besides my fear blocked my expression of deeper love. So in my dark depression I started to walk. And I kept walking.

My disease brought me to another level. One I didn't know about and didn't realize existed. My depression brought me to the point of attempting suicide. This brought me to a lower level. This awakened a new fear in me. This was not about love, this was about destroying those I loved. This became twisted and convoluted in the name of love. As difficult as this was for me at first, I surrendered to a God I did not understand because I was too afraid of succumbing to my disease. And in surrendering to my God of love, I found a strength to go on living and confront my darkness, to confront the deep fears I carried most of my life. Fear is controlling and not freeing. Something is anchoring me in the deep ocean. I keep returning to the darkness despite brief times of relief. It is time to pull up the anchor. I need to get to the shore and join my daughters and husband while there is still time to live life alongside them.

The real question is, where am I walking? Am I walking towards recovery or am I walking backwards to my childhood? Could I be doing both at the same time? I do not understand but I go where Jesus and my heart lead me now. I am walking with Jesus by my side and feel His presence. My heart physically hurts but I will not allow my fear to interfere. I can do this; I tell myself with the help I have. One step at a time. Trust. Love. I will allow myself to think and feel, and express these with someone I trust. That is the difference. Trusting God and someone else; allowing others into my life.

I thought back to love. I realized how little I really knew or understood about it. Just wishing or wanting things to be different does not make it so. Nor does pretending they didn't happen or didn't exist. Some things I cannot change no matter how hard I try. But there are some things that could be changed if I asked for help. I can see that now. Going it alone all these years has not been easy nor has it been helpful. Trusting parts of myself and my life with other people has been a good start. Some things people cannot change. God is ultimately in charge of my life. Learning to trust Him and accept certain things takes time, but I begin to realize that that is how I will truly grow and change. This is how I will be free to live. I need to put myself in God's hands. Trusting His love instead of my fear is the better choice for me. This is how I can provide a safe home for my children. I can only do so much. I am human and limited and flawed and I live in an imperfect world. As did my parents. I need to trust God to protect not only me but my children.

CHAPTER 29

RELATIONSHIPS

*G*od's love is the glue that put the pieces of my life together and He holds me together. Glue is flexible. Cement would have sunk to the ocean floor. I needed to reach the land, and I needed a bridge to get me there. I found that God was not rigid. My fear made me rigid and controlling. I needed something else. I needed to be connected and to learn how to communicate. Communication needed to flow freely. Being open to God and to his love was what connected me to my past and my present so I would have a future worth living. Being open to God connected me to people in my life. I needed to be open so I could hear and listen to what Donald said to me, so I could question what I believed about myself and others.

Just as God's love was the glue that connected the pieces of my life together, it was the glue that connected me to others. I needed to live in relationship.

I found that God's love was not controlling, not blaming or condemning. It was forgiving and caring. I wanted to live in this love. I could be secure in God's love for me and this helped me extend love to others. This was not easy but possible. I found that light was present amidst the darkness all along. Most of the time I was too absorbed in my darkness to notice this light, however there were moments of recognition, moments of hope or peace that inspired me to keep going; while there were other moments when I thought I could not go another step. The moments with my daughters as they grew healthily despite my illness touched and tugged at my heart, cementing the connection that challenged me to do my own healthy growing. Because I learned through this journey that I live, not in isolation, as my fear wants me to believe, but in connection with others. Although I might feel safer by myself, I am unable to experience the feelings of giving and receiving love and joy, and I am unable to connect with others in any meaningful way to any deeper extent that my humanness calls me to, unless I am in a relationship with others. For I have found that when I am in a relationship is when I am able to experience my most basic feelings of joy and sadness, insecurity and pain, and I am called to trust and be honest, even if it means exposing who I am. It is also when I am in these relationships that I am my best self and connected with others who are experiencing similar feelings. Our experiences may differ but our feelings are more similar than I ever realized. The act of sharing and connecting enabled me to survive this journey which could have destroyed me. Instead it enabled me to reach a more joy filled level of living. For by sharing my pain with others and receiving the help I needed, I was able to get the strength and resources needed to transcend the deep darkness and fear and live in the hope of recovery until that hope became a reality. My recovery started with a spark of God's love and grace within me which kept burning, and although I was seriously depressed and faced many desperate and lonely moments, by crying out for help, usually through my therapist who was a primary connection, I learned the importance of my relationship with

Jesus, my husband, my daughters, my family, my recovery group, my friends, and with anyone and everyone I met throughout each day. When I live in isolation, I live primarily in my fear. When I live in relationship and connection, I live in love and trust, which is much more difficult but far more fulfilling. When I am connected in love, I have a better chance of being the mother I want to be for my daughters. This is the wife I want to be for my husband. This is the person I always wanted to be growing up. This is the person I can be today. I am grateful for that. I am alive today because of the journey I took. I would not have necessarily planned this road for myself, but I am grateful for where I have ended up. For that I say, thank you God for the blessings of those years and for the blessings of my husband and daughters and for the ability to know You. This, I realize, is how to provide that safe and secure home for my family - to teach them of your unconditional love for them. The way I am to teach them is by the way I live, not only by what I say.

Help me to remember each day that your dawn follows the night. As I look back on those long and painful years, I have regrets at times. I regret the time lost with my daughters as they were growing up that I will never get back; I regret the memory loss and the loss of my profession; I regret the loss of family relationships. But when my thoughts go there, I try not to allow them to park there. If I do, my fear takes over and begins to control my thoughts and feelings. If I stay in that thinking too long, my fear begins to control my behavior. I will choose to isolate and not share my thoughts or feelings with a trusted friend. As my fear tells me to isolate; my thinking will become more negative and I will become more focused on the pain and sadness of those years instead of the joy along that journey. Today, because of that journey, I have choices I did not have before. I can see that there were extremely painful parts of that journey, but there was also joy along the way. And today, because of that journey I walked, I am able to experience joy and love more freely. I am free to be myself and experience life. So just for today, which is all I have, I choose to focus on the brighter moments of that time, which does not take away one moment of the pain, but instead I choose to celebrate it by choosing to focus on the joy of recovery, the hope that if I could recover, perhaps others can too.

Help is available. Hope is available. Love is available to any and all.

Sometimes I was rejected or misunderstood, or perhaps it was my illness that was misunderstood. But my life was worth fighting for even when I didn't feel like it was. I will be forever grateful that God and other people knew that, and those that did reached out.

CHAPTER 30

A CHANGE OF HEART

*A*fter my father died when Emily was six and Sarah was four, my mother was left alone to worry about what was happening to me. I knew she loved me, but she was unable to grasp what was happening to her daughter. How could she really? Especially when I attempted to end my life. This must have been too much for my mother. She was searching to understand, and in trying to make sense of something that one cannot begin to understand, my mother blamed my husband for my illness and suicide attempts. This caused many problems. I think my desperate situation was too painful for my mother to accept in her heart. Instead, she tried to blame someone, and the closest person was my husband. Talk about the lesson of forgiveness in our family! One day, as I was on the way to the psychiatric hospital after attempting to take my life, my husband called my mother to tell her of the situation.

My mother, upset, screamed into the phone, "What did you do to her to make her behave that way?"

He responded, "Nothing, I didn't do anything to her. I love her. It is because she is so depressed. She doesn't want to live anymore."

"How can she not want to live anymore? She has Emily and Sarah. She has so much to live for. You must have done something to hurt her. She would not have tried to kill herself otherwise. This is all your fault!"

My husband carried this with him for many years. Forgiveness came, but it did not come easily and it came with a great deal of pain, time and tears. It did not come until I was on the way to recovery and unfortunately, it did not come until after my mother died. I only know my husband's side. I do not know if my mother forgave my husband for an illness for which he had no responsibility. It no longer matters to us. I believe my mother was afraid for me. Worse, she was afraid because she could not understand what was happening and felt helpless to control my illness and protect me. I can understand that fear. As a mother, I was experiencing that same fear for my own daughters. I wanted to protect Emily and Sarah from my depression. Sadly, my mother and I could not share our similar feelings with one another. But even that was alright at the time. We had each other as we were able to be. I could finally accept her as she was, not as I wanted her to be. I think and hope she accepted me as I am, I know she LOVED me as I am; of that I am sure. I am also sure I loved her as only a mother and child can love. She gave me the gift to continue on with my journey for myself and my family. Perhaps unknowingly, but I know and recognize the gift she had been and was, and that was only because of my illness. I had been so consumed in the dark all these years that I was no longer able to recognize any light in my life. I had been so consumed with myself, even as I grew older, that I had not been able to see beyond myself, to my own parents, and that hurt all of us. Love is not contained but moves out to others, and as my heart and eyes opened, I was able to see the hurt I had caused others in my life, not necessarily by what I had done but by what I failed to do. And I failed to be the daughter I was meant to be. It was not too late. As areas of my heart were illuminated, I was able to reach out and take tiny actions to reach out and connect to those I needed to reconnect with. I was floating at sea but I needed to be safely at land. I needed to belong to a family, to a larger group. I needed support and connection and I needed love and care. I needed to be able to give love and support. When I was lost, I needed to know someone was looking for me. And I would look for others. What I did not know was that I could be an individual within my community. I was learning that now. Fortunately, it was not too late with my mother but it was too late for me and my father. I knew that my mother worried about me. As the years passed and my depression did not improve, I believe my mother tried to understand my illness. I did not know how much she understood, but I do know she made an effort. Today I believe she understood as much as she was capable of understanding. As I have mentioned, our relationship was always a rocky one, and honest and open communication was not something at which either of us excelled. I excelled at avoiding my mother and not telling her what she did not what to hear. As an adult, I was afraid of her reaction just like when I was a child. I wanted to please her and I could not handle her disappointment in me, so I avoided disappointing her at all. I did not tell her what I thought and how I felt, and so I hid; but now there was nothing to hide behind, so I gradually began to share honestly with her. It was not easy but it was my truth. It was me. This was all I had to share.

Perhaps I should have not let my fear stop me from reaching out to my mother all these years. I needed and wanted her to be a part of my life. Sadly, my life was broken. This was not how I wanted to show her my life but this was how it was. This was my reality. I talked to her frankly and honestly. Some things we agreed on, some things we didn't. It was okay. We didn't have to agree. We could be different. We were learning to accept one another. It was not ideal, but we were taking little steps in the right direction.

I was sure my mother loved me. I knew this because I felt her love. My mother stood by me. She came to the place that, despite what she said or believed or understood about my illness, she was my mother and I was her daughter, and she knew that I needed her love probably now more than ever. She gave me that love as best she was able; freely, with no strings attached. Each and every time I was hospitalized my mother called and said "I love you." My mother's calls meant so much to me during that lonely and scary time. She called me at home and ended each phone call the same way, "Don't give up. I know that you will get better. I am praying for you every day. I love you." A mother's love. That mother/daughter bond of love and connection at the time in my life when I needed it the most.

My pain touched her as only a mother's heart can be touched. Whatever mistakes happened in the past I needed to leave there. I needed to see what was happening in the present. My mother was here for me now in the way she was able to be. What a gift. Was I willing and able to accept it? That was up to me. Perhaps my gift to her was reaching out in my pain and being truthful about where I was in my life. Perhaps my darkness and where it brought me helped her look into her own pain and respond from that heart of love. Her gift was loving me as I was with a mother's heart. It was a true gift to me. She did not desert me during these years.

We had many disagreements but my mother did what she could for me and my family. My mother and I disagreed about many things but there was one thing we definitely agreed on — the mother/daughter connection of love formed at birth, or even before, was so strong; my voice reached my mother's heart and my mother knew my voice. She responded as only a mother could, she responded to me out of her heart of love. Just as I was walking through my depression for my daughter's life, my mother walked through this difficult time for me because she loved me. It was as simple and profound as that. I finally accepted her love not as I thought it should be, but as she was able to give it to me. Just as I thought I needed to be a certain type of daughter throughout the years, I thought my parents needed to be a certain way. I had pushed my parents away because I was too afraid to trust and accept them as they were. Now I not only needed my mother's love, I welcomed it.

My mom died before I recovered from that extreme depression. She died, however, knowing I was on my way, knowing we loved each other as best we could. For this I am extremely grateful. I was able to love her back for being my mom especially during these darkest years. In this way my illness brought us closer together. In my neediness I was finally able to look beyond past hurts and see the possibilities for connection despite the hurt, disappointment, and old patterns of behavior. For I found that my need for love was greater, and so was my mother's. The power of that love was waiting to be unleashed. It hadn't disappeared during the years; it was always there, waiting for me to be ready to accept it. I was ready and able. I needed my mother and longed to connect with her, as an adult child to her mother. I needed to get to know her and she needed to get to know me. I was willing, and it turned out my mother was too. We stumbled and made mistakes but it no longer mattered so much. We were in a relationship, a part of one another's life. We shared as honestly as possible. My mother could not fix my depression but she was able to help out. She could be a part of my life and her granddaughters' life. She was capable of being there in the way she could be and I realized and accepted that she was good enough. She was my mother and I LOVED her. I always had, but I didn't allow myself to feel that love for fear I would disappoint her, and in disappointing her I would disappoint myself. In denying myself that love for her, I denied myself feeling her love for me. I realize now I have denied both of us a most precious gift. It was not too late.

I learned from my mother that being a parent is not easy or simple. My mother could not keep me safe from my depression. Neither she nor my father could keep me safe from my addictions. Since I could not even be honest with myself I was not capable of being honest with my parents. As I lived many miles from home, I seldom visited my parents, and other than my food disorder, they did not know of my other addictions. I began to understand that parents can love and pray, but at times there are circumstances beyond their control. I thought about my own children. I wanted to keep them safe and protect them, but from the moment Sarah was born I was unable to do everything I had originally envisioned. Did this mean I was not a good mother? These thoughts were stirring in my mind as waves in the ocean. It seemed to me I had held fast to certain ideas but they no longer seemed so clear cut. The water seemed to be as muddied as when the bottom of the ocean floor is stirred up, blurring my vision.

I could sense that my views were changing, and ideas or beliefs I once thought safe were no longer secure. I felt my deep-seated fears and insecurities coming to the surface. I sensed, as in a coming storm at the ocean, the waves were gathering in intensity and force. I had better run to seek cover but where was I to go for shelter? No matter where I looked, I could not see any shelters that looked strong or safe enough to withstand the threatening wind and incoming tides.

To stay where I am would be a form of giving up, a form of suicide, and I cannot or I will not do that today. I have suffered enough from this disease and I have put my daughters and husband through enough suffering by my suicide attempts. They have been through enough, having to live with me and the effects of my disease daily. They do not need the added stress and worry of whether or not I will try to kill myself again. Thankfully, it has been at least four years now since my last attempt. I prayed that was my last attempt.

I must do something else. I cannot afford to stand still, waiting for the incoming storm and waves to overtake me yet again. That would be irresponsible. I am sick, but that does not give me a reason to avoid making necessary decisions for the good of myself and my family. Taking responsibility was crucial. It was a huge part of being an adult. It was also, I believe, a huge part of being loving. I couldn't afford to stand still and let this next storm come, and it will come. I can sense it. It could overpower me; it might even drown me. If that happened I would be allowing it to overtake my family. There was always the chance that my disease would overtake me when I do the right things. Sitting by and choosing not to do anything was making a decision to let my depression win, and that was a poor choice. That was irresponsible. That would be giving up, or perhaps being in denial of how powerful depression actually was. When I failed to accept my illness and take my medications on schedule, or I stopped going to therapy, I was telling my depression that I did not think it was powerful enough to destroy me, but I was wrong. I knew this because I took my medication and went to therapy and tried to stay connected, yet I still wanted to commit suicide. That, to me was extremely tragic, and extremely sad. If my disease had that much power when I was following the treatment recommendations, I could not begin to understand the power it would have if I weren't following treatment recommendations. Yes, I believed from my own experience this disease was serious and wanted me DEAD. It was relentless. Fortunately, God had another plan.

In the course of all this, the most innocent of all, my two daughters, and my husband, would have suffered the most. I needed my therapist's perspective to help me see how important other people were to me, and to see how my actions would affect them. I also needed help understanding how important I was to other people.

So here I am. What was I to do? Would I stand here paralyzed by fear, something I was well familiar with, or would I step out and respond in a new way for myself and my family? Would I take a risk and act out of faith?

As many thoughts whirled through my head, I practiced focusing on them in the moment. I tried to let the thoughts go as I had learned through my yoga classes and my mindfulness group. I attempted to slow my frantic breathing by focusing on it. My mind, body, and spirit were connected, and by actually doing the skills I had learned, I was able to calm my anxious mind and body. I realized that being willing to do them and not worrying about doing them perfectly was a gift. I reaped the benefit as my mind began to clear and my breathing slowed. As I focused on the remaining thoughts in my mind, three voices were attempting to be heard above the others. I recognized the loudest voice. This voice was the voice of FEAR. I knew this voice which had controlled me and most of my decisions for many years. As I attempted to let this voice go so I could hear the other voices, my heart spoke to me, "That voice belongs in the past. That voice belongs in the dark. Open your hands and push that voice away." So I did just that. Sitting outside in our backyard alone looking at the trees, I opened my hands and pushed the FEAR away.

Then I heard the other two voices, one voice gentle and loving, the other barely audible. The gentle voice was God saying to me, "Be not afraid. I formed you in my image. My plan is to bless you. I am with you always. I sent my Son Jesus to die for you. There is nothing you experience that He has not experienced. Through your relationship with Him you are in a relationship with me and my perfect love. Seek me and my love for you. This love bears all things. I have put people in your life. I work in many ways. Sit back quietly, take some time, and reflect on some of the ways I have been present to you in your life."

As I did this, I thought of how God had been in my life. I thought of the time Donald brought me to the dentist because I was too afraid to go. I had not gone in nine years. I refused to go. My fear was too great. Donald offered to go with me! I thought, "How can he do this and why would he?" I eventually realized the answer was he truly cared about me. The real grace was that I had no cavities after nine years! My husband and I brought our daughters to the dentist every six months to have their teeth cleaned. Once they were old enough to notice they began to say to me, "How come you never go to the dentist?" I feebly answered, "I don't need to go as often as you do," but as they got older I needed to tell them the truth. "I'm afraid of going."

I thought of the times I sat in silence in Donald's office and he offered to make me tea because I was too anxious to talk about anything. I thought of how Donald allowed me to call him at home when I needed to; I thought about how he reached out to my mother and Stephen numerous times. I thought of the times we sat and he read while I wrote in my journal, or I tried to read. He was willing to reach me by any means possible and he did not care what others might think of his methods. He was patient and gentle and caring. He showed me what God was like and I had no idea what his spiritual beliefs were. Donald taught me about honest and caring relationships and I believe God worked through Donald. He also worked through my alcoholic recovery group who accepted me.

I also had another friend from my teenage years who stood by me and consistently encouraged me and was there for the long haul. All these qualities taught me about God. He is faithful, even when I am not and loving and caring. He wants me to be in a relationship with Him. Most of all He wants me to be honest and not afraid of Him. He wants me to be MYSELF. This was the third voice that I could barely hear. God said to me, "That small voice that you hardly recognize is YOU! I gave you that voice, and by being in a relationship with me and my Son, and by completing this journey, your voice will become stronger. This is the voice you are meant to use when you speak. Anything else is not your truth. When you became a mother, you began searching for your voice to parent and it was time for your past traumas to surface and to heal, if you so choose. You are now a mother and not a child. If you stay connected to me, in love and not the fear you can choose to push away, you will find your voice and speak from whom you are. I made you and I know what I am doing. Just as I made Emily and Sarah, I made you."

"If you want to finish this journey and find your voice, Marcia, then continue surrendering to my love and embrace your darkness. Embrace it in love and not fear; as my Son is with you, so am I."

"I call you by name, Marcia, to enter your past darkness. Enter in Love. Enter with my Son. Faith and trust is not enough at times. As you become more aware of my presence you will know when and how to act.

Take His hand. You never need to be alone, unless you choose to."

The spark within me grew brighter and warmer. It was as if the waves in the ocean calmed down for a while. In the midst of this calmness I felt my raft switch to a sailboat. My boat picked up speed. It seemed to go with the wind and changed course.

Best of all, I gave up all control. I surrendered to God's love for me. I allowed the wind to take me where I needed to go. I was not in control, God was. The best thing was I was able to travel back to my past, but I was finally able to make my way to the safety of land. But to get there I had to allow the wind to direct my sails. I did not know the way, but I needed to trust that God knew. So I did just that.

I was no longer tacking back and forth as I had been doing for years, which resulted in being stagnant at times in the same waters. I had made some progress, but I had returned to the same area of the ocean like a ship trapped in the Sargasso Sea. I was safe in my sailboat, but I now had the power needed to get through the deeper waves that we encountered. With Jesus, my hope was renewed. I could now begin to move into the wind. I was at the point in my illness where I needed to step out in faith, as precarious as it seemed; because if I didn't, I felt like I would lose my family. I needed the wind to fill my sails so I could move into the blackest times of my life. It was time for me to rely on God's love, just as I trusted my love for my daughters. When God touched my heart through Jesus, I knew I needed to answer for myself. God loved me for who I was. I could no longer afford to be afraid He would not love me. He was my Father and He gave up His Son for me. My heart opened to that. My journey changed as I began to walk for myself.

I slowly learned that surrendering control of my life to God was not easy, but was what I needed. I realized that God not only provided the wind, He was The Wind. He loved me and He was Love Itself. He was in charge of my life, and my boat went where He directed it to go. I always had a choice. I did not have to go. I could drop anchor anywhere I wanted. I could say "No." I had done that many times in my life. But I knew where that had taken me. I wanted to end up somewhere different this time.

For quite a few years now, I struggled with trying to understand God's love. Now I realized it was more important that I believe and trust God than it was for me to understand Him. Perhaps this was faith. Perhaps I lost this when I was child. Perhaps I never had it. I did not know. I don't know if it matters.

Sometimes I felt like I was alone on my raft on the stormy seas, drowning, feeling as if no one in the world cared, and if they did they couldn't understand how I felt, or there wasn't anything they could do to help me. At times I felt like there were no words to express the daily terror and the horror I was living in. Other times I simply felt like "What's the use of trying anymore, I may as well give up. Others will be better off without me. I am useless like this anyway, who am I kidding." It was at times like these that I felt like I was thrown a life preserver that was too small. I was clinging to this life preserver for dear life and had been for far too long. My body temperature was below zero and I felt like I could not hold on another second. In the distance I heard someone yelling, "Just hold on a few more minutes! Help is on the way! The only problem was I had heard that for days. When would help arrive? How much longer could I hold on?

It was at times like these that I needed to look within, not without. I needed to listen to the still small voice of God, not the loud voices of my fears clamoring to be heard. I needed to still the pounding of my heart so I could feel the warmth of God spread throughout my chilled body. I needed to release the death grip on my life preserver so that I could take hold of God's hand and those of the people He placed in my life. I then needed to open my eyes to what lay in the dark recesses of my mind and heart and look with the eyes of an adult, with love and compassion at what lay there. I must if I wanted to come back to land to live my life as the woman, wife and mother I hoped to be. I did, so I released my tight hold and opened my eyes, and I went where my fear forbad me to go before.

When I went, I went with Hope in my heart.

Hope seemed like such a fragile thing until it became based on my faith. My hope grew as my faith grew. When I realized God was my Father and He sent Jesus out of love for me, I felt an incredible release inside of me. I let go of my fear that I was unlovable and that God could not love me. If God was my Father and sent His son to die for me - a love this great - I could not debate or argue with this. The truth was, I no longer wanted to argue. I felt so defeated by my illness, I was desperate for recovery. I was desperate to be that mother I longed to be to my daughters who were now teenagers. I felt desperate to feel the sunshine on my face, to dance in the rain, to go on a date with my husband, and to have a cup of tea with a friend. I was desperate to shop for clothes with my daughters and go to the movies; to go to a museum or to take them skiing (I would be a spectator); to go away for the weekend without my family worrying about me not sleeping or changing my mind about wanting to go.

I longed to be a bigger and more consistent part of my family's life. When I heard God's voice, I was relieved and I answered. I did not understand, but I believed and then acted on that belief. I trusted that love, and that made the difference for me in my recovery. As I trusted in that love for me, as I walked in that love, I had some difficult choices to make and pain to embrace, but I was able to do it because I was no longer debating whether or not God loved me. I felt it and I knew He sacrificed His Son for me. I accepted this and I decided I needed to do all I needed to do for my daughters out of love and that LOVE was within me. And so I embraced my darkness head on.

When I did, the repressed memories came flooding back to me from my childhood. Instead of destroying me, they eventually freed me! I did not like them, they hurt, but with Jesus by my side, His spark burning within me, my truth could be seen for the lies they were in the dark. My trauma did not make me a bad person or unlovable, it did not make me defective; it did not make me responsible; it did not make me a mistake or mean I was to be punished for life. It also did not mean my father was a bad person; to me it meant that he made a morally wrong decision which had horrible and far reaching consequences for me and probably for him too. My lies told me to keep silent because the silence loves the dark which blocks the sunlight of the spirit. But God's Love was stronger as was my need and desire for healing. For He had placed that desire within me the day I became sober, and I wanted that life, free from alcohol, free from substitutes, and I was learning that I needed to surrender to this God of Love for help. I did not understand Him or Love but I desperately wanted His help and gradually I realized how much I craved and needed and desired His Love and care. And each day as I move forward, I realize how starved I have been and how Good and Loving He is. It is my lack of trust that stands in my way of deeper relationship but even that is alright as He does not have a timetable. He Loves me with an everlasting Love!

CHAPTER 31

MY TRUE HOPE

*W*hy am I unlovable? This question haunted me the most. "What have you done that was so bad," echoed in my mind. Donald asked me many times, too numerous to count. My typical response, "I don't know" echoed right back. This had become like a mantra I could not shut off.

Did I still believe these things about myself? How would I ever resolve this?

When I was able to accept that God loved me and cared for me, I was finally able to begin recovering for myself along with my daughters and husband. I began to care about myself for perhaps the first time that I could remember. Connecting with God awakened a part of me that felt dead to life. I connected to a life-giving power; a source of love, but it was more than that for me. It was as if I had connected to an original part of myself, like I had just been reborn in a sense. I now had access to a power and strength I never had before. It was as if the film that covered my eyes had fallen off and I was able to view the world more clearly and accurately. I was able to see it through the light of God and His love.

I had been out in the deep ocean all these years, trying to get to shore. I was pushed back and overcome by the waves when they came, despite the medical help I had. More was needed. More power, direction, guidance, and strength to overcome the storms and the waves that sought to destroy whatever progress I seemed to make. Could it be that You, Lord God, are the source of that power and guidance? Will you lead me out of this deep dark powerful ocean that seeks to keep me underwater despite my attempts to get to shore? Will You be the light I need, and the One I can trust that will never fail me? Will you be the One that is that source of Hope that I can rely on, no matter what is happening in my life?

As these thoughts ran through my head, I realized I was speaking them aloud to God. It was as if He whispered back to me, "Yes, I am that One. Just walk with my Son, Jesus. I gave Him for you because I love you that much. He understands everything you feel. When things become too much for you, turn them over to my Son. Let Him carry them for you. That is the way out of your darkness. We can do this together. I am the source of Love. You need to be connected and in relationships. I can restore relationships."

God was telling me to use care and love to look with the eyes of my heart. God wanted me to begin seeing myself as He saw me— as he created me — with Love and compassion. Truth was important, but it was important how I viewed the truth and what I did with it once I saw it.

Most importantly, He told me to continue taking others with me, to remember what I have learned from my own walk. He whispered these things in my ear and talked to me about them in my mind. He reminded me of His love and His light, which exposed what lied in the darkness. He also reminded me of how much easier it was for me to walk now that I can see with His light shining through my heart, that it is starting to reflect His love for me. "Remember how much I love you," goes through my mind over and over again. "You cannot remember this enough. Trust my love. Just as you have trusted your love for your daughters, trust in my love for you. I am your Father. I made you in my image and in my likeness. Your true identity comes from me and from me alone. My love is not like human love. My love is perfect love.'"

So it is with this in my mind and heart that I continued on. It is still not easy, but I walk with renewed hope and a sense that I am not alone. I feel for perhaps the first time that whatever is preventing my recovery could be resolved.

As I move ahead, I recall those words. My fear attempts to take over my thinking but I am determined to place my trust in the right place this time. I not only sense it but I feel God's presence growing within me. I feel strengthened and more hopeful. I try to nurture my relationship with God as best I know how. I move forward, step by step. I have no idea where I am going to end up, but I let God lead me.

I return to my bench. I thought of my time sharing my more intimate thoughts and feelings with Donald as I reflected on my rawest feelings. Now, as I shared, I felt a deeper connection. Was it with Donald, or was it with God? Perhaps it was with both. Since I had become more aware of His presence in my life I had spent quiet moments with Him. I have allowed Him to see my pain and mistakes and even my secret fears. As I shared them, I found He comforted me and didn't judge me, similar to the way Donald accepted me. I am drawn to this God. I feel like I can rest while I am with Him. His love wraps its arms around me and encompasses me despite the darkness. HE tells me I am loved. He is with me. I feel safe with Him. I trust Him more and more. This is a love I never knew. The best part is that I can go to this bench whenever I want and sit with my God. I can be comforted and wrapped in love whenever I need it. There is no limit. He invites me to come. It is an open invitation. His heart and door are always open. I found He is always home. He knows all about me yet accepts and loves me as I am. His light is always on. He comes with me wherever I go. I can come to Him whenever I want.

It seems that my old best friend has been displaced with my new best friend. Fear does not like to leave so easily; but when God's invitation has been accepted, fear must leave. At least it left in this situation in my life. It was no longer welcome.

CHAPTER 32

FORGIVENESS

*A*s I carried my secrets with me throughout the years, I also carried a lot of unnecessary blame, shame, and guilt. As I continued in therapy I came to an unfamiliar place in my heart; a place called forgiveness. I needed to get to this place and it didn't come easily. It was a process, like the rest of my recovery, but it was necessary. I wanted to recover and move forward. I couldn't do this when I had an anchor attaching me to my past. It was as if I had one foot on land and the other pulling me back into the ocean. I could not live like this. At least not the way I wanted to and was hoping. My perspective needed to change, so I continued to press into my therapy and process my painful feelings. I tried to be honest. I tried to connect with my God of love.

Also, during this time I reconnected with my husband. I was able to talk to him. I drew comfort from him as I relived my past with him. This drew us closer to each other. I found that as I poured out my rawest hurts to him, he was able to love me through them and was able to understand me. It was as if we were talking and sharing as we did during our time together when we first met and were dating. We were sharing honestly and freely. This helped me to accept myself and eventually accept my past.

I needed to work through my emotional hurts to come to this place called forgiveness. I thought of it as a resting place, a place of peace and letting go. A place of acceptance and of love, not necessarily a place of understanding. I found that although I could easily say the words, I needed to forgive from my heart. I needed to be honest about this. This trauma ran deep, as did my illness. It took time, patience, tears, anger, and prayer. Finally, it took a willingness to let go.

I had previously heard that it was important to forgive people, not for the other person but for myself. I had absolutely no idea what this meant. Most times in my life I wasn't interested, or perhaps more accurately, I wasn't ready to forgive some people in my life. While I was so depressed, my heart and perspective were changing. I began to see my parents and myself with the eyes of compassion instead of blame or misunderstanding. I did not know much about my parents' lives. I did know that they, too, suffered their share of sorrow. Neither of my parents spoke much about the roads they travelled in their lives. I knew losing my oldest sister must have had a significant impact on their lives, and perhaps a part of their hearts never recovered. I could not know the depth of their loss. I recalled my oldest sister's picture on the dining room hutch in a silver frame. She looked beautiful and young. My mother said that was her eighth-grade picture. My mother often said, "The high school teachers came here to our house to teach her when she was so sick. They loved her."

I often felt sad when my mom talked about MaryAnn, but I inwardly cringed when these same high school teachers called me MaryAnn instead of Marcia. I knew how perfect my mother and these teachers thought MaryAnn had been. I knew how much of a mistake I was. These feelings were too difficult for me to handle. I could not discuss them with anyone. I did not eat my lunch again. I hid it and tried to excel at being the thinnest in my family.

I had seen pictures of my parents when they both looked more carefree and happier than I remembered them. I knew they loved me, they worked hard and provided and cared for me. Just as my wounds influenced my behavior, perhaps they were carrying things on their hearts that influenced what they said or did. Wounds that never healed and caused or influenced their thoughts or emotional, physical, or spiritual behavior. My mind opened to this possibility. My dad died long before I made peace with my past. I was sad about this, but I knew now that my dad and I were not meant to talk about those times. I had forgiven him in my heart. I had mourned the loss of the relationship we could not have, and I prayed God's blessings on him. I knew my dad loved me despite what happened. I knew my dad was not a mistake and neither was I. I took a long dark journey to come to that place. I choose to focus today on the good memories I have with both my parents. And there were good memories. The choice is mine today on where I focus my thoughts.

Forgiveness does not excuse behavior; it does not make something wrong that happened right. Just as I am responsible for my choices, my father was responsible for his choices, as was my mother. My daughters are also responsible for their choices. It is also not my place to judge anyone. I receive undeserved forgiveness from Jesus. This enables me to extend forgiveness. I can accept that some things happen in life that I do not or will not understand. What is more important is that I look with compassion. Perhaps as I have journeyed, I need to pause to think about where my father might be coming from, the roads he may have walked that I may not know about; the mountains he may have climbed; the storms of life that may have attempted to destroy him; the wounds he may ultimately have carried deep within his heart that perhaps he was carrying alone or was carrying in silence. Or worse, wounds that ran so deep he could not heal from them.

I needed to forgive my mother too. I overly focused on her most of my life because I could not look at the truth that existed between my father and me. I interpreted my mother's criticisms and responses to me and my less than perfect behavior to mean that I was not good enough. I internalized this and carried it with me wherever I went. I allowed it to influence my thoughts, decisions, and choices in life. I owed her an apology. She, too, had passed on at this point. I made my apologies to both my parents for my behavior in a letter and in my heart. I choose to believe they heard me and received my apology. Despite my parents' behavior I had to look at my own actions throughout my life. There was much I felt sorry for, especially for distancing myself from them.

Seeing my parents with the eyes of my heart, with the love of Jesus, allowed me to forgive them. I began to see beyond my hurt. I could see more than the mistakes they made. My mother had nine miscarriages in addition to losing my fourteen- year-old sister. These traumas must have changed her forever. As a mother myself I cannot begin to imagine suffering through that. As I remembered that World War II picture hanging in our basement, I realized my dad too suffered his share of pain in addition to all the losses he shared with my mom. I could not imagine the horrors my father witnessed or suffered while he served in the army. Perhaps both parents passed on to me much more than I realized. Despite their heartache, they continued to take care of my sisters and me the best they could. My dad went to work in a factory and worked overtime whenever possible so he could save for us to attend college. My mom did not work when we were young. She stayed home to be there for us when we came home from school. My sisters and I meant that much to our parents. My parents taught me the value of work, responsibility, and family. They brought me to church every Sunday. They believed in education. My parents were loving people. They worked hard. Life had hurt them deeply. I cannot begin to understand their deep loss after my oldest sister died and how they were changed probably forever. Perhaps fear began to grow as it did in my life although I believe God held their hearts in His loving hands.

The mistakes they made did not define who they were. They were responsible for them, but just as Jesus freely forgave me, He has freely forgiven them and I was to do the same. I have. It has not been easy but it was necessary. Having done so has freed me to move forward in my life. My heart has opened and I am willing to risk once again. For I now know that when I get hurt, as I will, I can go to Jesus and He will be there to comfort me. And when I hurt other people, as has happened, I can also go to Jesus and ask forgiveness, and He will be there for me. To comfort, to encourage, to strengthen me to ask others for forgiveness. I need help. Life is not easy when I live in relationship, connected to others, but that is when I experience some of my most joy filled moments.

By looking long and hard into my heart and letting God's light shine into the darkest corners, I could eventually admit and accept my truth. It was easier to blame my parents for everything. My parents had their part, but I also had my part. I am responsible for my own choices in life and for my own actions and addictions. I am responsible for my behavior. I am responsible for my decisions, the good ones as well as the poor ones. When I was able to accept my truth, I was able to forgive and also ask for forgiveness. Then I tried to let it go. I tried to let it go by giving it to God. I imagined myself placing my hurts, fears, pain, loneliness, lost dreams, anger and disappointment and the loss of my innocence and loss of faith in God's hands. I took my hands away. I pictured myself letting go of both of my parents' hands and putting their hands in God's hands. Then I pictured myself having two free hands. I placed one of them in God's hand and the other in my daughters' hands. I was free to move forward in my life. I could do this as often as I needed to or wanted to. I learned that I do not have to carry anything by myself anymore or hold onto things unless I choose. What a huge relief this was for me.

Then my mind and my heart and feet are free to move on. I am freer now to be the mother I want to be to Emily and Sarah. I want to spend more time with them and enjoy them more. I want to enjoy life more and cry less. I want to live more and sleep less. I want to look forward to what each day will bring and what we can bring to it. I am tired of living in the past. The best news is that I no longer need to. Because of the journey and the steps I have taken to heal, I can revisit my past when I want to but it no longer needs to control me or my daughters', or hopefully their children.

Forgiving someone releases their hold on my heart so that I am free to love once more. To me the very act of forgiveness is also an act of love.

Just as I needed to learn to forgive, I needed to learn to ask for forgiveness. Just as I am a parent, a wife and a friend in the course of a day, I make many mistakes. One of the best examples I can be for my daughters is to admit I make mistakes and ask for forgiveness. I have learned the important lesson that being a parent does not mean being perfect; it means being human.

Perhaps one of the hardest people I had to learn to forgive was myself. I thought I was to blame for my parents' unhappiness or mistakes. I thought I was to blame because I couldn't make them better. I felt like a failure. I couldn't live with my feelings. My addictions took over. These addictions took me to dark places all their own. I made many poor choices in my life. I could not forgive myself without help. Only by believing that God loves me and by accepting Jesus as my Savior could I start to forgive myself. I had to reconcile the image of God loving the unlovable me. I realized there are things I do or ways I think or things I say that are unloving, but God loves me as a person, unconditionally. I was also not responsible for a lot of things that happened.

I was not in control of other people. I was not to blame for my depression; I was not to blame for thinking like a child when I was a child; It was not my fault that my oldest sister died before I was born; I was not to blame that I was not my sister. I had to let go. I needed to seek a balance between what I held onto and what I let go. I learned this by being connected in quiet times with my God of love, by being still and knowing He is God. As I looked at the still waters they were calm and level. They were not churning. I wondered how they came to this place of peace or balance and maintained it. How could I come to a place of peace in my life? I knew it must came from allowing God to continue to live in my heart and life. Letting go was difficult for me. I liked to hang on. I thought there was security there, but as I sat on my bench and talked with God, I realized that it mattered what I held onto. Holding onto anger or blame or resentment or bitterness or unforgiveness kept me from peace. That kept me from finding the balance I was seeking. More importantly for me, it kept me closed from moving on to become the mother I longed to be for my daughters and the wife I wanted to be for my husband. It kept my heart closed to the sunlight of God's spirit. That kept me closed to God's Love.

When I have trouble getting to my place of forgiveness, as I do at times, I try to picture myself releasing a huge balloon into the sky. I try to picture doing this over the ocean. I have no control over where that balloon goes, provided I release my hold on it and give it over to God, the source of the Wind. The balloon will drift and my hands are then free. God will take the balloon out of my sight eventually and my hurt or resentment will be gone. I do not need to know where it went. That is trust. That is faith. I am then free to enjoy the rest of my day at the beach, where I would probably choose to read a book or daydream while watching the water. Or watch my husband and daughters jump the waves. Or my dog run, fetching a ball with my husband.

I finally realized that I was responsible for the decisions I did or didn't make in my life. It was my responsibility to be the person I was meant to be. I might not have control over many of the things that happened to me in life but I did have a choice how I chose to respond to what happened. I also had a choice how I responded to others that journey with me in life. I have no control over how others respond to me.

I spent a great deal of time in therapy focusing on my childhood trauma. I also needed to revisit the trauma of being raped in college and my feelings that came from that abuse. I had many emotional wounds closely related to suicide; my boyfriend's attempts as well as my own. I had emotional wounds from my mother's negative words that I took internally and my inability to communicate. I felt guilty about all of these things. I took on behaviors that were not mine to take on. My guilt, shame and fear added to my insecurity and inability to speak about my feelings. My perspective about myself became very dark indeed. I still saw the ground as dirty because that was a reflection of how I saw myself. I saw myself as damaged and useless and a mistake; as if I should never have been born. Worse, when I became depressed, I saw myself and my life as hopeless. I saw myself as dead. I not only saw myself as all these things but I felt these ways. But God saw me differently, as did my therapist, my husband and daughters, members of my recovery group, and a few good friends. That was enough for God to work in my heart as I was willing to believe that light existed, that love existed, and that God existed. Now I know He does.

Because He does, I was able to see myself differently, in time and with much work. Today I know I am meant to be here and I am not a mistake. I know I make mistakes and that others make mistakes also. I have found that forgiveness and asking for forgiveness has opened my life and heart to a new level of freedom. It is not easy at times, but it is possible. I know forgiveness does not mean what has happened was right, for me it means my debt is cancelled and that the other person is not holding anything against me. I am free to move on. Free to live and love. To try again.

It is my responsibility to make better choices today. I needed to forgive myself for my depression. I did this when I accepted that my depression is an illness and not a moral issue. I am responsible for taking care of my illness as it is capable of destroying my life and affecting those I love. I did not cause my illness just as I did not cause my father to molest me. Today (2019) looking back and being aware of much more about my life and remembering many more repressed memories along with intensive trauma therapy, I know that this depression which looked like postpartum depression was a symptom of my PTSD triggered by Sarah's birth and Emily's age. Giving birth to both our daughters has been two of the greatest moments in my life shared with my husband. To be their mom throughout all this time and to love them and be a part of both their lives as they grow and live life has been the light that has never gone out for me. I am truly blessed to be able to journey with both Sarah, Emily, and my husband, Stephen.

I came to a place where I no longer wanted to ask the walls what they had seen or heard. It no longer mattered to me. It was enough for me to know what I had experienced and what I had remembered. I was able to accept my truth. I was able to forgive and let go of the rest. Both my parents died before I remembered my trauma so I could not discuss this with either of them. I trust this is how God wanted it to be. I came to a place of peace in my mind and heart. I can move forward. I AM FREE TO DO THIS. Jesus invited me to do this. Jesus offered me a way out, and I decided to take it. It is a much better way. What happened will always be a part of my being but it does not define who I am. It no longer makes my choices or controls my perspective. The presence of Jesus in my life does that. I am at peace with my past. The presence of light and Love did that. Living in the moment did that. I needed to go back and relieve those traumas so I could be free of them. As awful as that was for me, that was my responsibility. But I did not do it alone. Jesus promises He will always come with me. His presence made the difference.

Today I understand that once a person has died there is no way to compensate for the loss of a person's life, and families must go on and carry that tragic loss with them as they attempt to move on or start over. I was so close to ending my life far too many times. I was unable to comprehend the value of my life while I was deeply depressed. I was also, tragically, unable to comprehend how taking my life would affect those I loved and those who loved me. Perhaps this is part of the disease itself. Perhaps this is what depression wanted from me. For only by allowing my therapist and my daughters and husband and God into my mind and heart was I able to move beyond those suicidal thoughts, feelings, and behaviors that dominated my life. When I was alone, my illness was so powerful and spoke too loudly to me. I was broken and in so much pain I could not see a way out.

How could I? The darkness encompassed me. I had no sense of time except for the passing of my daughters' birthdays. It seemed like eternity to me. I could not see any way out of my misery and constant suffering. When my pain intensified, it was as if any moments of pleasure were erased from my mind. I believe this is how depression works. Depression kept pulling me further down, unwilling to stop until it had all of me, including my life. Fortunately, I was connected to life-giving supports, to therapy and medications, even though they didn't seem to be effective, and to my family, to God and to His love and Hope that He offered. I believe this is what made the difference for me. For even with these supports, I went to the abyss many times. I wanted to end my suffering despite what I thought I knew I would be doing to others. For at that moment of what I call "complete despair" or "utter loss of hope" the light or spark of hope that was burning within me was also burning within others, and this spark prompted me to reach out to pick up my cell phone each and every time. When I did, there was always a person on the other end. This was God and His love for me. This was grace. This was God's love and connection breaking through the power of the darkness of my depression. I wish I could say I stopped after one attempt, but I did not. My disease was too powerful. But so was God's grace and love. I needed to go through five more attempts until I reached a turning point in wanting to take my life. I was not consciously aware of this. I prayed that my last inpatient stay at the mental hospital would be my last. It was. Perhaps as my relationship with God grew, so did my ability to start comprehending what my actions were doing to those I loved. (Perhaps as I started to appreciate the value of my life I could appreciate the value of all life.) When I attempted to kill myself, it was not that I did not care about my husband and daughters, it was as if they did not exist, or at times like I was doing them a favor. I thought they would be better off without me. In either case, these were lies my disease was telling me. They were not my truth. It was when I was alone the extreme suffering and darkness distorted the truth. The next part of my journey called me to embrace my truth or my recovery would remain questionable. God's love gave me the strength to push through the unrelenting darkness and the constant lies my disease told me. It was enough for me to rely on when the going became difficult. I found I could trust God to be there for me when no one else could be or worse, when I wanted to run away from my truths as my fear shouted to me that I could not handle it and never could. God's love was enough for what I found.

CHAPTER 33

THE MOTHER I AM MEANT TO BE

I am the mother I am meant to be, not the mother I thought I should be. I thought I could be the perfect mother, and that I could protect my daughters from harm. I thought I could control what life handed them. I wanted to provide them with the perfect home environment. I found that the perfect mother does not exist, and I am certainly not the perfect mother. I found that I can "try" to do my best. I am a real mother with real-life issues and real-life problems. I am also a real mother with faith and hope and some ability to live life. I have love to pass on to my daughters that I did not have before. I have experience that has come from living through my own pain and darkness. I have peace and joy filled moments that I experience as a result of that journey. I have learned to communicate and express my feelings. I try to confront rather than run away from difficult situations. I have learned the importance of relationships in my life with self, with God, with my husband, with my daughters, with friends, and with those I meet throughout each day.

I know in my mind and heart I was not the mother my daughters' needed or deserved many times, but the reality is I was the mother they had. I struggled to come to peace with this. How was I to embrace and ultimately accept my reality; a home environment that was less than perfect; a mother that struggled with coping with severe mental illness almost daily? What was I to do with these inner conflicts? How did I resolve them? Could they be resolved?

My connection to my daughters was special. It was this connection that called me to push through my darkness, if not for myself, for them. I believed in them and in their goodness and their precious lives. On some level I was hoping, that maybe, I could be the best mother I could be for them. I was not content with how things were going, but I came to a place where I realized that despite my emotional state, our daughters were thriving. They were happy and something was working in their life. I needed to trust others to help care for my family, often Stephen's family as they lived closer than mine. It was difficult for me at times, especially when my fear was shouting at me, "Emily and Sarah will like them better or that my daughters would forget me." I wrestled with these fears and realized how blessed I was to never lose my daughters throughout this period. As the girls grew up they had friends and participated in regular social activities and sports. Their world expanded, as it needed to. I also came to realize that sometimes it was not how much I did for my children but how I did it. There were many, many moments I was afraid that my daughters would resent the time I wasn't available for them. I realized it was more important the time I was with them I spent lovingly with them. It is more important that I do things motivated from a heart of love and that is what they will remember. The quality of our time together is more important than the quantity of that time.

When our daughters were born and even before, I thought that I could protect them from life. I did not want them to get hurt, at least not before they grew up and had to face life on their own. I was horrified when I became depressed. I thought my babies were touched by pain too early in their lives. Worse, I was the one causing their pain. This cut through my heart and caused me much grief. I spent many hours mourning the mother I could not be for Emily and Sarah. I mourned the loss of the ideal infancy and childhood they deserved. I thought "How can life be so cruel? This little baby and child did nothing to deserve this." These thoughts swirled through my mind and tore through my heart. They slowly diffused through the years as I faced my own demons. I realized just as I could not control the tide, I was not in control of many situations in life but I could control or change my attitude or perspective. I learned this by finally facing situations in my own childhood and resolving issues. I learned that even though I face painful situations in my life, I am not alone, and love from God and others helped me through them. When a mistake happened with my father I needed to talk about it. Perhaps my parents could not talk about it, or perhaps they thought they were doing the best thing. Maybe they were at that time, I do not know. All I know is that I needed to remember those traumas in order to heal and forgive so I was free to move on. I needed to revisit a few of those mistakes because they had a major impact on my life. I owed my parents a great deal for all they did and for all they sacrificed. As a mother, I learned that mothering from the heart is often difficult.

Perhaps one of my biggest challenges is when my daughters call me to grow, to look within my own heart to see what lay there, to see what fear is keeping me locked into my own small world that keeps me from stretching and growing with them, that keeps me from reflecting the light, that tells me to isolate myself in my room, alone in my pain or my problems, thinking no one else in the world could possibly have my problem or understand. My daughters keep me aware of the possibilities life has to offer; the opportunities of each day, the resilience of youth. My daughters remind me each and every day why I struggled with each step I took. To be a part of their lives and be connected to them is one of the greatest joys I have ever experienced. I get to experience it one day at a time. Problems come our way as in every family, but so do the sweeter moments. When they come, I retreat into the silent place deep within my heart and I praise God for the gift of my two wonderful daughters and the young women they have become in spite of or through my illness, and for my loving husband who remained my steady partner on my journey. Love connected us from the first moment. Love withstood the depths of despair and has called me to confront my past so that I might have a future with my family. I did not understand love because my concept of love was based on my limited life experiences. My fear had dominated my choices and thinking for most of my life. Only God in His love could change that. He entered my heart and changed me. I will never be the same. I walk as a free woman today without carrying the guilt and shame of my past. I walk carrying a mental illness but I walk responsibly with that illness. I am not my illness. I am not ashamed that I have an illness or of the fact that I need help with it. Sometimes I need more help than others. I am grateful that help is available. My life at times would be easier if I did not have depression but that is not my reality. My story has been about my truth and about facing that truth while being honest about connecting with painful and loving feelings and issues. Both were a part of my story. About life, illness and recovery. Fear and love. When I accept my illness

I am better able to do what I need to do to take care of it, which means taking care of myself despite, or in spite of what others may think of me or what they may think of my illness. Ultimately it is my responsibility. It is easier if others understand. If they do not, I must still get the help I need.

I believe the real tragedy with my parents was our inability to communicate or the fear that kept us separated, not just that day when I was molested, but throughout my life. I know I was afraid to talk to my parents. I was full of fear and guilt and shame and confusion. The true tragedy was to block out the sunlight of God's love. I found that God does not have a timetable for restoring relationships with Him or with others. Today I have something more to offer my daughters. I have connected with myself and with God, and I am learning how to connect or reconnect with others. I have myself to offer to my daughters. Hopefully I can help teach them to become who they are, and to celebrate who they are, the gifts they are. I have a new chance at my life, and for this I am grateful. When my world becomes dark, I try to remove my sunglasses and sit on my bench with Jesus, recalling his words; "Be still and know that I am God." As I am mindful of Jesus and His presence, my perspective often changes. My breathing usually slows down as if His presence calms my frantic pace and reminds me of His nearness and of what matters in my life. I am reminded I am not in charge. I am also reminded of how much He loves me. I think back and know His love covered and protected me all these years, and His love covers me now. We sit in the stillness, two hearts beating as one. As a mother and her child; as a father to his daughter. Intimately. I know I am loved just as I am. I know because He was present among me and He still is. A living, loving God, who continually invites me to come.

"I love you dad," I said to my father.

"I pray for you every day," my mom said to me as she hung up the phone.

"I love you more than a mother loves her child," Jesus said.

"When are you coming home mommy? We love you." Emily and Sarah said.

"In sickness and in health, for death do us part." Stephen and I stated in our marriage vows.

"Marcia, you are good enough." Donald told me many times.

My new mantra, "A life motivated by love not by fear."

For a long time, my biggest fear was that I was unlovable. Then my biggest fear became that I would not recover from my depression. I realized my true fear was I was afraid to live life.

I found that to live life I needed to trust that God loves me. This frees me to celebrate who I am and to live life each moment, embracing the joy as well as the pain. This enables me to connect with others freely and honestly and to share my heart, my true self. In the end, all that matters is my heart of love, my true self.

I learned that God was with me throughout my journey, good days and horrible days; days I cried and days I was able to feel the sunshine. My depression was long and severe but when I remembered the memories that were repressed for so many years my path for recovery was much clearer. I had much work to do. I still do. I know that I learned a lot about myself and about love and life during those dark years. I found my relationship with God restored through Jesus. I have a new perspective on life and a newfound sense of who I am. In these ways, my walk was worth it. I appreciate my life today as I never did before. Perhaps I needed to come so close to losing my life to realize what a precious gift it is. For in losing my life, I would have lost in sharing in my daughters' lives and in my husband's as well.

Worse, I would have wounded them for life and that would have been the real tragedy. That would have been an act of true self-centeredness. As I think back to my own childhood trauma I can see now how it affected me. I went on to make my own poor choices because I was unable to speak about it and handle my emotions. But my parents were alive and able to love me and share in my life.

I took on the responsibility for what tragic pieces did happen. I began to think about the horror I would be inflicting upon my own daughters if I committed suicide. That would surely kill their young and precious lives. No matter how much pain I was in, I could not do that to them. The time we missed or the loss of my profession paled in comparison to the loss of their precious lives and life journeys.

At the end of the day, I can rest easy, knowing God is in charge and is watching over me and my family, and that in His love we are blessed and cared for. He ultimately protected me, and in protecting me He has protected them; in blessing me He has blessed them. My journey has opened my eyes and heart and changed my perspective to what is most important for me in my life: LIFE and LOVE are most important. Life and the relationships or connections I have. These connections grow from my heart. I am called to live in relationship. Our family is a fundamental relationship. It is within this relationship that my husband, our daughters, and I try to share as honestly as possible, make mistakes, love, fall down and try again. Today I understand our home to be a safe home because the love and acceptance among us enables us to be ourselves. As I found on this journey, that is what matters. This takes courage. This takes trust. This takes love.

I have told my story here not my daughters. They knew what it was like to live with me daily with my illness. They also knew what it is like to live with me in my recovery. We have more social times and more laughter, more spontaneity and more joy. We have tears and fears, and some ability to walk through them, mine as well as theirs. We have dreams and goals and celebrations when they are accomplished. We are a family and have remained one. We have our scars like many families, and we continue to live life. I continue to try be open and available to my daughters. They are now young women pursuing their own life paths. When we share about life issues or college days I can be honest with them and be myself. Hopefully, this encourages them to be themselves, which is one of the best gifts they can offer the world. I found I could be open and loving and begin to face my fears when I was honest with myself.

Once I began to be honest about my fears I realized how many I had since I was a child. Many of these I had not communicated to my parents or siblings, instead I shared them with my husband or daughters. There are many, but several stand out including my fear of going blind. I started to wear glasses when I was four years old. I was the only person in kindergarten with glasses. Talk about being self-conscious! Every year my mother took me to the ophthalmologist, and each time I needed a new pair of glasses as my eyes continued to get worse. One year, when I was in the fourth grade my eyes changed so much I needed two pairs of glasses. I was scared and horrified. I thought to myself, "How long will it take before I go blind? My eyes are getting bad so fast. What will happen to me when I can't see anymore and who will take care of me? What will my world be like?" I never shared these fears with anyone. Little did I know I had become "blind " in other ways.

Teaching my daughters to risk and live in love and not be afraid of what others think of them is one of the biggest lessons my husband and I try to teach. We have found the best way to do this is by how we live. My daughters continue to call me to a higher level of responsibility, and learning and reaching my potential. For this I am grateful. If I was to stop learning I would grow stagnant and stop growing. I was there for many years. That was not life giving. Best of all, they call me to be open, to live, to love, to try new things, to adventure.

As difficult as my depression was for us, Stephen and I tried to be honest with our daughters. We tried to express our feelings and teach them the truth about my illness. Perhaps being part of my healing will be healing to each of them. That I do not know, only time will tell. "I" had changed to "we" in my thinking, and we as a family came through this, and we as a family continue to live life today. We struggle at times like many other families do, but we remember our past and walk forward as a family unit. My illness is part of our daughters' childhood but it does not control our family today. That is not to say that our daughters have not been affected from that time. Issues may come to light for them at any point in their lives. If and when they do, I hope I can be there for them if they choose for me to be.

They include me at times, as they walk in their own journey, to share moments alongside them. What a joy and blessing! It is moments like these when I know in my mother's heart that every step of that dark journey was worth it.

CHAPTER 34

A CHANGED LIFE

I am a changed person and I continue to change. Life is dynamic, changing. When I return to my favorite spot on the beach, the ocean does not look the same. It is constantly changing. I try to teach my daughters to be motivated by love and not fear. Not fear of what their friends will think of them for the choices they make in their lives. For myself, not fear of what choices my children make. Not fear that my children might make a mistake. Not fear that I will make a mistake. Not fear that I will not be a good enough mother or that I will not look like a good enough mother to other people. I have lived in fear and fear destroyed my chances of joy and of living life. Mistakes will happen, and trying to control what other people think or do is not possible.

I have no control over any of that. My responsibility is to love my family and to try to grow with them daily. I try to be present physically, emotionally, and spiritually. I try to be available and to have a heart that is open. To do that I have to continue to be in a relationship with God and do my own work and walk my own life path. My recovery continues. Life continues to happen.

But today, so does love. And at least for today, which is all I have, this moment I choose *Love*.

To be the mother I wanted to be I had to start believing in myself, in life, in goodness, in love, and most importantly, in God. All the things I had stopped believing in so long ago I had to believe in again. I had to believe that my life was worth living; that I was meant to be here and that I was good enough. When I looked into my heart and embraced what was truly living in there I had a lot of work to do.

Many people did not understand me and what I was experiencing, but despite this, there were those who were able to love me. Perhaps that is one of the truest examples of love. We are all so much more alike than I thought. We share the same feelings; feelings and love connect us. Fear divides us but love and forgiveness heal us. At least it did for me.

I have described my life and my thoughts and feelings. I have described what I found in the depths of my heart. It was not easy to share, but the price of severe depression can be costly. Severe depression leads to suicidal thoughts and acts, causing a person to cut themselves off from their family and friends for years. It causes one to lose their profession and ability to provide for their family. Severe depression has the potential to cause someone to remain in that darkness. All of that and more is possible. Depression is painful enough, but what is sad is when suffering in silence adds to that pain. There was a way up and out and it was worth taking the chance. I was worth taking the chance. My life depended on it.

I didn't think I was worth it or that I was lovable but I know differently today. I needed to stay around long enough for my thinking and feelings to change. God's love changed me. He worked through different people and in many different ways in my journey. Some of which I am probably not even aware of yet.

I accept that today. I keep walking on the road I am on, which is the road of my life not someone else's. I am called to be myself. That is ultimately what this journey was all about for me. Living my life to the fullest one day at a time, no matter what each day brings because I no longer have to face each day alone. I am loved by God and my husband and daughters and friends, and I am able to love them back — freely from my heart.

A life motivated by love or a life motivated by fear. What a huge difference this has made for me and hopefully for my daughters and husband. This is hope. When I was controlled by my fears I became closed to living life. Fear shut me down and kept me locked in my own prison of darkness. I could not come outside because my fear told me that life was not safe and I dared not step out of my self-constructed prison and attempt anything new and exciting, anything life giving or fulfilling. Perhaps worst of all, I began to lose the desire of even thinking that my life could contain anything different than the loneliness, complacency, repetition and mediocrity that it contained in the last days of my drinking.

While I was depressed I found my security to be in my relationship with God and in His unfailing love for me. My feelings change all the time, but today I trust that God loves me. I believe this because He showed me His love, and I experienced this love personally in different ways and at different times. His love brought me to a place where I could live.

Fear was constricting and drained the life out of me. I have found God's love to be freeing and life giving. God's love frees me to live life one day at a time and to face whatever comes my way. I am no longer alone.

My approach to living life is different. I try to keep my life simple. I can complicate anything without trying too hard and that gets me into trouble. When I wake up in the morning I am grateful to be alive. I ask God for help to stay away from one drink and for help to live the day trying to do His will. I try to live one day at a time, and in the moment. I have found that the majority of the time, my attitude is what determines how my day goes. I try to spend some quiet time in the morning with God. Like any relationship, I have found that my relationship with God needs to be nourished. God speaks to me in different ways throughout my day. Today I can rest in His love, but this does not mean that I am to do nothing. Love calls or tugs on my heart to respond. People responded to me when I was depressed and love calls for me to respond to others. It is usually my fear or pride that tells me I need to do great things for them to matter. God tells me that I need to act from my heart, to act out of love, and then they will matter.

I realize whatever I do throughout the day, whether I speak to my daughters on the phone or write a note or go grocery shopping, if I do not act from a heart of love, these things are meaningless. What touched me most during those desperate days was kindness, gentleness, and love. I needed to face my truth with a loving perspective or it would have destroyed me. It would have kept me a prisoner of my past. I am to reflect the light. The way I am to do this is by extending love to others.

When I reflect on those years, I remember the pain, the isolation and the desperation, but more importantly I remember the love of the people who reached out to me time and time again. I remember their kind eyes, their gentleness, their patience, and their concern. I remember their kind words, "Is there anything I can do to help you feel better today?" I remember their hope. I remember the touch of God over and over. God met me where I was. He understood me and wanted to help me. I was too afraid to ask for help. God is all powerful and all loving and defeated my fear. I needed to walk through it but I learned I didn't need to walk alone.

I needed to walk with God and let Him direct me. Today, I need to remember where I came from but I also need to look ahead to where I am going. I often do not know where that is but I trust that it is good. I walk with one hand in God's hand and the other held out to life and the opportunities God has waiting for me. When they present themselves, hopefully I will step through and not hold back from fear.

As my ability to trust grew, I was able to trust our daughters. I needed to allow them the freedom to grow and make mistakes. That is how they learn. I could not be afraid of this or I would be impeding their growth. Emily would ask, "Can I go over to my friend Sandy's house Saturday night for a sleepover?" I had never slept over at a friend's house. I said, "Who else will be there, Emily?" She replied, "My friends, Julie and Lizzie." "Of course you can go. I hope you have a great time. It sounds like it will be fun. I can't wait to hear all about it when your dad brings you home Sunday morning."

Learning that I am not the mistake, but that I made a mistake was a huge lesson for me. When I learned that, I experienced a new freedom. This released me, allowing me to try new things. This gave me the permission I was looking for all my life to be myself. This allowed me to explore, to attempt, to dream, to fail, to hope, to risk, to be open, and to walk through fear. My identity was not tied to my failure as a human being. My identity was no longer tied to my shame. My identity was not tied to people's opinion of me. My identity was based on God's love for me. Who I am is a reflection of that love. As I started to grow more secure in this belief, I was able to make better choices based on love and not fear. My fear led me to make choices that did not allow me to grow or live life. Now I was free to begin interacting with people and my world from the love I felt and I believed. I wanted my dad to tell me that he loved me but I needed to let go of that. I could not move forward while I was living in the past. I needed my dad to say these words to me when I was a child and a teenager. Now I realized that while I still wanted that, I no longer needed it. I knew in my heart my dad loved me. I also knew so much more. I was now consciously aware of what had happened that day when I was a child and I understood a lot more about myself and the choices I made in my life. Understanding did not make things better or change what happened, but it led to forgiveness and acceptance; it helped me to let go and to walk in more freedom.

I can now see that that day so long ago in my childhood was like I had died. I began to mourn the loss of myself and the loss of all that I had once believed in and hoped for as a child. I lost my dreams, which caused me to begin searching for those needs in material things. What had really happened was that my spirit had died. I no longer believed in goodness, love, promises, joy or happiness for myself. Instead I listened to my fears and let them control my life and my choices. True to my fears, I had no true joy or happiness or goodness or love. I felt abandoned and alone. When I became sober by the grace of God, I began to realize that what I had really lost was my faith that God loved me. I had felt unlovable and been searching for my identity for many years. I thought it came from people in my life and I was searching for it in substances. I finally found that my identity comes from God who made me in His love. Today, I know that and believe that. No one and nothing can take that from me unless I let them. I also know that all I have is today, this moment really.

Life is precious. Life is fragile. My life is a gift to be unwrapped each morning. Like any gift, it is only useful if I accept and use it. Each night before placing my head on my pillow I say thank you for that gift, whatever the day brought and whatever I brought to that day. For me, an alcoholic in recovery, and a person suffering from a chronic emotional illness, I will always be in recovery and I will never be cured. I know and accept that, at least for today. But instead of that limiting me, my daily acceptance of my illness and whatever its treatment requires, together with my surrendering my life to God's love and care, makes me freer today than I have ever been in my life. I am free to live, free to love, free to be me; the person I never wanted to know because I was too afraid.

Fear can still play a part in my life but fortunately for me, God in His love is much more powerful. Some days I like myself, some days not so much. In any case, I am okay because before my head hits my pillow I discuss this with my God and say Thank You for another day of sobriety and for another day of life. Then I close my eyes and let my mind wander, but not too far. Perhaps back to that ocean, to that boat, to that beach, but this time I am enjoying the sea with all its beauty and wonder. I can sit on my bench or I can go out on that boat. I am safe on the boat. I am wearing a life preserver, a sunhat, sunscreen, and I have brought some snacks. I am relaxing in a beach chair, listening to music, while watching for a sighting of whales, wearing my daughter's old pair of sunglasses, covered in two towels and a sweatshirt. I am prepared this time! Of course I also have several books in my beach bag; I rarely go anywhere without a book or two! But despite how prepared I think I am, I can be surprised. That is the beauty and wonder of my life today. I remain open, otherwise my fear is again controlling me. As I look up at the evening sky, the colors begin to change. It turns to a landscape of oranges, reds and purples; too beautiful to express in words. One almost has to be there to adequately experience the beauty. I am there not only in my mind, but I experience the beauty. It has touched my heart and soul. I feel the warmth spread throughout me, reaching those now healed scars that are woven into the fabric of my being. The scars do not repel the warmth of the setting sun, instead they welcome it, as I do. I know, as surely as the sun sets in all its majesty and beauty, that the night will follow in its darkness but the wonderful news is the dawn will always follow. The sun will rise again with new promises, new potential, and new work for the day ahead. But for now, for this night, in the darkness and silence, while I cannot see the sun, I know it is not gone forever. I carry the hope that it will rise again in my heart. The warmth it gave me before it went down is all I need for this night until it rises again. I can picture it, sense it, feel it, and share it. This is my true hope, this is my faith, this is my story. That is true love from God.

Some journeys I take in life I take and return to the same place while others take me to a new place. My depression took me to a new place. What was the price? I do not think I know the answer. I certainly lost my ability to work. I lost my dignity, I lost precious time with my daughters that I can never get back, I lost years of my memory from the failed ECT treatments, and damaged relationships with family members; but the true cost of those things pale to what I have gained — unconditional love. How can I put a price on that?

CHAPTER 35

ANOTHER PERSPECTIVE

*T*oday I am free to feel all my feelings, not only pain. Just because I am open to God's love does not mean that I no longer feel afraid because I do. I am a person trying to walk through my life journey like others, but today I also know that whatever I feel, I can go to that place in my heart where I connect with God and share what I am feeling. I know that He will always be there for me whenever I invite Him in. The more I do, the more I trust that He will be there. That is how trust grows for me.

My perspective has also changed towards God and myself and life. In my family at dinner, we usually sit in the same chairs. One day when Stephen and I were eating dinner I sat in a different chair and an amazing thing happened. Sitting in a different chair, my view of the kitchen changed. As I thought about this, I thought about my journey through depression. I thought that perhaps my journey could be seen as a journey *up and out!*

Perhaps the day I gave birth to Sarah I was catapulted to the bottom of a steep mountain and my task was to climb up it instead of falling farther and farther into despair. What would those years have looked like if I had seen them from this perspective?

From this perspective of the mountain, maybe I was walking up and out of the darkness and just didn't realize it. Maybe the road seemed so difficult because I was walking up a mountain that was steep and snow-covered and I was out of shape. I couldn't breathe very well. I needed to stop often along the way to rest, to eat, and to drink water. Maybe I wasn't wearing the right shoes for the walk. Perhaps I needed to drop some of the excessive weight I was carrying. Maybe the climb took such a long time because there were some detours along the way, necessary ones, but still bothersome. Maybe I wasn't prepared for the trip. I had no rain gear, sunscreen or bug repellent, and what was I to do when I forgot to bring my tent, never mind my sleeping bag? In my heart, when I dared to look, I brought fear, insecurity, guilt, shame, blame, mistrust, and unforgiveness. As I climbed, I slowly and painfully realized I needed to reach out if I was to have any chance of surviving this trip. The first person I met was my therapist, Donald, who seemed to know a lot about walking this road, as if he had travelled a similar one before. He reached out and offered to make the journey alongside me. Wait. Don't I do most things by myself? I really don't trust anyone. Yet something inside me tells me to take his hand. My life depends on it. I reach out. We join hands and that is how we make this climb. *I am no longer walking alone.* The climb is steep but we are now in this together. This is so different from how I have always walked in my life. The climb is still risky but now we have each other to hold onto and I am less afraid. At least I can keep climbing.

I also know I must keep moving. If I were to lay down where I am, I would risk dying from the cold or risk being eaten by the wild animals. Even in my emotional state, I do not want this. I continue to climb.

Along the way, most of the mountain is totally shaded from the sun, keeping us in darkness for quite a while, most of the day and all night. The snow and the ice on the mountain make for even tougher climbing than I expected. I start to be grateful that Donald is with me. As the time passes, I begin to enjoy Donald's company. We begin sharing stories or enjoy the silence. We rest. Donald seems to know the way, even in the dark. I begin to sense that I can depend on him. We share the warmth of getting to know each other. Fortunately, he has brought provisions. A blanket which feels so soft and warm against my cold skin and bruised feet. He covers me with his blanket of gentleness, patience, kindness, and acceptance. He offers these to me freely, and I accept. We rest often because I get extremely tired, especially at night. Sometimes we stay up late and watch the stars in the night sky and the moon which looks so bright. Before the sun rises each morning, we wake up and begin our climb for the new day. As we continue our ascent, I become more aware of the great love I have for my daughters, Emily and Sarah, and my husband, Stephen. It is this love that propels my feet up that steep mountain. I concentrate on this love and ignore how tired I am and how I miss all the comforts of home. It is this love, although it feels inaccessible to me at times, and my contact with them that keeps me going.

Unfortunately, at times, I became disconnected from my ability to focus on my love for my daughters and my husband. The force of this disease was too strong and powerful for me. My feelings of self-loathing and deep despair overwhelmed me. I was unable to share my innermost feelings of loss and emptiness with my companion. I lost sight of the mountaintop and began focusing on my innermost darkness. I lost sight of love and the summit. I was focused on the bottom and of falling backward. At these times, I ventured to the precipice of the mountain. I stepped out, alone, in the darkness of the night. I looked down instead of up at the bright stars. I thought I could, or I should, take a step out into nothingness because I had become nothing, or perhaps I would feel better if I felt nothing. Whatever the truth was, it was lying because when I stepped out, the truth exposed itself to me as Love. I cried out screaming, "Donald, I need you, where are you," and fortunately he heard me and came running. He tugged at my fingertips that were hanging on to a branch overhanging the edge of the mountainside and edged me back to solid ground. Donald wrapped his sturdy arms around me and pulled me back to safety. He gently looked into my eyes. "What was that?" I asked myself, "if not the loving hand of God?" The closer we got to the mountaintop the more aware I became of the self-loathing I have always experienced. I do not understand where this comes from or why I feel this way. Donald told me not to worry about it, that what was important was for us to keep on our path. He tells me it is important that I continue to love my daughters and husband despite the steep climb, despite the blisters on my aching feet and how cold I am. He tells me to be gentle with myself. To be myself? I do not understand. He tells me I am good enough, that I always was and that I still am.

I have no idea what he means but he repeats this as we climb. He tells me I will understand one day.

Eventually I share more of my life and my feelings. They seem to come to me more easily as we continue to walk together and get closer to the top of the mountain. Perhaps it is the lack of oxygen at this higher altitude that enables me to talk more freely. But then a strange thing happens. Instead of getting easier the climbing gets more difficult as the angle of the mountain gets steeper. Donald listens more intently. My daughters and my love for them. I feel warmth as I speak about them and my husband. This is what we are walking towards; my new life with them.

My love for them and my inability to love myself and to accept love comes up repeatedly. Donald says, "Marcia, why don't we consider these thoughts more deeply." I know he is right. The light at the top of the mountain is visible now. The sky is brighter at the top of the mountain. We must keep climbing towards the sun.

Suddenly, out of nowhere it seems, storm clouds appear. The ominous sound is followed by a torrential rain that soaks us to the skin as lightning flashes around us in a menacing dance. Memories from childhood flash across my mind, clear as day. I was there. I can feel it. I know these memories are true. I remember them now as if they happened to me yesterday. Donald listens as I retell the horror of that day at the cottage when my dad molested me. He listens and takes me in his arms as I cry tears of relief and sadness. I begin to mourn a childhood I never had. Donald has brought two raincoats and a red-and-white striped umbrella to help shield us from the pouring rain.

He opens the huge umbrella. I ask, "Donald, why didn't you bring two umbrellas?'

He replies, "Why do you think I only brought one?"

I think about this for awhile. The answer comes to me.

I say to him, "You brought only one because this way we can share it."

I think about how Donald is sharing in my journey and pain and how I am sharing in part of his life journey. This is what life and relationship is about.

At this point in the journey something more is needed. The elements we are attempting to confront are too violent and the trauma is too fresh. Donald unfastens a backpack he has been carrying since we began. He takes out some items I am not too familiar with: willingness, honesty, forgiveness, acceptance, letting go. He tells me to pick them up, one at a time, and he will help me understand them. It will take time but they will help me with the rest of my journey. We still have to reach the summit. The top of the mountain seems even steeper. He tells me it is alright to be afraid as long as my fear does not control my actions or choices.

As I continue climbing to the summit, putting one foot in front of the other, sometimes haltingly, I become aware of the warmth of the sun on my face and my back. This feels good to me after so much time on the cold and dark mountain. I have almost forgotten how good the sun feels when it warms my body on a cold day or when I go to the beach. The closer we get to the top, the brighter and warmer the sun becomes. I need to stop and remove my coat.

When we finally reach the top of the mountain my heart is open to more fully receiving the love I desperately needed and wanted all my life. I was looking in the wrong places. It is the warmth of this brilliant sun that warms my heart and my tired and aching body and soul from this seemingly endless journey I began when Sarah was born. Is that when my journey of darkness really began? That is a better question for me to think about. My severe clinical depression began with Sarah's birth but the deeper darkness that I carried with me began a very long time ago

We reach the top and the view is breathtaking! Magnificent really. I do not know if I can express it in words. Not just the view but how I feel. As I stand there, I can't help myself. I start to dance. My body is filled with a feeling that spreads from my feet up to my head. I cannot contain it and I do not try. I feel like I need to release this new energy within me. What is this feeling I am experiencing for perhaps this first time in my life? Could this be JOY? I made it, or more accurately, we made it. We are at the top, and not only my body dances with joy, my HEART bursts open and lets out a SHOUT for JOY!

As I look down, up, and around, I try to take in my surroundings. My fear subsides and I am able to take in the beauty around me. The pain and heartache and the long days and even longer nights begin to fade from my memory in the brilliance of this sunlight. But I cannot forget them: they have become a part of me. I know I cannot afford to forget them. I am to learn from them and integrate them into my life, into myself. But how am I to do this? As I look back on my journey, I reflect on different experiences, but in the presence of the sunlight they begin to look different to me. Perhaps these are some of the ways I am to integrate this depression and my childhood trauma into my heart and mind.

Along the climb I have come to experience the love of God in my heart through the people and the love and compassion I experienced. God was with me as I walked up that mountain through my therapist in his gentleness and acceptance, warmth and caring for me; in his willingness to be with me when most other people in my life had moved on; when my darkness had become so dark I was at my lowest moments.

I went to some very dark and lonely and desolate places. My depression brought me to suicide attempts and mental institutions. My depression brought me to financial losses and loss of my profession. My depression brought me to years of social isolation. But worst of all, for me as a mother, my depression brought me to a loss of precious quality time with my daughters when they were infants and toddlers and preschoolers, and then in grammar and middle school; a loss of time that can never be recaptured. I went to dark places in my heart. I wasn't alone; I believe that made the difference. I always felt so alone in the world and like no one could or world ever understand me. Here I was in this hopeless situation which was indescribable, but Donald was willing and able to walk beside me each step of the way. That was a gift from God. I could not have made this journey by myself. I had to walk my path but I learned that it was alright to ask for help. I not only needed help, I wanted it. By allowing Donald into my life I was able to allow God and love and healing to enter. I am not saying that Donald had the power to heal me by himself because he didn't. I am saying that God was able to work through him. I was so alone in life because I was too afraid to trust people. I didn't want to get hurt again. I didn't think I could handle it.

I needed to learn to let people into my life. And God. But I had to learn. This took time. A lot of it. There were other people who walked with me. My husband walked with me and stood by me. I needed Stephen's presence and love in a different way. Stephen and I were living this nightmare together with our daughters, and we were too closely connected for Stephen to help in an objective way. This is not to say that Stephen could not or did not help me, because he did. But we were living through this together. This had become our nightmare in many ways. But just as Donald's help was so essential, so was Stephen's presence and love in my life. Stephen was my partner and we shared this journey together as only a husband and wife can.

My thoughts and connection with Emily and Sarah also keep me walking up this mountain. I remember feeding them, holding each one of them so close to me, feeling their little hearts beating against mine. This is what I want to be able to do. I want to be connected to them in a deep way. I want to be able to give them more than milk to drink. I want to give them the best I can offer for their lives. But they will need more than milk and food. Before very long they will need much more. The world can be a very frightening place. I want them to grow up secure in love, but how will that happen if I am full of fear? The gift of life is so precious. The gift of life is a gift from God. The gift of being a mother is a gift from God. I want to be responsible. I want Emily and Sarah to feel safe and secure. I want them to feel loved and to trust love. At least I want to provide them with that opportunity before life touches them. They are just babies. There are conflicts stirring inside of me that I do not understand. Where are they coming from? I love my daughters so much. But before I know what happened to me, a darkness envelops me for thirteen long years. But something else happens to me too. That mother/daughter bond, that connection I felt nursing them, their hearts beating against mine and mine beating against theirs; being able to look into Emily's blue eyes when I nursed her or being able to feel Sarah's tiny soft hands and arms around my neck as I rubbed her back before putting her down in her crib for her nap; the smell of their hair after their bath so fresh with baby shampoo and both Emily and Sarah so cuddly in their pink or mint green fuzzy sleepers getting ready for a bedtime story. These are the images I try to focus on as I climb. I see them through the darkness, sometimes blurry, but always there. I hear their voices calling "mommy when are you coming home?"

"Soon" I say to myself and to them, "I'll be home soon," or at least that is what I begin to hope. That becomes my hope. Soon I will truly be home for my daughters and husband. Present as the mother I always wanted to be but too afraid to become. To mother from a heart of love and not a place of fear.

The Sun in this perspective of my journey represents Jesus, the Son of God. Jesus was the warmth and the light that entered my life. I was walking towards this light and I was walking with Him all along in some ways. When I was discouraged and tired of trying, and ready to admit defeat, I heard God's voice above all of the confusion in my mind. I surrendered to Him and to His love. When I did this, I found my true hope and freedom to move forward in and through my darkness to the other side. God's love frees me to go where He leads me. I may not always like the journey but I can walk in love. My depression was relentless, but so was God's love for me.

Another freeing and loving gift from God was my ability to forgive. Forgiveness frees my heart which allows me to move on from my past.

I realized that being aware of love is not enough. I need to act in love. My journey taught me that I need to love others, first my daughters and husband, and then others who are placed in my path. If my heart and perspective had not changed by my journey, my trip would have been hopeless. That time would then have been wasted time and my disease would have won.

Others told me I was worth it and my life was worth living for a long time. I couldn't believe them but I held on to a dim spark inside me that was the love of God, a hand that reached out to me, a gentle voice that welcomed me; the kindness and acceptance of my therapist, the love of my husband, the connection and bond with my daughters, any and all of these added up to hope for me to go on for just one more day. When that seemed too difficult, I walked one more step, putting one foot in front of the other. I made many mistakes along the way and yes, I regret the time, the years really, that I missed more quality time with my daughters and husband and my dogs, who brought much joy to our home that I will never get back. I have mourned those losses but I cannot stay there in that loss. I have moved on. Life is too precious. Today I can have quality time with my family and I am grateful for that. The way I am able to move on is to make the most of each day with my family. My past will always be a part of my life but it no longer needs to control me. It can be a piece that fits into that picture of me but it doesn't have to be turned and squeezed and made to fit, or worse, ignored or be a missing piece. My past fits into the story of my life, and acceptance of it enables me to be myself, the only person I can be, the person I was trying to avoid being all my life. The person I was too afraid to be, too afraid to face, the person I was too afraid to allow the world to see. My therapist saw me, in all my humanity, at my lowest, and he accepted me and loved me. That opened the door for me to start to love and accept myself, a little bit at a time. Today, I know that God loves and accepts me, and today I struggle with my acceptance of myself on a different level.

I am no longer in the extreme darkness. I walk in the light.

I can look at these years from any perspective I choose. Today I have options I did not have before because my mind and heart were closed from fear and the lies my fear and illnesses told me. I also lived in darkness from my inability to form relationships with people. Depression certainly was not like climbing a mountain, but my perspective throughout my life and when difficulties occurred is what matters for me. How I look at things makes a difference. My attitude and my viewpoint and my approach to living life make a difference.

I have a choice today. Some days I do better than others. I can choose to look up at the sky or down at the ground. I will see different things. I will still be walking.

CHAPTER 36

RECONNECTIONS

I could look as this journey in many different ways. One way I see this is as a story of reconnection with myself; a connection that was severed forty years ago by tragic circumstances beyond my control. A chain of events started that led me to connect to substances and things which would ultimately betray me. I then connected with new things in an attempt to form a permanent connection with something I thought could give me fulfillment. This was illusive because my initial disconnect was so severe and came from the source of life and of love. As a child, I was totally dependent upon my parents. When that connection was severed, my world fell apart. I was no longer connected to the source of my protection and security, identity and love. My world became frightening and lonely. I no longer lived to play. I survived to live. I was not consciously aware of what was happening. My reality had become too traumatic. My memories were repressed. I detached from my painful feelings. I became isolated in my own world. Overnight I had grown years older, much too old for my young body. This survival world eventually became my real world.

When I became depressed, I needed to reconnect and trust in love and to connect and form relationships with people. I could no longer trust the false promises that my fear gave me. I needed to trust love and God again, but a side of God I never knew. I needed to risk. I needed to step out. Love was calling and inviting me. I needed to respond out of love for my daughters and husband. I wanted to connect more fully with them. I wanted to be a better mother to them, but something was blocking me. My depression certainly was, but so was something else. Whatever it was needed to go. God was calling to me to connect. I never considered a relationship with Jesus before. I had heard of Jesus, but I had never heard of how much he loved me. Truthfully, I was afraid of His love. What would that mean? What would I have to do? How did I earn it? I did not understand love. I was tragically hurt too many times. I was confused about Love. I was no longer open. I stepped out with Stephen, but only to a limited degree. *Then look what happened after Sarah was born and look at me now*, I thought to myself. I was beginning to understand Donald's interaction with me as well as my husbands. They respected and cared for me. This felt good at times. My love for my daughters and their love for me motivated me to respond to God's call to accept Jesus as my Savior. When I did, I began to experience what God's love was really like. Forgiving love, accepting love, healing love. I did nothing to earn it. It was freely given, I just had to accept it as a free gift. I loved to get my daughters gifts for their birthdays and make them gift bags, especially when they were young. I loved to get them small gifts and wrap each one separately. I watched then unwrap each gift and throw the carefully wrapped paper onto the floor. They were so excited. I was too. Seeing them unwrapping each gift was almost more fun than getting the gift! Perhaps because I am a mother, it gave me pleasure to see their joy. The surprise was part of the gift. I felt such joy being able to give the gift. I saw from my daughters how to be gracious receivers!

God truly surprised me with the goodness of His gifts to me. I still learn how good He is and I am still learning what love means. God's love was the only thing that was more powerful than my fears and illness. My love is a reflection of His love. I am not perfect. I fail many times and I make many mistakes; but it is God's love that enables me to get back up today and try again and again. Fear kept me from even trying. That is a huge difference.

I also needed to connect to my memories of long ago. It was time for my repressed memories to return so I could begin to deal with them with the correct support. The traumatic events will always be a part of me. As much as I wish those times never happened, they did. I needed to acknowledge that they happened and I needed to feel my feelings and see what I could do about that trauma. While I was not to blame for what happened to me, I was responsible for what I was going to do about it. As an adult, I had choices available to me. I chose to forgive my parents, Tim, and myself. I chose to let go of my hurt once I had dealt with the pain but I could not do it before then. After I did that, I was then able to connect with a new part of myself. A part that was like a child, a part of myself that I discovered when my daughters were younger but felt restrained, now I felt freer, to explore the world and connect with myself in a new way. I was starting to discover parts of myself that were lost or never came to life.

I always enjoyed reading ever since I was a child, but there was little else I enjoyed doing or that I would try to do. Now I found myself willing to try other things. Certainly part of this was from the depression improving, but part of this was from me being released from my past. I never felt free or interested in playing games. I didn't like to play. Now I wanted to learn how to fly a kite and I wanted to play more with our daughters. I wanted to walk the dogs on the beach. I wanted to run barefoot in the sand and let my hair grow long. My world was opening up. My fear was stepping aside as I made new choices to walk through my fears.

I learned that although my thinking needed to be mature, it was good for me to be like a child in other ways: to wonder, to explore, to dance, and to run more; to read, to play, and to have more childlike faith; to try again, and again and to get up when I fail; to be open to people and to the world and it's opportunities and to GOD. I found that I needed the sunlight of the Spirit. I had been hidden in the dark for many years of my life, not just these past 13 years. I needed to come outside and explore the world. I have seasonal affective disorder and I need to use a light in the winter. I need to get out of the house all year, especially during the spring and summer and get natural sunlight for my mood and my body to function properly. Just as importantly, I need the sunlight for my spirit to feel God's presence.

I eventually found the sun to be healing. Certainly the warmth was healing as I felt it spreading through my cold body, but the sunlight also warmed and cleansed my cold spirit. My spirit seemed to be barren after I gave birth and needed to be awakened. Sitting in the sun or allowing sunlight into the house helped immensely. There was something about letting in the light that awakened me. A tiny bit was a start. I found that I liked it and was attracted to it. I wanted more, just as when I bite into a warm oatmeal raisin cookie, I cannot stop, with one bite. My spirit began to awaken to the presence of God. I began to carry it with me. I was not often aware of this presence but that did not mean He was not there.

I realized I was too serious and I took myself and all of life too seriously. I had lost the ability to discriminate between work and play. More importantly, I had little ability to bring childlike qualities to my approach to everyday activities and my approach towards life.

I was able to connect to my daughters and my husband more fully. All relationships slowly and gradually began to open for me. Today I still have damaged relationships from my past, but I am moving forward in my life as the person I am; learning that no one is perfect, especially me, and that relationships are fragile and changing and involve two people. Much about a relationship involves communication and honesty and commitment, and often a willingness to go places that are uncomfortable but necessary. As I think about my marriage I can see the periods of difficulty and times of great joy. Only a commitment of sharing the pain of our true feelings instead of running or avoiding them has enabled us to grow and remain together as a couple.

I am learning how to be in a relationship with myself, God, and others; and I believe I will continue to learn as long as I remain open to love and to life. When my fear takes over I am much less open. My past will always be a part of me and will be woven into the fabric of my being, but it no longer has to control or terrify or lie to me. I cannot erase it and I no longer want to. Today, when I look into the mirror I see the person I am instead of the person I was, or the person I feared I would be. I have some hope for the person I might become instead of fearing who I need to keep hidden from the world and from myself and from my children. My daughters have the chance to know the real me, not the person I wanted them to see. They have seen me at my worst moments and at some of my best moments. They loved me through all of them and I was able to love them back. I found out that this is real love, unconditional love; seeing past my illness or what one does not understand, or looking past one's differences and loving them anyway, always being present. Seeing past one's disappointments and hurts and mistakes and hugging one's mom anyway, hugging one's child, hugging one's husband or wife. Ultimately I learned about true love from my daughters, and hopefully they have learned something from me.

CHAPTER 37

AN EQUAL CHALLENGE

*P*erhaps an equally difficult challenge for me had been "Could I embrace the joy in my life as well as the pain?" I learned throughout this time it was important for me to embrace my darkness or inner truths. It was equally important that I awaken to the presence of joy in my life. Often JOY was staring at me. I was unable to recognize her or often I did not take the time to acknowledge her. As I reflected back on this journey, I realized that the births of my daughters brought more than depression, they brought JOY into my life. Often both were present together, side by side, and it was up to me to recognize each of them. It was this embrace that allowed me to keep going, to experience life more deeply; enabling me to laugh and cry, and to be in relationship and have some balance without completely falling apart. Just as pain connected me to others, so did joy. While I was in the depths of depression, it was this awareness of JOY that started to awaken and stir within me. This JOY awakened with the birth of our first daughter, Emily, and kept growing despite the darkness. This became my challenge as my depression continued. Could I recognize the JOY through the darkness and the pain? Or would I lose sight of it completely? I learned that experiencing joy connected me on a deeper level to my creator, and through this connection to all of creation. When I was connected to my creator I was freer to create and express myself. I became reenergized. It was as if I experienced a creative force flowing through me, which allowed me to keep going. This was what I craved from substitutes. This, however, was real. This was loving. This was from God the source of all Life and light.

This was also the source of the new life I held in my arms and nursed at my breasts. I began to hope and believe in new life as I looked intently at my daughters. Their little fingers and toes, as I counted them to be sure they were all there. Their fists uncurling, their first words spoken, "mama, dada." All these were miracles in front of my eyes daily. They were a source of joy even though I was struggling to keep up with the daily needs of our little family. Running after them as they began to walk and run, seeing their wonder at life. I wanted to experience life as they experienced life. They were JOY FILLED! And the miracle was I could see this, and their joy seemed to flow into me, as if we were still connected in the womb, mother to fetus. This intimate connection could only be from God. I sensed it, although I could not find words to express it. There was much I could not express at that time. That is okay. I have expressed what has come from my heart at this time; what has come to the light to be shared as a gift to be unwrapped in love.

Today, I no longer experience my world as a series of grey or black days. Rather, they are splashed with color. Certainly there are shades of grey and even times of black, but my challenge continues to be to find the color amidst the darker tones. For it is in finding this color, however tiny it may be at times, that enables me to keep my perspective. This enables me to remember there is HOPE despite how black my world looks to me. I need to remember that I see a small picture and that my feelings change, but God sees the big picture; and I need to trust Him. It is more difficult on some days to find JOY. That is alright. It is often by connecting with someone that I recognize her, but I also have learned not to discount my pain.

Moments of joy were staring at me many times, although I often did not recognize them as such. Many times I felt a connection and called it the mother/daughter bond of love. Joy dotted my otherwise grey landscape and gave my life not only color but meaning. In the seemingly endless sleepless night hours or dark lonely moments, JOY pulled me forward for another step and another day. These moments of JOY were expressed in my life and looked like this:

The look of wonder in Emily's eyes as she swam in the pool without her arm floats for the first time.

The sound of Sarah's laughter as I tickled her in bed before bedtime.

Picking Sarah up when she fell off her tricycle. Then hugging her, and telling her she could do it and watching her get back on and ride down the driveway!

The sounds of giggles and laughter and barking as both girls, Stephen, and the dogs built a snowman in the backyard.

The sounds of all four of us screaming on the roller coaster at Disney World.

The clicking sound of the hospital door where I had been after my suicide attempt as Stephen and I left for what turned out to be the last time.

Being able to see the sunrise as we camped together as Stephen and I enjoyed our morning cup of coffee with each other after an uninterrupted night's sleep.

The sound of Donald's voice on the phone when I called him endless times during those years, especially those six crucial times.

The sound of Stephen's and the girls' voices when they came home each day and called out "Are you home," and the sound of my voice back "Yes, I'm home, I can't wait to hear how your day was. I'll be right there." Buddy and I came rushing into the kitchen. Buddy often got the first hug!

Today I experience a range of feelings. Many exist at the same time. I am not true to myself if I do not acknowledge and feel all of them. Joy was a gift of this journey.

CHAPTER 38

AN UNEXPECTED GIFT

I made amends to my father in a letter because I had been absent from his life when I was actively drinking. One day he spoke to me on the phone, "Thank you for your letter." I simply said, "You're welcome, dad." About one year later at his bedside, I bent to give my dad a kiss. I said to him, "I love you dad" as tears fell down my face. My dad whispered something back to me. I bent closer to hear him as I put my ear next to his mouth. I stood, sobbing, and left the room minutes later. My dad had died. My heart was broken.

It was late at night or extremely early in the morning. It was early in the month of April, springtime, a time for new life, not a time for dying I numbly thought to myself. Our daughters were sleeping along with their cousins upstairs in my childhood bedroom. How would I tell them their grandfather had died when they woke up in the morning? Emily was five and Sarah just three. It was not yet morning. I cannot believe my dad is gone. I try to remember the words my dad said to me, but this was early in my depression. I was severely impaired cognitively and emotionally. I can't remember. I sat in the living room and looked at the green walls. I think to myself, "Some things never change. My mom still loves this color, but this green always seemed to drain the life out of me." This night, there is no life left to drain out of me. Since I have been so severely depressed, there doesn't seem to be anything else my illness can take from me. As I sit here in the living room of the home where I grew up, I realize this is not true. My dad just died. I feel numb inside. I am afraid to feel. I am trying to protect myself the only way I know how. I push my feelings away. I begin to feel like sharks are circling me, coming way too close, waiting for the right moment to attack me.

What DID my dad whisper to me minutes before he died? He whispered words that spoke volumes to me but I was in a place where I was unable to hear them. They rolled off of me. I did not know what to do with them. I had waited all my life to hear them.

I was too emotionally sick. This was my issue, not my fathers. My heart could not absorb the reality of those words and what they meant because of my broken state. But they weren't wasted. I took those words into my mind and absorbed them into my heart and carried them with me. Just as my mind had repressed those traumatic memories years ago, my mind repressed these words. But my mind, heart, and spirit used these words to encourage and anchor me each day. When the rudder of my boat seemed to get stuck it was my father telling me to STOP and LOOK. It was my dad telling me not to run away again. It was my dad telling me to listen to his words to me, to unlock their meaning. He was saying from his father's heart to his daughter, "You want to sail ahead, but before you do you must look behind at your past with me and know that I loved you." Maybe I needed to listen more closely to him…

Perhaps I needed to hear these words through my therapist first. Perhaps the relationship I had with Donald was a substitute for the relationship I could not have with my father. My heart was closed to my father for good reason at the time. But today is not my past. Today is my present. I now believe my father loved me. I learned that through my own pain.

My life is not a fairy tale. I rely on some people today but my trust is in God. I need both in my life. My true security comes from my God who loves me and that is my faith, not a fantasy or a fairy tale. It is not even a hope at times. It is my faith. When I look back on this journey of darkness and where I have walked, I know in my heart that I should have died. God saved me. He saved me in love and he saved me through love and through loving people He put in my life.

I realize that telling someone I love them is never wasted nor is it too late. Nor is it too late for someone else to tell me they love me. It may be risky but so are many things worthwhile in my life. I may never know if I don't try.

I can absorb my father's words today as a result of sharing my written expression of what lay in my heart with all of you. This was one gift I received as I shared my story. Thank you for allowing me to share. The eyes of my heart opened further to my dad.

I carry my dad's last words to me, "I love you, Marcia," each day as I live. I trust he knows what a tremendous gift he gave me that night. I know today what a gift he gave me and what a gift he was.

It amazes me how similar these words from my father, my mother who ended each phone call to me, and the words from my God of Love are. "I LOVE YOU." Perhaps when I was at one of my lowest points in my life I needed love the most. It was at this time that it was the most difficult for me to accept love. I did not think I deserved to be loved. I felt unlovable. I felt ashamed. Guilty. Desperate. I became willing.

I was holding in my arms a precious gift of love. My heart had connected and opened a tiny bit. That was enough. I was attracted to this light and love and new life. Hope became a tangible thing for me. My daughters were present. My husband. My therapist. My recovery group. God was present among my life through love and I began to feel Him. Today I live and breathe because of this Love.

"I love you." Three words that can change a life. I know they changed mine. With time and perserverance. It is an open invitation; one too important for me to ignore then or now. My life depends on it.

When I walk through dark experiences or dark moments today, I need to remember those years. I need to recall those moments when God touched me and called me, when people reached out to me, and I remember how loving and gentle, kind, and faithful God is, even when I am not. I remember the light and the love. I remember my babies' birth. I remember goodness and new life.

I remember as surely as night follows the day, that the dawn follows even the darkest of nights. Many times I may not be aware of the dawn because of the emotional pain that seems all consuming, or my thoughts seem too jumbled and overwhelming, but when I stop for even a moment to lift my head to the sky, or I stop long enough to notice the sun or the stars, I can remember where I have come from and say "Thank You." I can ask Jesus for help and uncurl my fisted hands and extend them to someone else or ask for help for myself. Either way, it is in honest connection with others, self, and God, that I have the best chance of continuing my journey in the light. I try to face each day with hope in my heart despite any fear I may feel. Wherever you are on your journey, thank you for allowing me to be a part of your walk.

EPILOGUE

Three years later
SEPTEMBER, 2015

*L*ast night we decided to go to the beach as summer was rapidly coming to a close. My husband, Stephen, and our dog, Dakota, were walking on the nearly deserted beach as it was after Labor Day. The beach was formally closed for the season. I stayed behind to sit on my bench and relax. While watching the tide come in, I was mesmerized by the rhythmical sound of the waves coming into shore and receding. I sat in my favorite place, my sandals off, my feet in the cool sand. A few flies were out and I began to think about our former camping days with our daughters. We hadn't gone now in quite a few years. Stephen would have bug repellent with him this evening, he never did tolerate mosquitoes!

Our house was noticeably quiet this September as both our daughters had left for college. Emily, now a junior, and Sarah a freshman. As I sat and reflected on our transitioning family, a Cub Scout troop of approximately twenty boys and several leaders came onto the beach carrying kites. One leader passed me saying, "I hope you didn't come here looking for peace and quiet. If so, that ship has sailed."

I smiled and shook my head no. I realized that many ships had sailed with or without me in my life. For now, I am at peace, knowing my life has a rhythm like the tide with it's ebb and flow. My God of Love is in control. I continue to entrust our daughters to His love and care and pray for our relationships as our lives continue to grow and change.

I proceeded to intently watch the boys as did others at the beach. Before long the sky was filled with colorful kites in varying sizes and shapes. I was quite taken aback by the colorful display in the evening sky.

I was more overcome by the conversations I overheard between the leaders and the young boys. "You need to try if you want your kite to fly," and "If you hold onto the string too tightly your kite will not be able to fly very high." As a different leader walked past me I asked him, "Do you do this regularly?" He answered, "No, but it was such a beautiful night we decided to buy the boys kites and come here to enjoy it."

His responses touched a place within me. I had needed to learn these lessons myself these past twenty years. I wished I had learned them as a child. My life desperately needed color but I also needed to learn to take risks and how to let go.

As a child I did not have a desire to fly a kite but this is a new day and I am a changed woman! I still my urge to jump in and join the class. After all, I have my "new" blue and yellow kite, three years old, in the original wrapping with the clearance tag, in the trunk of my car. I guess I was waiting for the right time to take it out and I think I found it!

As I watched these boys, I felt the freedom and peace I was now familiar with; a sense that I was no longer alone. This presence filled me. So much about that evening touched me. Obviously taking the opportunity to enjoy the moment was important enough to these leaders to teach this to these boys. I needed to relearn this too, to enjoy each moment and make the most of each day. These young boys were embarking on an important road this evening. I thought of Emily and Sarah as they were pursuing their own life journeys and my heart filled with love and a longing as I missed them. I knew in my heart of hearts, my mother's heart, that we were connected, as only a mother and daughter could be, and I sent a loving thought to each of them and to God. Although I missed them at times, I recall many of our shared times especially those of recent years. But it is the unconditional love that connected us during our past that continues to hold strong in our present. This is what I hold onto, this is what gives me peace and encourages me as my life changes and situations arise. This is what I connect with in times like these when I feel several emotions and I can be still and sense God's presence and guidance.

As I focused inward, I was touched with the kind words the leaders spoke and the gentleness of their voices. I thought about my therapist, Donald, and his gentleness. "These scout leaders remind me of you. I can picture you here with children flying kites. Because of you, I am able to be here, enjoying this beautiful night. Thank you so much for all you did for me. It feels so good to be alive. I miss you so much, but I think you know that. I know you know that. Because of all you taught me, I am able to get up and choose to come here and enjoy this moment. Life is too precious. Thanks again. I miss you lots! I need to go now; I have some playing to do!"

"Wait up, Stephen, Dakota, I'm coming," I shouted into the wind as I ran slipping in the cool sand, barefoot, trying to catch up, trailing my colorful kite behind me. "WIND, WE NEED MORE WIND!" I shouted as I ran laughing. I attempted to lift my kite into the night sky.

"Don't struggle so much" I heard a voice say to me as if it came down from the sky. I turned around. A young cub scout trailed behind me telling me to let go, to surrender to the

WIND. So I released my grip on my string and the cub scout and I watched my kite soar into the evening sky!

"Awesome!" he said.

"Awesome indeed!" I replied.

"Our God Is Great!"

THE DAWN

*L*iving through, remembering, dealing with, and sharing about sexual abuse is extremely difficult, dark and personal.

The Dawn, The Light, however, has truly come into my life, into my darkness, and that, I hope and pray, is the message that comes through this book.

Jesus is The Light - He is for me. He continues to enlighten my mind and my heart. He helps me see there is another way to live - His way. His love frees me to make better choices in my life; He frees me to surrender to Him; He frees me to walk through my fears.

God has shown me through my darkness that love is a choice. His love is not forced. I am safe in His presence.

With the dawn of each new day God gives me, I arise and invite God into my life, my mind and my actions. I ask Him for help. I invite Him in as He continues to invite me into a deeper relationship with Him, myself, and others. This gives my life deep meaning.

I have moments of deep peace. At home. With myself.

May it be so for you too.

September, 2019

ACKNOWLEDGMENTS

I thank the following people for their support and encouragement to me in the writing, publishing, and republishing of this book. In many cases they supported both me and the sensitive issue of this memoir as they are so closely related.

Each knows of their unique contribution. I say thank you to the following and to all the others that I cannot remember: Dr Donald McNeil, Rev. Anthony Kuzia, The Writer's Group of Halifax Massachusetts, Bridgewater Tale Spinners Writing Group also of Massachusetts, Don Brown, Jack Minor initial editor.

I thank my team at Book Trail Agency for their guidance, patience, and support during the reediting and republication of my memoir. So happy to have their expertise!

I thank my parents and sisters for their presence in my life. Our deepening relaonships as the years pass mean so much to me.

Thanks, also, to my dear friends Jack and Ellie Walker who have been a special presence in my life these past ten years. They have encouraged me through their prayer and presence to seek the truth in my life, to grow in my faith, and to live in the light.

I thank my dear friend, Rose Kennedy, who is like a sister to me. Her love and presence in my life remind me daily what a gift true relationship is.

I thank Stephen and my daughters, Emily and Sarah, for their unconditional love and patience. I loved them from the beginning but my illness prevented me from showing them the depth of my love. Their love and acceptance of me has helped me to come to love and accept myself, a true gift, a journey well worth it. A lifetime journey so wonderful to take with them my dear family. I am truly blest!

I thank ALL of the friends I have met in various stages and places of recovery and healing throughout the years. Through sharing some extremely difficult times together, we have grown with God's grace and love holding us and leading us to the next step, often with a box of tissues and a cup of coffee and talks on the telephone. Where would I be without each and every one of you, many who are like my second family?

Thanks, also, to those professionals, who, despite being short-staffed or overworked were willing to take that extra step that meant so much to me.

As I mentioned, this past year has been extremely difficult as I have embraced many new, remembered, traumatic memories in therapy. I questioned many aspects of my growing faith in God and in Jesus, His Son. My road of recovery has not been easy however I am still on it and it is worth every step. I extend my deepest gratitude to Fr Jason Giombetti for his willingness to be that guide in my darkness that Dr McNeil had been. I thank him for his ability and willingness to be present, to encourage, to support, to be a voice of reason, and to consistently direct me to The Truth of Jesus present in the Sacraments of my faith. The grace and strength I receive through these sacraments has deepened my relationship with Jesus which has allowed me to be more open to questioning and learning, to think differently, to discern God's voice and presence more fully in my life, and to risk following where God leads me.

Most of all I thank God. I don't understand His immense love for me but I trust He loves me and wants the best for me. He has encouraged me when my pen has faltered to speak the truth from my heart. I am safe in His presence. He has guided me through the darkness and continues to help me face my truth so I may embrace The Truth of His Son, Jesus, who frees me to live in the light.

May it be so for you too.

Marcia Orcutt
April 29, 2021